MADE *in* AFRICA

MADE *in* AFRICA

Learning to Compete
in Industry

CAROL NEWMAN
JOHN PAGE
JOHN RAND
ABEBE SHIMELES
MÅNS SÖDERBOM
FINN TARP

BROOKINGS INSTITUTION PRESS
Washington, D.C.

The Brookings Institution is a private nonprofit organization de-
voted to research, education, and publication on important issues
of domestic and foreign policy. Its principal purpose is to bring
the highest quality independent research and analysis to bear on
current and emerging policy problems. Interpretations or conclusions in Brookings publications should be understood to be solely
those of the authors.

Library of Congress Cataloging-in-Publication data are available.
ISBN 978-0-8157-2815-3 (pbk : alk. paper)
ISBN 978-0-8157-2816-0 (epub)
ISBN 978-0-8157-2817-7 (pdf)

9 8 7 6 5 4 3 2 1

Typeset in Officina and Sabon

Composition by Westchester Publishing Services

This book is based on the results of a four-year, multi-country research project jointly sponsored by the African Development Bank, the Brookings Institution, and the United Nations University World Institute for Development Economics Research (UNU-WIDER).

B | **Global Economy and Development**
at BROOKINGS

AFRICAN DEVELOPMENT
BANK GROUP

UNITED NATIONS
UNIVERSITY
UNU-WIDER

Contents

Part IV

HOW AFRICA CAN INDUSTRIALIZE

Preface and Acknowledgments

Africa is rising. Since 1995 it has grown faster than many other parts of the developing world. Per capita income has been increasing steadily, and with six of the world's ten fastest-growing economies of the last decade, Africa has been branded the developing world's next "frontier market" by Wall Street and the World Bank. Yet Africa's experience with industrialization has been disappointing. In 2012 sub-Saharan Africa's average share of manufacturing value added in GDP was about 10 percent, the same as in the 1970s.

This book presents the main results of Learning to Compete (L2C), a research program jointly sponsored by the African Development Bank, the Brookings Institution, and the United Nations University World Institute for Development Economics Research (UNU-WIDER). The L2C program tried to answer a seemingly simple but puzzling question: Why is there so little industry in Africa? Given Africa's recent economic success, one may reasonably wonder why we chose to focus on industrialization, an area in which the Continent has not performed well. It is not because we wanted to return to the "Afro-pessimism" of earlier decades. Rather, it is because we want to see growth in Africa sustain itself. One worry that motivated us to undertake the project was that since 1995, growth in Africa has taken place without the changes in economic structure that normally occur as incomes per person rise. This raised concerns in our minds about the durability of the "African growth miracle."

When we began Learning to Compete in 2010, not many observers of Africa—academics and policymakers alike—were concerned with its lack of structural change. That certainly has changed. Over the last five years, the African Development Bank, the UN Economic Commission for Africa, and the African Union have all voiced concerns with the pattern and pace of structural change. A new Africa Center for Economic Transformation, led by one of the region's most distinguished economists, K. Y. Amoako, has been established in Accra and has published its first "Africa Transformation Report." At the urging of African nations, the new Sustainable Development Goals of the United Nations appear likely to contain structural change, employment generation, and industrialization as global development objectives. This book is in part our contribution to that ongoing discussion.

Historically, industry has been a driving force behind structural change, but Africa has abundant land and natural resources. Perhaps it does not need to industrialize to maintain the pace of economic progress. While it is certainly possible for economies to grow based on modern agriculture or natural resources, we are convinced that there is something special about the role of industry in low-income countries. At the most basic level industry is a high-productivity sector into which a large number of workers can flow. This is good for growth, for job creation, and for poverty reduction. It is also the only sector in which poor countries are catching up to rich country productivity levels, regardless of geography, institutions, or policies. This makes industry a potentially powerful driver of economy-wide productivity growth. All of these good things depend on the size and the rate of growth of industry. That is why we have written this book.

We have subtitled it *Learning to Compete in Industry* because setting out a new agenda for industrial development in Africa is our key objective. Yet, for Africa to succeed, it is critical to understand why few manufactured goods have been made in Africa for the last forty years. To understand this better we asked national researchers to undertake eleven detailed country case studies—eight from sub-Saharan Africa, one from North Africa, and two from emerging Asia. The eight sub-Saharan studies document industrialization efforts and outcomes in Ethiopia, Ghana, Kenya, Mozambique, Nigeria, Senegal, Tanzania, and Uganda. Tunisia was included both to extend the coverage of the research to the Continent as a whole and because—in light of the events of the Arab Spring—it is of considerable interest in its own right. The emerging Asian countries—Cambodia and Vietnam—were chosen because they are East Asia's newest industrializers. They also had per capita income levels and structural characteristics similar to the African economies studied, as recently as 2005 in the case of Cambodia and 2001 in the case of Vietnam.[1]

Made in Africa is mainly a story about firms. For Africa to industrialize its firms must be able to compete in global markets. Successful industrializers have been those that over time have managed to raise the productivity of the "typical" firm. For this reason we wanted to understand better what makes firms more productive in low-income countries. We were particularly interested in the roles of exports and industrial agglomerations in firm-level productivity. To address these questions the research team carried out a total of seventeen econometric studies of the drivers of firm-level productivity using statistical data from our eleven case study countries. Much of this book is based on that research.

We were also interested in the role of foreign direct investment (FDI). There is an extensive literature—most of it based on studies of middle-income countries—which suggests that foreign firms can be an important source of knowledge for industrial development. We wanted to understand the interactions between foreign-owned and domestic firms in low-income countries. To address this question

---

1. The country studies are available as Brookings Learning to Compete Working Papers (www.brookings.edu/about/projects/africa-growth/learning-to-compete) and as WIDER Working Papers (www.wider.unu.edu/research/current-programme/en_GB/L2C-2010/).

we carried out qualitative surveys in Africa and emerging Asia in which we asked the owners and managers of foreign and domestic firms how they interacted and whether they explicitly or implicitly transferred knowledge to their purchasers or suppliers.

We are not alone in our concern that Africa has failed to industrialize. At the same time we carried out our research two other important research projects were taking a close look at African industrialization. The first project, spearheaded by Justin Lin, then chief economist of the World Bank, studied light manufacturing in Africa. The second, led by Professor John Sutton and sponsored by the International Growth Centre, produced a number of Enterprise Maps for African countries. Both projects add substantially to our knowledge of African industry, and we have drawn on them.

This book is an attempt to persuade African policymakers, aid practitioners, and those interested in Africa's future that Africa can industrialize. For that reason we have tried to write a book that is accessible to a wide range of readers. While a mass of technical research—ours and that of others—underpins the writing, we have tried here to minimize the use of technique and jargon. Those interested in the finer technical details can find them in the publications and working papers to which we refer.

The book is organized in four major parts. Chapter 1 takes up the question of why industry matters. Part II (including chapters 2 and 3) provides a brief history of industrial development in Africa, gives our assessment of past industrialization efforts and outcomes in the countries we studied intensively, and outlines the challenges faced by African economies in breaking into the global market for industrial goods today. Part III (chapters 4, 5, and 6) presents the main results of Learning to Compete. The three chapters discuss the key drivers of firm-level productivity in low-income countries—exports and competition, firm capabilities, and industrial agglomerations—and their relevance to Africa's industrial development.

In Part IV (chapters 7, 8, and 9) the focus shifts to policy. While traditional concerns such as infrastructure, skills, and the regulatory environment are important, our research suggests that addressing these factors alone will not be sufficient. Chapter 7 presents a new industrialization strategy for Africa, grounded in that research, while chapter 8 takes up the question of industrialization in Africa's growing number of resource-abundant countries. In chapter 9 we suggest changes in donor priorities and practices to support the new approach to industrialization.

Before closing, a final note: the idea that governments can successfully develop and implement strategies for industrial development is at the heart of the decades-long controversy over industrial policy. Often overlooked in that debate over "picking winners" or "leveling the playing field" is the reality that governments make industrial policy every day through the public expenditure program, institutional and regulatory changes, and international economic policy. These choices—sometimes inadvertently—favor some enterprises or sectors at the expense of others, and in Africa they often lack a coherent strategic focus. The relevant question is not: will governments make choices? It is: will they make the right choices? We wrote this book with a view to helping to inform those choices.

Many people worked with us during the five years of Learning to Compete's implementation. Our greatest debt is to the country-based research teams who carried out much of the case study and quantitative research that underpins this book. They are:

Cambodia: Sokty Chhair (Team Leader), Sophal Chan, and Luyna Ung

Ethiopia: Mulu Gebreeyesus (Team Leader) and Eyerusalem Siba

Ghana: Charles Ackah (Team Leader), Charles Adjasi, Festus Turkson, and Adjoa Acquah

Kenya: Peter Kimuyu (Team Leader), Jacob Chege, and Dianah Ngui

Mozambique: António Sousa Cruz (Team Leader), Dina Guambe, Constantino Pedro Marrengula, Amosse Francisco Ubisse, Søren Schou, and José Cardoso

Nigeria: Louis N. Chete (Team Leader), John O. Adeoti, Foluso M. Adeyinka, and Olorunfemi Ogundele

Senegal: Fatou Cissé (Team Leader), Ji Eun Choi, Mathilde Maurel, and Majda Seghir

Tanzania: Samuel Wangwe (Team Leader), Donald Mmari, Jehovanes Aikaeli, Neema Rutatina, Thadeus Mboghoina, and Abel Kinyondo

Tunisia: Mohamed Ayadi (Team Leader) and Wided Mattoussi

Uganda: Marios Obwona (Co-Team Leader), Isaac Shinyekwa (Co-Team Leader), and Julius Kiiza

Vietnam: Nguyen Thi Tue Anh (Team Leader), Luu Minh Duc, and Trinh Duc Chieu

We are grateful to the late Gobind Nankani, then head of the Global Development Network, for early encouragement. We are indebted to Louis Kasekende and Mthuli Ncube, former chief economists of the African Development Bank, and Steve Kayizzi-Mugerwa, currently the acting chief economist, for their sustained support for the project. Kemal Dervis, vice president and director of the Global Economy and Development Program at Brookings, was a committed supporter. We are also indebted to the UNU-WIDER Board, headed by Professor Ernest Aryeetey, for its support and guidance.

We benefited from the thoughtful advice of Ernest Aryeetey, Arne Bigsten, Howard Pack, and Tony Venables in designing the research program. Over the years, we have engaged in many discussions with colleagues who also study industry and development. These conversations helped shape our thinking and test our assumptions. Without implicating any of them in the perspectives offered in this book, we would like to thank Paul Collier, Hinh Dinh, Ann Harrison, Mark Henstridge, Justin Lin, Margaret McMillan, Celestin Monga, Benno Ndulu, Keijiro Otsuka, Tetsushi Sonobe, Joseph Stiglitz, John Sutton, and Francis Teal.

The African Economic Research Consortium (AERC) and the Economic Commission for Africa (ECA) helped us to organize preparatory workshops with the country teams in Nairobi and Addis Ababa, respectively. We are grateful to the participants in numerous meetings, seminars, and lectures, including the June 2013

WIDER Development Conference in Helsinki, for comments, critiques, and advice.[2]

An anonymous donor helped to support Brookings contributions to the joint work program. The African Development Bank recognizes the financial support provided by the Government of the Republic of Korea through the Korea-Africa Economic Cooperation Trust Fund. UNU-WIDER acknowledges the support of its donors— the Ministry of Foreign Affairs of Finland, the Swedish International Development Cooperation Agency (Sida), the U.K. Department for International Development, and the Danish Ministry of Foreign Affairs (Danida).

2. See (www1.wider.unu.edu/L2Cconf/) for a summary of the conference proceedings.

PART I

WHY INDUSTRY MATTERS *for* AFRICA

CHAPTER 1

Why Industry Matters for Africa

Economic growth in Africa has been on an accelerating trend for more than thirty years. The average annual growth rate of real output increased from 1.8 percent in the period 1980–89 to 2.6 percent in 1990–99 and 5.3 percent in 2000–09. Since 2010 it has remained in the range of 4.5 to 5.5 percent per year. One of the enduring "stylized facts" of economic development is that structural change—the movement of labor from low productivity sectors into higher productivity employment—is a key driver of growth, especially in lower income countries.[1] Despite two decades of solid economic growth, however, Africa has experienced relatively little structural change.[2] The region's growth turnaround beginning in 1995 was largely due to making fewer economic policy mistakes, rising commodity prices, and natural resource discoveries.[3]

1. See, for example, Lewis (1954), Kuznets (1955), and Chenery (1986).
2. In general we use the terms Africa and sub-Saharan Africa interchangeably in this book, following the regional classifications of the World Bank and common usage. Where we wish to discuss only sub-Saharan Africa or North Africa we use those terms explicitly.
3. Arbache and Page (2008, 2009).

3

In both theory and history, industry has been a key driver of structural change, but it has only played a minor role in recent structural change in Africa. Since 2000, a growing share of African workers have been leaving agriculture and moving to higher productivity sectors. This positive structural change has contributed to overall growth, but the shift in employment has primarily been from agriculture into services for domestic consumers. Only about one in five African workers leaving agriculture has moved into the industrial sector.[4] To us, these trends raise the question: How important is industry to Africa?

As we attempt to answer this question, the definition of "industry" is critical. When the economic statistics used today were first drawn up in the 1950s, there was little confusion over what industry meant. At the broadest level it encompassed mining, manufacturing, utilities, and construction. Of these, manufacturing—"smokestack industry"—was the subject of central interest. However, changes in transport costs and information and communications technology have shifted the boundaries of industry. A wide range of services and agro-industrial products have become tradable and have many features in common with manufacturing.[5] Like manufacturing, they benefit from technological change and productivity growth. Some exhibit tendencies for scale and agglomeration economies.[6] For that reason we take a broad view of what constitutes industry today. It is manufacturing and those tradable services and agro-industrial value chains that share the firm-level characteristics that are the subject of this book. Put more straightforwardly, we are interested in industry both with and without smokestacks.

In an attempt to understand industry's importance to Africa, we begin this chapter with a snapshot of the magnitude of Africa's industrialization challenge. We compare the structure of Africa's economies with a number of benchmarks and with the cross-country patterns relating the size of the industrial sector to the level of per

---

4. McMillan and Hartgen (2014).
5. See, for example, Baumol (1985) and Bhagwati (1984).
6. See Ebling and Janz (1999) and Ghani and Kharas (2010).

capita income. The output and employment structure of a "typical" African economy is quite different from these comparators. The main gaps lie in the much smaller shares of output and employment in industry.

Although the numbers suggest that Africa has too little industry, it has managed to grow without industrialization for nearly two decades. Perhaps it does not need to industrialize. In this chapter we make the case that industry matters for Africa. We show that the slow pace of industrialization is at least partly responsible for the region's disappointing performance in translating growth into good jobs and poverty reduction. Lack of industrial development may also have closed off important opportunities to raise women's welfare. We end by arguing that industrialization has some special characteristics that can sustain growth.

Africa's "Manufacturing Deficit"

Most African countries have national visions that call for achieving middle-income status over the next decade. One measure of the extent of structural change that might be needed for the transition to middle income can be found by comparing Africa's current economic structure with that of a "benchmark" middle-income country.[7] The World Bank defines lower-middle-income status as falling in the range US$1,045–4,125 in 2012 purchasing power parity (PPP) prices.[8] The lower bound of this range would seem to be a reasonable target for Africa's national visions.

We constructed a benchmark economy by identifying a group of currently middle-income countries that have crossed the US$1,045 threshold.[9] We selected the following benchmark countries and

7. This idea was proposed in a single-country context by Bevan and others (2003).

8. The World Bank Atlas method of currency conversion is used.

9. Because the World Bank only provides GNI per capita in current terms, the GNI per capita in 2012 was projected backward using the GDP per capita growth rate to the US$1,045 threshold, thus giving the benchmark year for

years: China (2000), India (2007), Indonesia (2004), Korea (1968), Malaysia (1968), Philippines (1976), and Thailand (1987). The economic structure of the benchmark is simply the average of the shares of value added and employment in four broad sectors—agriculture, manufacturing, other industry, and services—for these seven countries in the relevant year.

The differences between Africa and the benchmark are substantial (table 1-1). The largest difference is in industry. The manufacturing value added and the labor shares in low-income African countries are about half of the benchmark values. Even Mauritius and South Africa, the middle-income countries represented and arguably sub-Saharan Africa's two most successful industrializers, fall short of the benchmark in terms of the share of manufacturing value added in GDP. This is the region's "manufacturing deficit" relative to other lower-middle-income countries.

Table 1-2 gives another view of the manufacturing deficit. It compares selected indicators of industrial development for Africa with other developing countries in 2010, the last year for which we have reasonably comprehensive data. By any measure Africa's industrial sector is small relative to the average for the developing world as a whole. The share of manufacturing in GDP is less than one-half of the average for all developing countries, and in contrast with developing countries as a whole, it is declining. Manufacturing output per capita is about 10 percent of the global developing country average. Per capita manufactured exports are slightly more than 10 percent of the developing country average, and the share of manufactured exports in total exports is strikingly low. Moreover, these measures have changed little since the 1990s.[10]

Because economic structure reflects an economy's level of development, it is possible that the "manufacturing deficit" reflects nothing more than the lower per capita incomes of African countries.

---

each country. Small island economies and economies with populations of less than one million were excluded. Countries for which labor force data near the benchmark year were not available were also excluded.

10. See UNIDO (2009; 2013).

Table 1-1. *Africa's Manufacturing Deficit, 2010*

	Value added share				Labor share			
	Agriculture	Other industry	Manufacturing	Services	Agriculture	Other industry	Manufacturing	Services
Benchmark middle-income country	21.7	12.2	21.9	44.2	45.2	6.6	11.6	36.6
Africa low-income country	27.8	11.8	11.1	49.3	63.1	5.1	6.6	25.2
Africa middle-income country	4.8	10.9	17.1	67.2	8.6	11.9	16.8	62.7

Sources: McMillan and Rodrik (2011) database; World Bank World Development Indicators (WDI) database; de Vries, Timmer, and de Vries (2013). Authors' calculations.

Notes: Middle-income benchmark as described in text.

Africa low-income sample ETH, MWI, GHA, KEN, MAD, MOZ, SEN, TZA.

Africa middle-income sample MUS, ZAF.

Table 1-2. *Selected Indicators of Industrial Development, 2000–10*

	Manufacturing value added				*Manufactured exports*		
Region	*Share of GDP 2000 (percent)*	*Share of GDP 2010 (percent)*	*Per capita 2010 (US$2,000)*	*Per capita growth 2000–10 (percent)*	*Share in total exports 2010 (percent)*	*Per capita 2010 (US$2,000)*	*Per capita growth 2000–10 (percent)*
Sub-Saharan Africa average	8.1	7.0	36.7	2.69	30.0	61.8	10.3
Developing countries average	20.5	21.0	400.2	3.01	74.0	579.6	7.1

Sources: UNIDO (2009); UNIDO (2013); UNIDO Industrial Development database. Authors' calculations.
Notes: Sub-Saharan Africa average excludes South Africa.

This is where cross-country patterns make a useful reference point. The relationship between manufacturing and per capita income has an inverted U shape. In the early stages of development when most economies are concentrated in agriculture, growth in income is associated with very rapid increases of the share of manufacturing in total output. As incomes and real wages rise and skills develop, the relative importance of manufacturing peaks and countries moving toward upper-middle-income levels diversify into more skill-intensive activities, including services.

Globally, the share of manufacturing in total output rises with per capita income until countries reach upper-middle-income status and then declines. While African economies generally conform to this global pattern, the vast majority are below the global average in terms of the relationship between per capita income and the share of manufacturing in GDP. Only Madagascar, Mozambique, Lesotho, and the Ivory Coast have shares of manufacturing in total output that exceed the predicted values for their levels of income. Many of the region's recent growth success stories—Ethiopia, Ghana, Kenya, Tanzania, and Uganda, for example—have shares of manufacturing in GDP that are well below their predicted values. Controlling for the level of income, Africa faces a larger deficit in terms of manufacturing than other countries at the same level of development.[11]

Structural Change, Industry, and Growth

Because developing economies are characterized by large differences in output per worker across sectors, there is a substantial growth payoff when factors of production move from lower productivity to higher productivity sectors. Africa is the developing region with the most to gain from structural change. It has the greatest differences across sectors in output per worker. The average ratio of highest to lowest productivity sectors in Africa is more than twice that for Latin

11. Dinh and others (2013).

America and Asia.[12] This shows the large potential for structural change to boost growth of income per person in Africa, although recent research finds that this potential has not been fully tapped.[13]

Economywide changes in output per worker over time can be decomposed into two components.[14] The first component reflects productivity growth within individual sectors. It is the weighted sum of changes in labor productivity in each sector of the economy, where the weights are the employment shares of each sector in the beginning period. Not surprisingly, it has come to be labeled the "within sector component" of productivity change. The second component captures the change in economywide labor productivity of labor reallocations across different sectors. It is the product of individual sector productivity levels in the end period with the change in employment shares across sectors. This is the "structural change component." Among developing countries and across regions, the contributions of these two components to overall productivity change are strikingly different.

Between 1990 and 2010 the movement of workers from lower to higher productivity sectors—mainly industry—in Asia added substantially to economywide growth of output per worker. In this sense structural change was growth enhancing. Latin America was the polar opposite: there structural change was growth reducing. The share of workers in low productivity employment increased between 1990 and 2010, offsetting productivity improvements within sectors and reducing overall productivity growth.[15]

Africa's record of structural change is mixed. From 1990 through 1999 Africa looked more like Latin America. Output per worker increased within sectors while the share of workers employed in high productivity sectors declined. Up until the turn of the

12. Page (2012a).
13. McMillan, Rodrik, and Verduzco-Gallo (2014); de Vries, Timmer, and de Vries (2013).
14. McMillan and Rodrik (2012) and de Vries, Timmer, and de Vries (2013) present differing decompositions reflecting different choices of weights. The exposition here follows McMillan and Rodrik.
15. McMillan, Rodrik, and Verduzco-Gallo (2014).

twenty-first century, structural change in Africa reduced growth of income per person.[16]

After 2000 labor in Africa began to move out of agriculture into more productive employment, but not into industry. Eight out of ten African workers who left agriculture ended up employed in the "market" services sector, mainly in trade, restaurants, and personal services.[17] This amounted to movement from very low productivity employment to only slightly higher productivity jobs. Output per worker in services in Africa is only about two times higher than output per worker in agriculture. Average labor productivity in manufacturing is more than six times that in agriculture.[18]

Africa has a rapidly growing labor force, but employment in manufacturing and in other activities with high value added per worker is growing slowly. This pattern of structural change has some important implications for job creation and poverty reduction (as we explore in the next section). In addition, there is a risk that structural change in Africa will run out of steam. Services have been absorbing workers faster than the services sector has been increasing output. The relative productivity level of market services fell from 3.0 times the total economy average in 1990 to 1.8 times in 2010, suggesting that the marginal productivity of new services workers is low and possibly negative.[19] This raises the risk that without a more robust growth of industry, the structural change component of growth in Africa may diminish or once again turn negative.

Jobs and Poverty Reduction

Africa has enjoyed twenty years of sustained economic growth. Yet there are many worrying signs that this has not resulted in robust

---

16. McMillan, Rodrik, and Verduzco-Gallo (2014).

17. De Vries, Timmer, and de Vries (2013); McMillan and Hartgen (2014).

18. McMillan and Hartgen (2014).

19. De Vries, Timmer, and de Vries (2013).

growth of "good" jobs—those offering higher wages and better working conditions—and rapid reductions in poverty.[20] Africa's structural pattern of growth during the last two decades is at least partly responsible. The sources of growth in the region's most rapidly growing economies have not been employment intensive. Lack of employment-intensive growth, together with the absence of progress in transforming traditional agriculture, are largely at the root of the region's slow pace of poverty reduction. Industrial development offers a high employment, high productivity path for job creation, and evidence suggests that it can accelerate the pace of poverty reduction.

Industry and Africa's "Employment Problem"

On the face of it, sub-Saharan Africa does not have a severe "employment problem." In 2013 the overall unemployment rate for the region was 7.6 percent, compared with a global average of about 6 percent, and youth unemployment rates in many sub-Saharan countries are relatively low compared to world averages.[21] Unemployment is low in Africa's lower income countries—falling in the range of 1 to 5 percent for countries such as Ethiopia, Ghana, Tanzania, and Uganda. But the averages are misleading. For the great majority of Africans the employment problem is more about the quality of the job than the absence of a job. Low unemployment frequently signals poor quality employment.

When an African worker finds a job it is likely to be of low quality in terms of wages, benefits, and job security. Where unemployment in Africa is low the informal sector is large, and many workers are forced into household, family, or self-employment because of

20. See World Bank (2013).
21. ILO (2014). Unemployment rates in Africa are likely to be underestimated because the ILO excludes people who were not working or were not actively looking for work, but say they would take a job if one were offered.

the absence of a wage-paying job. The International Labor Organization (ILO) estimates that three out of four jobs in sub-Saharan Africa can be labeled "vulnerable" due to workers working on their own account or as unpaid family workers. In 2011 nearly 82 percent of workers in Africa were classified as working poor, compared to the world average of about 39 percent. The overwhelming majority of young workers in both rural and urban areas are engaged in informal self-employment. Fewer than one in five of Africa's young workers find places in wage employment.[22]

Africa's poor employment outcomes largely reflect the reality that the region's fastest-growing economies—Ethiopia, Rwanda, Tanzania, and Uganda, among them—have the lowest responsiveness of formal employment to growth (figure 1-1). In fact, there is no statistical relationship in Africa between economywide growth and the rate of growth of formal employment.[23] This is a highly unusual finding. Globally, there is a statistically significant relationship between growth of GDP and employment growth. Between 1991 and 2003, for every 1 percentage point of additional GDP growth, total employment grew between 0.3 and 0.38 percentage points.[24]

The case of Tanzania, one of the countries we studied under our Learning to Compete (L2C) program, makes the point more concretely. Tanzania has a young and rapidly growing population. Approximately 800,000 new workers enter the domestic labor market every year. The economy, however, is not creating that number of "good" jobs. In fact, Tanzania's performance in job creation has been among the most disappointing of the region's "growth miracle" economies. As the supply of workers seeking nonfarm employment has outpaced demand in the wage sector, many labor force participants have been left with no choice but to create their own jobs. Today, 5 million nonfarm businesses operate in Tanzania. This is one of the highest rates of business formation in the world (one

22. ILO (2011).
23. Page and Shimeles (2015).
24. Kapos (2005).

Figure 1-1. *Employment Elasticities and Growth in Africa, 2010*

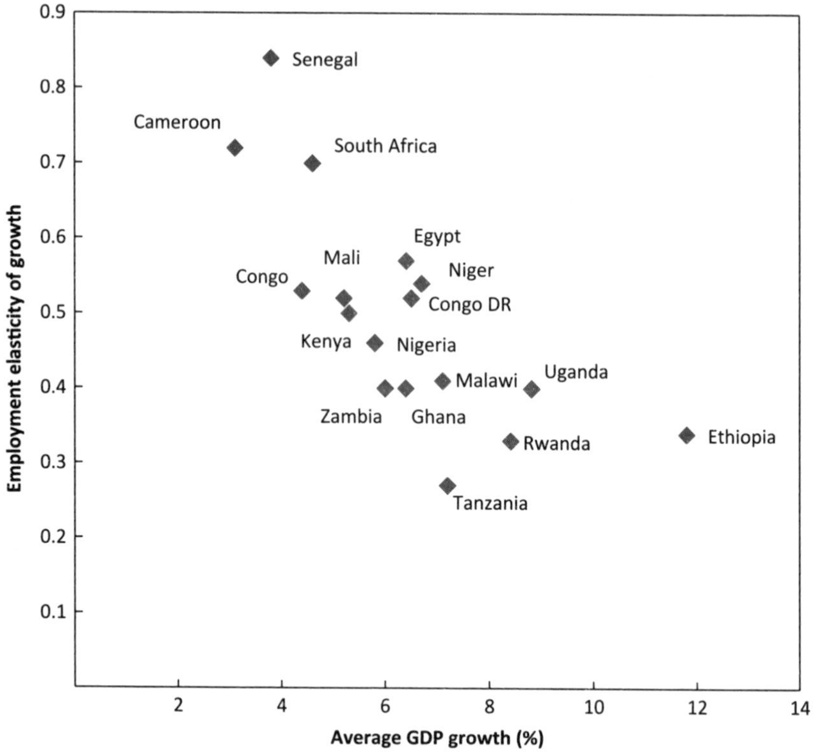

Source: Page and Shimeles (2015).

for every four people), four times higher than in the United States and ten times higher than in France.[25]

The vast majority of these enterprises are in the household sector. Between 2000 and 2006, employment in the household enterprise sector grew by 13 percent, exceeding the overall growth in the labor force and the growth of wage employment. These are tiny firms consisting of a single entrepreneur, perhaps working with unpaid workers who are likely to be family members. The vast majority of household business owners tend to be subsistence entrepreneurs who have minimal business skills. More than two-thirds of household

25. World Bank (2014c).

enterprises in urban areas were formed because of lack of any other job opportunities.[26]

It is perhaps no surprise, then, that the political conversation in Africa often turns to the problem of "jobless growth." Industry, including manufacturing, tradable services, and agro-industry, is a high productivity, employment-intensive sector into which labor can potentially flow. As we shall see in chapter 2, it is a sector that has been growing more slowly than the economy as a whole for more than twenty years. The failure to industrialize is clearly a major part of Africa's employment problem.

Industry, Structural Change, and Poverty

Poverty in Africa is something of a puzzle. We know that while individual country experiences vary, growth is good for the poor; poverty declines as per capita incomes rise. And we know that the pace of poverty reduction for any rate of income growth is affected by the distribution of income. The puzzle is that Africa has both the lowest responsiveness of poverty to per capita income growth and the lowest responsiveness of poverty to changes in income distribution of any of the world's developing regions.[27] The answer to the puzzle lies in part in the structural changes that have accompanied Africa's recent growth. Both cross-country evidence and country-level simulations suggest that Africa's performance in reducing poverty would have been better had the region started its structural transformation earlier and had it experienced more robust growth of industry.[28]

Our first piece of evidence comes from cross-country econometric work. Standard cross-country analysis of poverty reduction assumes that the poverty headcount ratio—the share of poor in the population—is a function of per capita income growth and income

26. Kweka and Fox (2011).

27. Page (2015a).

28. Africa's poverty challenges are also related to initial conditions reflected in basic economic structures. See Arndt and others (2012).

distribution.[29] To examine the influence of structural change on poverty we can modify this relationship to test whether the poverty headcount ratio is affected by variations in the share of employment in agriculture, services, and industry, controlling for per capita GDP and the income distribution. We performed such a test for a sample of all developing countries, and the results support our intuition that industrialization can play an important role in accelerating the pace of poverty reduction.[30] Controlling for income growth and income distribution, a 1 percent increase in industrial employment is associated with a 0.8 percent reduction in the poverty headcount ratio.[31]

While the cross-country evidence is suggestive that industrial development can accelerate poverty reduction, it is unlikely to convince skeptics. Another way to get at the same question is to undertake some simulations. There are twelve African countries where sector-specific poverty headcounts at the level of three broad sectors—agriculture, industry (including manufacturing), and services—are available. We can use these data to estimate what the outcome in terms of poverty would have been, had these countries gone through a pattern of structural change more in line with other countries moving from low to middle income.

Because economic structure is itself a function of per capita income, we need a "counterfactual" distribution of employment for each of the twelve African countries at their current levels of development. To arrive at such a counterfactual we again identified a sample of non-African countries, mainly in Asia, that had achieved or were rapidly transitioning to middle-income status. We averaged the shares of employment in agriculture, industry, and services of the benchmark countries at the time they were at the level of per

29. See, for example, Fosu (2011).

30. For those interested in the econometrics, we also controlled for unobserved time-invariant, country-specific effects To address possible endogeneity of the sectoral shares of employment, per capita income, and the Gini coefficient, the model was estimated by the generalized method of moments (GMM) using internal instruments (two period lags).

31. Page and Shimeles (2015).

Table 1-3. *Actual and Counterfactual Employment Distributions*

Country	Share of total labor force		
	Agriculture	*Industry*	*Services*
Least developed countries (US$600–700)	70.0	12.0	18.0
Ethiopia 2005	83.2	5.6	11.2
Malawi 2004	77.6	6.0	16.4
Low-income countries (US$900–1,100)	60.9	14.4	24.7
Mali 2005	66.0	6.0	28.0
Rwanda 2010	79.0	4.0	17.0
Tanzania 2005	76.7	4.8	18.5
Uganda 2005	72.0	5.0	23.0
Zambia 2005	72.9	6.5	20.6
Transitioning and lower-middle-income countries (US$1,200–1,500)	57.9	16.7	25.4
Ghana 2005	48.1	15.1	36.8
Kenya 2010	48.3	16.4	35.3
Nigeria 2010	59.6	5.9	34.5
Senegal 2005	52.8	13.0	34.2
Upper-middle-income countries (US$10,000)	14.0	29.0	57.0
Botswana 2005	39.2	14.3	46.5
Mauritius 2010	7.2	30.3	62.6
South Africa 2010	15.0	23.2	61.8

Sources: McMillan and Rodrik (2011) database; World Bank World Development Indicators (WDI) database; de Vries, Timmer, and de Vries (2013). Authors' calculations.

Notes: Least developed country benchmark: BGD (1994), CAM (1996), CHN (1987), IND (1989), IDN (1982), VNM (1992); Low-income benchmark: BGD (2003), CAM (2002), CHN (1992), IND (1994), IDN (1986), THL (1980), VNM (1996); Transitioning economies benchmark: CAM (2005), CHN (1995), IND (2000), IDN (1992), PHL (1982), THL (1985), VNM (2001); Middle-income benchmark: CHL (2003), KOR (1993), MYS (2004).

capita income of each of the twelve African economies at the time the poverty statistics were collected. The distributions of employment for the African sample and the counterfactual distribution appropriate to their level of income at the time the poverty rates were estimated are shown in table 1-3. In general the African economies have a higher share of their labor force engaged in agriculture and services and a lower share engaged in industry than the counterfactuals at each income level.

Table 1-4. *Structural Change and Poverty Simulations*

Country	Observed poverty headcount	Simulated poverty headcount	Percentage change in headcount
Ethiopia 2005	41.6	39.7	−4.6
Malawi 2011	65.6	63.5	−3.2
Mali 2005	47.4	47.4	0.0
Rwanda 2005	52.8	48.5	−8.1
Tanzania 2007	62.6	55.2	−11.8
Uganda 2005	36.2	34.0	−6.1
Zambia 2003	64.9	63.4	−2.3
Ghana 2005	22.6	22.9	1.3
Nigeria 2010	66.8	66.6	0.0
Senegal 2005	31.1	40.3	29.6
Botswana 2005	34.4	30.7	−10.8
South Africa 2006	15.9	11.6	−27.0

Source: Authors' calculations as described in text.

We then carried out our simulations using the sector-specific poverty headcount data and the counterfactual distribution of employment based on the structural characteristics of the non-African economies.[32] In effect we asked: What would the poverty outcome of the countries in Africa have been if structural change had been more in line with the observed experience of other economies at the same level of per capita income? The results of these simulations are given in table 1-4.

While there is considerable variation in the country-by-country results the main takeaway is clear. Had Africa's economies gone through patterns of structural change that were more in line with those of the counterfactual economies—a faster decline in the share of the labor force in agriculture and a more rapid increase in the employment share of industry—poverty reduction would have been greater. The median poverty headcount for the twelve countries in the sample falls by about 4 percentage points in the simulation. The reductions in the headcount are largest for the country groups—

32. For a more detailed description of the method, see Page (2015a).

high-income economies and low-income economies—that most diverge from the structural characteristics of their benchmark.

Creating Opportunities for Women

In addition to generating good jobs and accelerating poverty reduction, industrialization has the power to transform women's lives. Manufacturing growth has been known to be associated with increases in female labor force participation for a long time. This adds to household incomes and may increase women's independence. More recently, evidence has begun to accumulate that manufacturing improves the welfare of women workers in other ways. There is some evidence that access to factory jobs increases the chances that girls will stay in school and postpone marriage by increasing the returns to education and by raising the opportunity cost of being married.

The garment industry in Bangladesh currently employs more than 3 million women, about 15 percent of women between the ages of sixteen and thirty. It was the first industry to provide large-scale employment opportunities to women in a country where traditionally they have not worked outside the home. In addition to creating jobs, the arrival of the garment factories has affected women's school enrollment, marriage, and childbearing decisions. Young women are entering school in greater numbers, staying in school longer, and postponing marriage and childbirth.[33]

Because garment manufacturing jobs reward basic literacy and numeracy, school enrollments in villages within commuting distance to garment factories have responded strongly to the arrival of textile plants. Enrollment rates in villages near textile plants increased by nearly 40 percentage points compared with villages that did not have a garment factory nearby. Women appear to be seizing these

33. Rivoli (2005) points out that in the United States at the turn of the twentieth century, textile factories in the South played a similar role in women's decisions to stay in school and postpone marriage.

educational opportunities in higher numbers than men. Girls living in a "typical" (median) village near a textile plant stay in school for an extra 1.5 years relative to their brothers. In these villages there was a 50 percent increase in girls' educational attainment compared to nonfactory villages. Access to manufacturing employment has also helped to reduce early marriage and childbirth. Girls in villages near factories are choosing to work when they are about seventeen to twenty-three years old instead of getting married.[34]

A similar transformation in the working lives of women has taken place in Lesotho. From the early 1980s to 2010, Lesotho's manufacturing sector expanded from about 6 to 18 percent of GDP. This was driven mainly by strong growth of apparel exports, and it was accompanied by a significant increase in female wage employment. In recent years the garment industry has employed between 35,000 and 43,000 workers, and women make up between 70 and 75 percent of the workforce. In some activities, such as cutting and sewing, women represent between 90 and 95 percent of workers.

Apparel exports have created a large number of new jobs for relatively unskilled women, more than 60 percent of whom come from rural areas. While wages are low, they exceed earnings in agriculture and self-employment. Core labor standards regarding working conditions are respected by the industry. Little is known yet about the impact of employment on women's education, marriage, and fertility decisions, but employment in Lesotho's garment industry has affected their welfare in another very important way. In a country where, by some estimates, as many as 40 percent of workers are HIV-positive, women working in the factories have access to innovative workplace health programs that provide free HIV care and treatment. The fact that workers can go to the clinics while they are on the factory premises is of great importance. It means that they do not miss a working day.[35]

34. Heath and Mobarak (2014).
35. UNCTAD (2012).

Manufacturing and Convergence

In an open world economy, poor countries should grow faster than rich ones. Conventional economic theory suggests that the return to investment will be higher in poor, capital-scarce economies, and global export and capital markets in principle break the constraints imposed by domestic markets and national savings. Thus, investment rates in poorer economies should rise, and over the long run as capital per person grows, income per person in developing countries should increase to the levels of the world's richer economies. This is called convergence.

In reality, convergence has been the exception rather than the rule. Except in East Asia, sustained rapid growth in poor countries has been rare, and only a handful of low-income countries have reached high income levels. Economists have accommodated this reality in two ways. In theory, new growth models have evolved that do not impose diminishing returns to capital.[36] In empirical work, convergence in developing economies has been shown to depend on a variety of country-specific factors that range from weak institutions to poor geography to inappropriate policies. The argument is that these hurdles must be overcome for investment to increase and become more productive. Only once the constraints are removed will developing nations begin to converge to rich-country income levels. This has come to be called "conditional convergence."

Manufacturing is apparently the exception. In manufacturing, convergence is "unconditional." Dani Rodrik has found that since 1960, output per worker in manufacturing has increased to advanced economy levels, regardless of country-specific or regional factors. This turns out to be as true for Africa as for any other region. An equally important finding of Rodrik's research is that unconditional convergence is not characteristic of agriculture or services.[37]

Unconditional convergence in manufacturing opens up two channels for economywide growth. The first is productivity growth within

---

36. For a survey of these "endogenous growth models," see Romer (1994).
37. See Rodrik (2013).

manufacturing itself. Its importance to overall productivity growth depends on the size of the manufacturing sector, the economy's distance from best practice productivity levels, and the rate of convergence. The second channel is structural change into manufacturing.

Because the manufacturing sector has the potential to converge unconditionally to high levels of productivity, a shift in employment out of agriculture into manufacturing—the pattern of structural change seen in Asia—can be strongly growth enhancing.[38] Economywide growth depends crucially, however, on the size of the modern manufacturing sector and its rate of growth—in short, on the pace of industrialization. This is not good news for Africa. Africa's manufacturing sector is small and its pace of industrialization has been slow for more than forty years.

What You Make Matters

Two more stylized facts related to the structure of industry itself add to the case for industrialization. First, more diversified production and export structures are associated with higher incomes per capita. As income per person rises, the range of industrial activities becomes more diverse until quite high levels of income are reached.[39] Second, countries that produce and export more sophisticated products—those that are primarily manufactured by countries at higher income levels—tend to grow faster.[40] We have found that differences in diversification and sophistication are strongly related to differences in long-run growth in developing countries.

We divided a large sample of low- and middle-income countries into a four-way classification based on growth performance and income level. Slow-growing countries were defined as those with average growth below the median for all countries in the sample between

38. Rodrik (2014).
39. See, for example, Imbs and Wacziarg (2003), Hummels and Klenow (2005), and Cadot, Carrère, and Strauss-Kahn (2011).
40. See Hausmann, Hwang, and Rodrik (2007) and UNIDO (2009).

1975 and 2005. Fast-growing countries are those with average growth above the median. The countries were split between low- and middle-income status on the basis of their ranking in the World Bank classification system in 1975. We then estimated the level of sophistication of production and exports in three groups of products for each country grouping between 1975 and 2005.

Next, we used the four-way classification to explore the relationship between sophistication in production and exports and long-run growth. Figure 1-2 shows how the production structure of developing country manufacturing evolved in terms of sophistication between 1975 and 1985 and 1995 and 2005. Our focus is on two classes of industrial activity, low- and high-sophistication products.[41] The vertical axis gives the average share of the country-product group in total production relative to the world as a whole. This is defined as "production intensity." A value of one means that the average share of the product group in total output is equal to the global average; values less than one indicate that the product represents a smaller share of national production than of global production, and vice versa.

Each vertical bar shows the average production intensity for the periods 1975–85 and 2000–05 for the country-product group. Increases in intensity indicate that the share of the product group in national output is increasing relative to its share in global output. Thus, changes in this ratio show whether an economy is entering or leaving a sector relative to the evolving structure of global production.

The results strongly support the assertion that "what you make matters." Between 1975 and 1985 and 1995 and 2005, fast-growing low-income countries diversified their production structures by increasing the production intensity of both low-sophistication and high-sophistication manufactured goods. Production among the slow growers—mainly countries in Africa—on the other hand became

---

41. Manufacturing activities are classified as "sophisticated" if they have an index value of US$13,500 or above for the period after 1995 (regardless of their values in the earlier periods). Unsophisticated activities are classified as those with values below US$10,000 in 1995. The omitted category of products lies between those two bounds.

Figure 1-2. *Production Intensity by Country and Product Group, 1975–85 and 1995–2005*

Low sophistication products

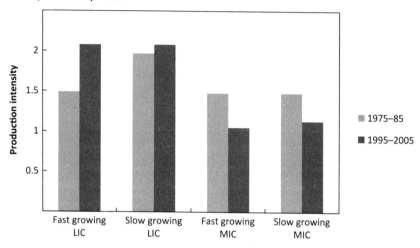

High sophistication products

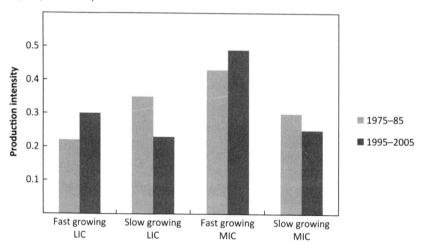

Source: UNIDO (2009) Production Sophistication database. Authors' calculations.
Notes: The vertical axis represents the production intensity; a value of one indicates world average intensity.
The division between low and high sophistication is based on the sector rankings presented in UNIDO (2009).
The high-sophistication group is made up of the Fabricated Metals (381), Machinery (382), Electrical
Machinery (383), Transport (384), Equipment (385), Furniture (332), and Printing and Publishing (342) sectors.
The low-sophistication group is made up of the Food (311), Beverages (312), Tobacco (313), Textiles (321),
Leather (323), Footwear (324), and Rubber (355) sectors.

more concentrated in low-sophistication products. They also became less sophisticated. Production of high-sophistication manufacturers in slowly growing low-income countries declined dramatically in relation to the structure of world manufacturing output. Middle-income countries tell a similar tale. Fast and slow growers have quite distinct patterns of production intensity. Fast growers that were highly concentrated in high-sophistication products in 1980 became more sophisticated; slow growers did not.

Figure 1-3 repeats the analysis for exports. The interpretation of export intensity is the same as for production intensity, except the base is the global structure of exports. This is analogous to calculating revealed comparative advantage. The results for export intensity indicate that what you export matters as well. Fast-growing low-income countries showed a strong revealed comparative advantage in low-sophistication exports, as they moved decisively into the export space vacated by the rapidly growing middle-income countries. The fast growers also nearly doubled the intensity of high-sophistication exports. Slowly growing low-income countries only modestly increased the intensity of low-sophistication exports, and export intensities of high-sophistication manufactures were virtually unchanged over two decades. Fast-growing middle-income countries exited low-sophistication exports and rapidly increased the intensity of high-sophistication exports, in marked contrast to their slow-growing counterparts.

Our results suggest that economies that succeed in moving up in terms of the diversity and sophistication of their manufacturing sector have greater prospects for sustained long-term growth. One reason may be that more diverse economies are better able to take advantage of opportunities in global markets. Industrial diversification appears to take place at lower levels of per capita income than export diversification.[42] This is consistent with the idea that firms build competence in new activities locally and then enter global markets.

Diversification into more sophisticated products provides an additional advantage. Because sophisticated products embody advanced

42. UNIDO (2009).

Figure 1-3. *Export Intensity by Country and Product Group,*
1975–85 and 1995–2005

Low sophistication exports

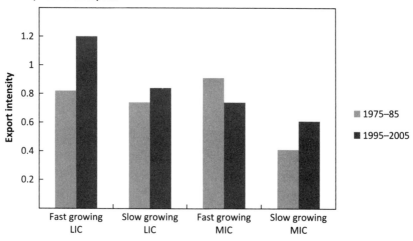

High sophistication exports

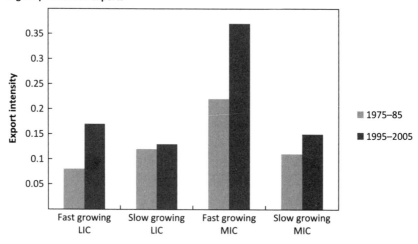

Source: UNIDO (2009) Production Sophistication database. Authors' calculations.
Notes: The vertical axis represents the export intensity; a value of one indicates world average intensity.
The division between low and high sophistication is based on the sector rankings presented in UNIDO (2009).
The high-sophistication group is made up of the Fabricated Metals (381), Machinery (382), Electrical Machinery
(383), Transport (384), Equipment (385), Furniture (332), and Printing and Publishing (342) sectors. The
low-sophistication group is made up of the Food (311), Beverages (312), Tobacco (313), Textiles (321),
Leather (323), Footwear (324), and Rubber (355) sectors.

country productivity levels, the ability of firms in lower income countries to produce and, especially, to export such goods indicates that they have mastered both the technology and the management practices required to be globally competitive in price and quality. These are "high capability" firms in the sense that we shall discuss in chapter 5, and economies with large numbers of high capability firms have a strong base for productivity change and long-run growth.[43]

Like many of the structural characteristics that we discuss in this book, the roles of convergence, diversity, and sophistication appear to change during the process of economic development. At low levels of per capita income, unconditional convergence to best practice productivity levels, driven by better knowledge of production and technological catch-up, is likely to be the primary source of productivity change in manufacturing. Because the impact of convergence depends on the size of the manufacturing sector and the rate of its growth, structural transformation driven by the expansion of industry, even in relatively unsophisticated activities, can be a significant source of productivity growth in low-income countries. As incomes rise, productivity growth from sectoral reallocation is eventually exhausted, and firm-level sources of productivity growth become increasingly important.[44] Diversity and sophistication are then likely to play a larger role in sustaining productivity growth in manufacturing and overall economic growth by contributing to the accumulation of firm capabilities.

Summing Up

This chapter has presented our case for industrial development in Africa. We believe it is a strong one. Africa has seen a "growth

43. Sutton (2012).

44. One strand of the literature on "middle-income traps" explores the implications of this shift for economies trying to break into high-income status. See, for example, Eichengreen, Park, and Shin (2011) and Gill and Kharas (2007).

miracle" over the last two decades. However, until quite recently this remarkable growth took place without the kinds of changes in economic structure that were the hallmarks of the economic transformations of today's high-income industrialized economies and, more recently, of the rapidly growing economies in East Asia. In fact, until the turn of this century structural change in Africa may have reduced its overall rate of growth of output per person. The missing player in Africa's growth story has been industry. Even for its level of income, the relative size of Africa's industrial sector and especially manufacturing is smaller than expected. Given the aspirations of Africa's economies to place themselves solidly among the ranks of middle-income countries by 2025–30, this deficit will need to close.

Industry matters for Africa in multiple ways. Africa has only recently begun to experience growth-enhancing structural change, but these changes have been unlike those experienced elsewhere. The shift in employment has been from agriculture to services, where output per worker is less than a third of manufacturing. Africa's inability to create enough higher output per worker jobs in the face of a rapidly growing labor force has reduced the impact of growth on wage employment and poverty reduction. Industry can make a positive contribution to solving these problems. Industry is an engine of growth-enhancing structural change. Manufacturing, tradable services, and agro-industry are all labor-intensive, high productivity sectors into which workers leaving agriculture can move. This movement is critical for the growth of wage employment and poverty reduction.

Manufacturing also has a special role to play in sustaining growth. Modern manufacturing industries converge to best practice productivity levels regardless of geographical disadvantages, poor institutions, or bad policies. This provides a powerful engine of productivity growth and increases the potential for growth-enhancing structural change. When productivity growth within the manufacturing sector and structural change work in tandem, the growth payoff can be large. Within the manufacturing sector what a country makes matters. At higher levels of income per capita, more diverse and sophisticated production and export structures increase the chances for sustained growth.

While these characteristics of industry open up new possibilities for growth, job creation, and poverty reduction, success mainly depends on the pace of industrialization. That is not good news. Today, sub-Saharan Africa is more or less where it started in terms of industrial development half a century ago. The policy choices and external circumstances that helped to shape this trajectory are the subject of the next chapter.

PART II

REALITIES *and* OPPORTUNITIES

CHAPTER 2

Industrialization Efforts and Outcomes

The idea that Africa should industrialize is not new. The Continent's postindependence leaders—like those in many developing countries in the 1960s and 1970s—looked to industrialization as the key to rapid economic growth and transformation of their societies. Those aspirations have not been fulfilled. Both regionally and at the individual country level Africa has ended up in 2015 more or less where it started in terms of industrial development in the 1970s. Today Africa stands out as the least industrialized region of the developing world.

This chapter begins with an overview of Africa's industrialization since independence. It then surveys the industrialization experiences of ten African countries in greater detail. Nine were the subjects of our Learning to Compete (L2C) country studies: Ethiopia, Ghana, Kenya, Mozambique, Nigeria, Senegal, Tanzania, Tunisia, and Uganda. We chose to add a tenth country, Mauritius, because it is, apart from South Africa, sub-Saharan Africa's most successful industrializing economy. The eight sub-Saharan countries that we studied were among Africa's early industrializers, and they are some of its current growth leaders. Six of the eight have been among the region's fastest-growing economies since 2000. In many ways they are representative of sub-Saharan Africa as a whole.[1] Together they account for 54 percent of the region's GDP and 56 percent of its population. They are all making the transition from low- to lower-middle-income status. Ethiopia is the poorest. Nigeria—an oil exporter—is the region's largest economy. Tunisia in North Africa, like Mauritius, has had a very different industrialization experience from the sub-Saharan countries.

Despite major differences in history, language, and political structure, the sub-Saharan countries that we studied share a striking uniformity in their approach to industrialization. These experiences are described in this chapter. Broadly, policies to encourage industrial development were implemented in three phases: state-led import substitution, structural adjustment, and investment climate reform. Industrial performance has also taken place in three phases, albeit with some variations across countries: a postindependence boom that ended in collapse, retrenchment and stagnation, and more recently modest growth that in most cases has failed to keep pace with overall GDP growth. We conclude the chapter by posing the question: Is Africa's failure to industrialize due to bad luck or bad policy?

Ending Up Where It Started: Industry in Africa since Independence

Beginning in the late 1950s, newly independent governments virtually everywhere in Africa sought to promote state-led industrialization. Protected from international competition and pushed by public

1. Except where specifically noted, the country narratives and statistics in this chapter are drawn from these country case studies. To avoid excessive referencing, case studies and their authors are listed in a separate section of the references. The country studies are available as Brookings Learning to Compete Working Papers (www.brookings.edu/about/projects/africa-growth/learning-to-compete) and as WIDER Working Papers (www.wider.unu.edu/research/current-programme/en_GB/L2C-2010/).

investment, industry took off in the 1960s. The boom was short-lived. By the 1980s growth of industrial output, manufactured exports, and manufacturing sophistication across Africa had all begun a long decline.

From Boom to Bust

Figure 2-1 traces the share of manufacturing in GDP for sub-Saharan Africa (excluding South Africa) from 1960 to 2012. Manufacturing boomed in most African economies in the decade following independence. For sub-Saharan Africa as a whole, manufacturing growth averaged 8.3 percent per year between 1960 and 1970, about twice as fast as overall output growth. The share of manufacturing in GDP increased from 6.3 percent in 1960 to around 11 percent in 1970.

In the 1970s manufacturing growth decelerated, failing to keep pace with the rate of growth of total output. This abrupt break in momentum was not the result of a fall in investment in industry. It was the result of a major decline in the productivity of investment due, in large part, to underutilization of capacity because of shortages of imported intermediate inputs. Industrial performance—especially in the state-owned sector—was also compromised by policies that emphasized large investments and employment at the expense of firm-level productivity.[2] A short-lived recovery of manufacturing took place in the 1980s. Between 1980 and 1988 the region's manufacturing share of GDP rose to a peak of about 12 to 13 percent, but since then Africa has deindustrialized. The share of manufacturing in GDP declined continuously from 1990 to around 2006, when it stabilized at about 10 percent of GDP, the same level as in 1965.

The long decline in manufacturing production was reflected in a similar decline in manufactured exports. Over the past thirty years, despite rapidly growing global demand for manufactures produced in developing countries, African manufacturing has been unable to maintain its share of global markets. While developing countries as

2. Meier and Steel (1989).

Figure 2-1. *Manufacturing as a Percentage of GDP in Sub-Saharan Africa, 1965–2012*

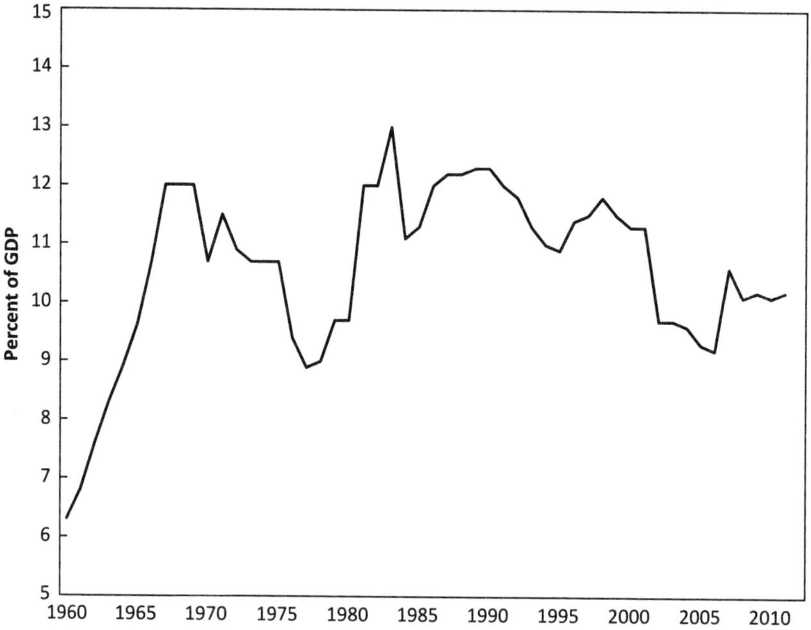

Sources: UNIDO Industrial Development database (2015); World Bank Africa Development Indicators (2014).
Note: Series excludes South Africa.

a whole increased their share of global manufactured exports from about 10 percent in 1980 to 29.6 percent in 2011, Africa's share of global manufactured exports fell from about 3 percent to 2.8 percent, about half of which was produced by South Africa alone.

The main reason the region has been unable to keep pace with the rest of the developing world is that global manufacturing capacity has moved out of Africa. Export growth can be decomposed into three parts: global growth of demand, shifts in the location of global production, and changes in export orientation. In the 1980s and 1990s, despite growing global demand and increasing export orientation of Africa's economies, industrial export production was moving out of Africa. It was the only region in the developing world in which the geographical shift of production capacity for manufactured exports was consistently negative.[3] Manufacturing was moving "out of Africa."

Declining Diversity and Sophistication

In chapter 1, we showed that diversity and sophistication of production and exports are important predictors of long-term growth. As manufacturing output and exports declined between 1975 and 2005, Africa's manufacturing base became less diverse and less sophisticated. Production became increasingly concentrated in low-sophistication goods, and the region exited high-sophistication activities. Using the data from chapter 1, we have computed the economywide average level of production sophistication in eighteen African countries in the 1980s and in the 2000s.[4] We also estimated the cross-section "average" level of manufacturing sophistication associated with a given level of per capita income from the global UNIDO database in the same years.

Figure 2-2 presents the results. Because the relationship between per capita income and production sophistication rises with income, it is best to compare each country's observed level of sophistication in manufacturing with the predicted value based on its per capita income from the global sample.[5] Countries above their predicted values, those with a ratio greater than 1, produce a basket of goods typical of economies at higher levels of income. We are most interested in these "positive outliers." The basic premise of "what you make matters" suggests that countries that consistently produce goods that are more sophisticated than predicted from their level of income will grow faster.

---

3. Page (2013).

4. The level of sophistication of each economy's industrial sector is the weighted average of each country's individual product sophistication measures, where the weights are the share of manufacturing value added of each sector.

5. Because the indices of product and export sophistication are measured in current U.S. dollars, it is not possible to compare sophistication levels from year to year directly, because they are affected by price changes.

Figure 2-2. *Country-Level Production Sophistication in 18 African Countries, 1995–2005 and 1975–85*

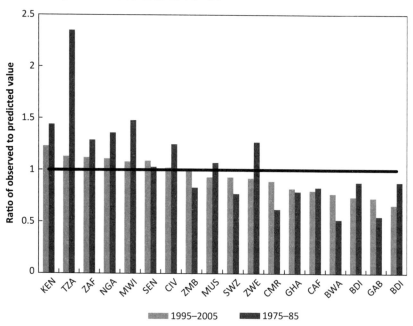

Source: UNIDO (2009) Production Sophistication database. Authors' calculations.
Notes: Countries are ordered by their percentage of the predicted value of production sophistication in 1995–2005.
Values greater than one indicate that the observed level of sophistication exceeds the predicted value at the level of
per capita income.

The African economies in figure 2-2 stand out in two important respects. First, a majority of countries are either at or below the level of sophistication predicted from their level of per capita income in the years from 1995 to 2005. Only seven of the eighteen countries exceeded their predicted values. The majority of African countries were producing manufactured goods that were characteristic of countries at lower levels of income than their own. Second, the sophistication of the manufacturing sector declined in eleven of the eighteen economies between the 1980s and the 2000s. The fall was especially sharp in several of Africa's early industrializers—Ivory Coast, Kenya, Nigeria, Tanzania, and Zimbabwe. By way of contrast, over the same period the Asian countries in the UNIDO sample were all producing goods typical of economies at higher levels of per capita income.[6]

Industrial Policy and Performance: 1960 to the Present

Broadly speaking, industrial policy in the African countries we studied has gone through three phases: state ownership and import substitution, structural adjustment, and investment climate reform. Industrial performance has also been broadly the same across countries: a postindependence boom that ended in collapse, retrenchment and stagnation, and more recently modest growth. Here, we review these three periods of industrial development efforts and outcomes.

State Ownership and Import Substitution (1960–85)

When Africa gained independence, leaders in former English, French, and Portuguese colonies shared similar views on the key role of industrialization, strongly shaped by a desire to modernize their mainly agrarian economies and reduce dependence on the former colonial powers.[7] The centerpiece of the industrialization effort was the development of large-scale, often capital-intensive manufacturing industries owned and managed by the state. Protection of the domestic market against imports was viewed as necessary for successful industrial development and was particularly appealing to postcolonial leaders as a way of securing "economic independence." The state became the central actor in the industrialization story for a variety of reasons, some reflecting political ideology.[8] Nationalism was certainly a key motivation. Newly independent African governments invested heavily in state-owned enterprises (SOEs) for the

6. UNIDO (2009).
7. See Killick (1978) for an excellent survey of the strategies pursued by Africa's postindependence leaders.
8. See Ndulu (2007).

domestic production of intermediate and consumer goods and to process exports of primary products.

Arguably, Ghana took the lead. When it gained independence from Britain in 1957, President Kwame Nkrumah embraced industrialization to transform the economy and to reduce dependence on the United Kingdom. His industrial development program emphasized import substitution, supported by high levels of tariff protection. It was Nkrumah's belief that every imported item that could be manufactured locally added to Ghana's continuing economic dependence on the colonial system. The government invested heavily in infrastructure and manufacturing, including producers' goods. The electrical, electronic, and machinery industries in particular were viewed as essential to provide the inputs needed to expand the industrial sector. Four other countries—Nigeria, Senegal, Tanzania, and Uganda—followed very similar approaches upon gaining independence in the 1960s. Kenya, in contrast, adopted a postindependence industrialization strategy that while relying on import substitution gave a smaller role to the state. State ownership and management was limited to a few "strategic industries."

Two governments followed more explicitly central planning approaches to industrialization. In 1974 the Ethiopian Revolution brought the Marxist Dergue government to power. It nationalized most privately owned medium- and large-scale manufacturing enterprises and increased protection of the domestic market. After independence in 1975, the Frelimo government in Mozambique introduced a set of policies designed to make the public sector the leading economic actor. Both countries invested heavily in SOEs with widespread donor support and sheltered them from competition through domestic regulations and control of imports.

Tunisia and Mauritius were the outliers on the Continent. At the beginning of the 1960s the Tunisian government embraced import substitution and state ownership, but by the 1970s it had adopted an *infitâh* policy that combined import substitution and export promotion. The economy was divided into an offshore sector, dominated by foreign investors and geared toward exports, and an onshore sector, shielded from competition and regulated by the state. The onshore private sector primarily consisted of small factory units that focused on production of simple consumer goods for the domestic market. Heavy industry, transport, water, and electricity were state-owned sectors.

By the time of Mauritius independence in 1968, an incentive regime designed to encourage import substitution by private investors had yielded very little industrial investment. In 1970 the government shifted gears and began attempting to attract local and foreign private investment into exports.[9] An export processing zone (EPZ) was created that offered duty-free entry of inputs, free repatriation of capital, and greater flexibility in labor relations. EPZ factories were scattered throughout the island in small or individual industrial sites. The government provided infrastructure and factory spaces as part of an incentive framework designed to increase cost-competitiveness. These policies attracted both foreign and domestic investors to the EPZs, mainly in the production of textiles and clothing.

A Short-Lived Boom

Protection from import competition and public investment strongly pushed industrial development in the postindependence period (table 2-1). Between 1965 and 1970 manufacturing output grew at more than 7 percent per year in all countries (except in Mozambique, which was still in its liberation struggle). In Ethiopia and Ghana, manufacturing grew at more than 8 percent, and in Tanzania and Uganda at nearly 10 percent per year. As early as 1970, however, the industrialization drive was beginning to lose steam in some countries, and by 1975 growth of the manufacturing sector had begun to lag total output growth in Ghana, Senegal, and Tanzania. Kenya and Nigeria, in contrast, maintained robust manufacturing growth throughout the 1970s.

9. Rodrik (1997).

Table 2-1. *Average Annual Growth of Value Added in Manufacturing, 1970–2010*

Country	1965–70	1970–75	1975–80	1980–85	1985–90	1990–95	1995–2000	2000–05	2005–10
Ethiopia	8.45	3.20	4.56	3.91	1.51	1.03	3.92	5.00	9.48
Ghana	8.22	1.43	–4.74	–4.36	7.53	–7.38	4.68	4.54	2.60
Kenya	7.43	7.67	11.46	3.84	5.75	2.52	–0.03	3.09	4.38
Mozambique	n.a.	n.a.	n.a.	n.a.	n.a.	–1.31	18.97	15.17	3.01
Nigeria	5.52	12.20	13.59	–0.99	4.10	–1.07	0.25	8.85	8.43
Senegal	n.a.	3.17	1.27	2.64	4.05	3.19	2.90	3.11	2.02
Tanzania	9.95	4.73	2.36	–5.01	2.43	–0.02	5.73	8.09	8.61
Uganda	n.a.	n.a.	n.a.	2.14	6.38	12.81	13.45	6.13	7.13
Mauritius	n.a.	15.53	18.47	8.49	11.09	4.95	5.69	–0.59	2.83
Tunisia	–0.74	20.50	13.63	6.39	0.50	5.66	5.78	2.79	4.88
Cambodia	n.a.	n.a.	n.a.	n.a.	n.a.	8.86	21.04	13.86	8.70
Vietnam	n.a.	n.a.	n.a.	9.50	2.42	10.35	11.26	11.66	9.33

Sources: 1965–90: de Vries, Timmer, and de Vries (2013); McMillan and Rodrik (2011); 1990–2010 UNIDO Statistics (2014) manufacturing value added database; Uganda 1980–90, Tunisia 1965–90, Vietnam 1985–90, Tunisia 1965–2010, Vietnam 1985–2010, World Bank World Development Indicators (WDI) database. Authors' calculations.

Notes: All growth rates in constant prices. n.a. = not available.

Lagging output growth and underutilization of capacity in manufacturing became more widespread in the early 1980s. Between 1980 and 1985, manufacturing growth turned negative in Ghana, Nigeria, and Tanzania. In the remaining countries growth of manufacturing failed to exceed 4 percent per year. The countries in industrial decline shared a number of common characteristics. Levels of effective tariff protection to the manufacturing sector were very high and the efficiency of production, measured in terms of international prices, was low. In some cases final-stage consumer goods were produced at negative value added in international prices—the cost of the imported intermediate inputs actually exceeded the border price of the fully manufactured import.

Contrary to the intent of the import substitution strategy, dependence on imports actually increased. This was largely due to two characteristics that were widely shared: (i) the import-substitution manufacturing industries were heavily dependent on imported intermediate and capital goods, and (ii) the relative neglect of agriculture led to rising food imports. Public investment had begun to exceed the fiscal capacity of the state and, perhaps more important, the state's capacity to manage the enterprises. There was substantial excess capacity in public manufacturing enterprises, many of which were heavily constrained by lack of imported intermediates and working capital.[10]

Only Tunisia and Mauritius with their two-track approach were able to sustain the pace of industrial growth. In Mauritius, manufacturing value added grew at about 17 percent per year between 1970 and 1980. Manufactured exports increased from zero to nearly 25 percent of total exports over the same period, and by 1985 apparel exports from the EPZ had overtaken sugar as the island's main foreign exchange earner.[11] In Tunisia, manufacturing grew at more than 15 percent per year throughout the 1970s. Between 1972 and 1977, 85,500 new jobs were created in manufacturing.

10. Steel and Evans (1989).
11. ACET (2014).

The *"Washington Consensus" and Structural Adjustment (1985–2000)*

In the early 1970s economists began to document the efficiency costs of excessive protection of the domestic market, and state-owned enterprises came under critical scrutiny.[12] Import substitution was increasingly viewed as a high-cost path to industrialization and public enterprises were widely found to be less efficient than privately owned firms.[13] Mainstream development economics moved from a focus on the potential failings of markets in developing countries to embrace a "market friendly" approach to public policy.[14]

A consensus—at least among the U.S. Treasury, the Federal Reserve, the International Monetary Fund (IMF), and the World Bank—emerged on the policies considered appropriate for developing countries. These included:

—Fiscal discipline
—Tax reform (to reduce marginal rates and broaden the tax base)
—Interest rate liberalization
—A competitive exchange rate
—Trade liberalization
—Liberalization of foreign direct investment
—Privatization
—Deregulation (ending barriers to entry and exit)
—Secure property rights
—Public expenditures focused on primary health care, primary education, and infrastructure

12. The major contributions to this literature were from Little, Scitovsky, and Scott (1970) and their colleagues at the OECD Development Centre; Balassa (1971) and his colleagues at the World Bank; and Bhagwati (1978) and Krueger (1978) at the NBER. For a recent contribution to the analysis of the complex measurement issues involved, see Jensen, Robinson, and Tarp (2010).

13. See, for example, World Bank (1983).

14. The term "market friendly" is from former World Bank chief economist Larry Summers. For a summary of the mainstream views on the role of markets in development, see the World Bank (1991).

John Williamson famously termed this list the "Washington Consensus," and it became the playbook for stabilization and structural adjustment lending by international financial institutions (IFIs), mainly the IMF and the World Bank.[15]

The Washington Consensus quickly found its way to Africa.[16] External shocks had left Africa's early industrializers with flagging economic growth and chronic foreign exchange shortages. Governments attempted to sustain growth through expansionary macroeconomic policies leading to widespread loss of fiscal and monetary control. Exchange rates became seriously overvalued, and most governments responded to the lack of foreign exchange by introducing exchange controls and rationing. Growth ground to a halt, and African governments turned to the IFIs. By 1988, eighteen African countries had initiated stabilization and structural adjustment programs with the World Bank and the IMF, and an additional fourteen had borrowed from the World Bank to support reforms at the sector level.[17]

The initial focus of public policy advice and conditionality in Africa was on macroeconomic stabilization. Better macroeconomic policies were defined as "keeping budget deficits and inflation low, establishing fully convertible currencies and competitive exchange rates, and increasing public savings."[18] Policy reforms designed to improve resource allocation—liberalization of trade and finance and regulatory reform—followed closely behind stabilization. Between 1985 and 2000, more than thirty African countries adopted adjustment programs that incorporated exchange rate and trade policy reforms.[19]

Privatization also became a major policy objective. Divestiture of state-owned enterprises was viewed as important for two reasons. First, it reduced the actual or contingent drain on the budget

15. Williamson (1990).
16. See Tarp (1993).
17. World Bank (1992).
18. World Bank (1992, p. 184)
19. World Bank (2000).

imposed by poor investment choices. Those enterprises that failed to elicit interest from private investors would be closed and liquidated as part of the fiscal consolidation. Second, the state had proved to be a poor entrepreneur. Even where firms were breaking even or providing a positive return to capital, the opportunity cost of the scarce managerial resources committed by the state to the public enterprises was high.[20]

In 1979 Senegal was the first to turn to the IFIs for a stabilization and structural adjustment program. Ghana, another pioneer, introduced its economic recovery program in April 1983. In Tanzania, an economic recovery program was adopted in the mid-1980s with the twin objectives of restoring macroeconomic stability and accelerating structural reforms. During the 1980s and 1990s, Kenya implemented several structural adjustment programs, and between 1986 and 1993, the IMF and World Bank supported a full range of Washington Consensus reforms in Nigeria. Mozambique began an economic rehabilitation program in 1987. Extensive trade and exchange rate reforms began in Uganda in 1987, and soon after it seized power in 1991, Ethiopia's new government announced that it would return to a market-led economy, supported by a structural adjustment program.

Even Mauritius and Tunisia did not escape. Between 1980 and 1986, Mauritius entered a stabilization and structural adjustment program with the IMF and the World Bank. The island's economy had combined the EPZ with a domestic manufacturing sector that was highly protected. Starting in the early 1980s, the government began to dismantle most of the quantitative restrictions that had sheltered the non-EPZ part of the economy from foreign competition. In the early 1990s there was significant tariff reform as well.[21]

At the end of the 1970s, Tunisia's foreign debt ballooned and the economy began to slow. Growth decelerated further in the period 1981–86, reaching its lowest average rate in decades, 2.8 percent per year, and productivity declined. Faced with growing internal im-

20. See Nellis (1986).
21. ACET (2014).

balances and ballooning external debt, Tunisia negotiated its first structural adjustment program in 1986. The program, which was in place from 1986 to 1990, featured tariff reductions, elimination of quantitative restrictions on imports, devaluation of the Tunisian dinar, and negotiations with creditors to extend the maturity on the country's foreign debt.

Structural Adjustment without Structural Change

Perhaps no episode in Africa's contemporary economic history generates as much debate and strong feeling as the structural adjustment period. Many countries—including those covered by our country studies—made major gains in macroeconomic management. By 1997 fiscal deficits in the thirty-one countries covered by the World Bank's Special Program of Assistance for Africa had dropped to 5.3 percent of GDP and averaged only 2.5 percent of GDP net of grant financing.[22] According to one estimate, the median African currency was 82 percent overvalued in purchasing power parity (PPP) terms in 1980. Between 1980 and 2000, there was a steady trend toward real devaluation of the exchange rate in most countries (including a major devaluation of the French-supervised CFA franc in 1994). By the early 1990s, the currency in the median African country was at PPP parity or undervalued.[23]

Across the Continent, governments liberalized trade, engaged in some deregulation of the domestic market, attempted to restructure state enterprises, and finally turned to privatization. Quantitative restrictions, once widespread, were replaced by tariffs. Tariffs were steadily lowered in most countries and their dispersion reduced. Average rates of 30 to 40 percent in 1980 had fallen to trade-weighted average tariffs of 15 percent or less by 2000.[24] Privatization was more controversial—and less vigorously pursued—than either macroeconomic stabilization or trade liberalization.[25]

22. World Bank (2000).
23. Easterly (2009).
24. World Bank (2000).
25. Nellis (2003).

The relationship between structural adjustment and industrial development was remarkably consistent across countries. The decline in industry—and in particular manufacturing—occurred in every country before structural reforms were undertaken. Indeed, the need to respond to a shortfall in manufacturing production was often one of the motivations for governments to undertake reforms. The early liberalizations of the foreign exchange market and the adjustment of exchange rates provided a temporary stimulus to industrial production, as firms increased utilization of capacity that had been heavily constrained by lack of imported intermediates and capital goods. During the period 1985–90, manufacturing output growth shifted from negative to positive in Ghana, Nigeria, and Tanzania, and growth accelerated in the remaining countries except Ethiopia and Tunisia.

The recovery was short-lived, however. Increased competitive pressure from imports and rising production costs due to reforms in the foreign exchange and financial markets put considerable pressure on manufacturing enterprises.[26] Import competition, lack of technical expertise, and the shortage of working capital resulted in most government-owned firms operating at as little as 10 percent of capacity. This trend was particularly acute in Ghana, Nigeria, and Tanzania and continued until the late 1990s when most state-owned firms were shut down awaiting privatization. By 1995 manufacturing growth rates had fallen below their 1985–90 averages, in some cases quite dramatically. In Ghana, for example, average growth of manufacturing went from 7.5 percent in the late 1980s to –7.4 percent in the early 1990s. Tanzania and Uganda were the exceptions. In Tanzania, average manufacturing-sector growth accelerated from –0.02 percent in 1990–95 to 5.7 percent in 1995–2000, and in Uganda manufacturing growth exceeded 10 percent per year throughout the 1990s.

In Mauritius the reforms, combined with active programs to support exporting firms, gave another boost to exports. Manufactured exports grew on average about 5 percent per year in the 1990s.

26. Meier and Steel (1989).

Local investors operating as contract manufacturers set up apparel businesses clustered around larger, mainly foreign firms. The Development Bank of Mauritius, a public development bank, provided capital to domestic EPZ investors. The government also built several industrial estates around the island and leased sites to investors at subsidized rates. By 2000, Mauritian companies owned about 60 percent of the apparel industry, and garments from the EPZ had reached 76 percent of total exports. Some firms had started to integrate their businesses vertically by producing textiles—spinning and weaving—as well as garments, and a few firms began to "offshore" their most labor-intensive manufacturing processes to neighboring countries such as Madagascar.[27]

Spurred by anemic manufacturing growth in the late 1980s, the government in Tunisia began the process of entering into a free trade agreement (FTA) with the European Union—one of the Euro-Mediterranean agreements—in the early 1990s and concluded the FTA in 1998. Liberalization of the domestic economy put increased competitive pressure on firms serving the local market. The government encouraged the modernization of the industrial sector through the EU-supported *Programme de mise à niveau,* launched in 1996. An industrial modernization program followed. The industrial sector responded with modest growth of about 6 percent per year during the period 1995–2000, led by rapid growth of exports. Exports to EU countries grew more than 10 percent annually.

Investment Climate Reform (2000 to Present)

By 2000 the stabilization programs in most countries had restored unified and appropriately valued exchange rates. Fiscal deficits were coming under control and inflation was beginning to subside. Africa began to experience its first positive per capita income growth around 1995, a trend that would accelerate through the first decade of the twenty-first century. Improved economic performance and increasing criticism of the Washington Consensus led to a retreat

27. ACET (2014).

from structural adjustment lending. The World Bank and many bilateral donors shifted their focus to the "investment climate"—the policy, institutional, and physical environment within which firms operated.

As defined by Nicholas Stern, the World Bank's chief economist in the early 2000s, the investment climate included (i) macroeconomic stability and openness; (ii) good governance and strong institutions, including the rule of law, control of corruption and crime, regulatory quality, and the effectiveness of public services; and (iii) the quality of the labor force and infrastructure.[28] In principle, programs to improve the investment climate would help consolidate the macroeconomic gains of the structural adjustment period, strengthen policy and institutional reforms, and allow some space for governments to set new priorities in public expenditure in the areas of infrastructure and education.

Most African countries have implemented a number of investment climate reforms since 2000. Ghana's industrialization strategy has prominently featured investment climate reforms focused on macroeconomic policies, trade policies, and reforms to the regulatory framework. In Kenya, investment climate programs were undertaken to improve power supply, liberalize the overall regulatory climate, and introduce tax reforms. Ethiopia's Industrial Development Strategy, formulated in 2003, focused on macroeconomic stability, access to finance, dependable infrastructure, and skilled and effective human resources. Since completing its adjustment program, Nigeria's approach to industrial development has sought to make the industrial sector internationally competitive, reduce the role of the government in the direct production of goods, and strengthen its role in regulation and export promotion.

The 2005 Senegal Accelerated Growth Strategy set as its principal objective establishing a business environment consistent with international good practice. In 2007 Mozambique adopted a new Industrial Policy and Strategy in which a significant role was assigned

28. See Stern (2001, 2002).

to promoting private investment. Uganda's National Industrial Policy, published in 2008, highlights reforms such as development of efficient and reliable infrastructure, promotion of entrepreneurship, and development of a skilled labor force, and in 2010 Tanzania introduced an Integrated Industrial Development Strategy aimed at creating a competitive business environment, improving existing development corridors, and concentrating infrastructure development on constraints to industrial growth.

Investment climate reform also played a prominent role in Tunisia. While the government continued its programs of gradual liberalization of the domestic economy and industrial upgrading, the World Bank, the African Development Bank, and the European Union engaged in a series of joint development policy lending operations in the mid-2000s, designed in part to improve the investment climate. As in Africa south of the Sahara, the centerpiece of these investment climate reforms was regulatory reform and, to lesser degree, upgrading of the institutions dealing with the private sector.[29]

Mauritius chose to continue to take a more active approach to industrial development. Beginning in the mid-1990s the export strategy came under severe stress from rising wages and the phasing out of the Multi-Fiber Arrangement. Many Asian-based investors left when their tax holidays lapsed. In response, the Mauritius Export Development and Investment Authority increased efforts to find new markets and new investors for the EPZ. The Mauritius Standards Bureau and the Industrial and Vocational Training Board responded to the needs of the textile and clothing sector, and the University of Mauritius became involved in developing skills and technology for clothing. Computerized sewing and stitching machines, backed by rigorous quality systems like ISO 9000,

29. Ironically, the World Bank (2008b) praised the Ben Ali government, now widely condemned for its legacy of crony capitalism, as a leading reformer in its *Doing Business* report the year before the Jasmine Revolution. See Page (2012b).

became a priority for most companies. A Mauritius Technology Diffusion Scheme provided grants to firms that wanted to procure technical services to improve productivity, quality, and design and promote quality assurance standards and systems in garments. Mauritian textile and clothing exports grew 25 percent between 2005 and 2012.[30]

Not Yet a Turning Point

The widespread adoption of investment climate reforms has not reversed the decline in African manufacturing. Since 2000 industrial performance in the countries covered by L2C has been uneven. The good news is that there appears to have been some acceleration in the growth rate of manufacturing in Ethiopia, Kenya, Nigeria, and Tanzania. On the other hand, growth of manufacturing in Ghana and Senegal has remained low and has lagged the overall growth of the economy. Mozambique had very rapid manufacturing growth during 2000–05, driven mostly by the Mozal Aluminum Smelter Mega Project, which came to an abrupt end during 2005–10. In Uganda, manufacturing growth averaged more than 6 percent per year during 2000–10, but this represented a major slowdown from the pace of industrialization in the 1990s. For sub-Saharan Africa as a whole, manufacturing growth has been less than the growth of GDP since the turn of the century.

In both Mauritius and Tunisia there are indications that the structural shifts in sectors and industries that we would expect of a middle-income country are taking place. The manufacturing sector in Mauritius has been growing more slowly than GDP since 2000, and the share of manufacturing has declined to about 20 percent of total output. The service sector, including tradable services, has now become the dominant sector of the economy. In Tunisia manufacturing growth after 2000 slowed to the range of 2 to 5 percent per year. This was accompanied by rapid development of the service sector, including information technology (IT) based services and tourism.

30. ACET (2014).

Bad Luck or Bad Policy?

Africa's failure to industrialize is partly due to bad luck. The terms of trade shocks and economic crises of the 1970s and 1980s brought with them a twenty-year period of macroeconomic stabilization, trade liberalization, and privatization. Uncertainty with the outcome of the adjustment process and low or negative economic growth meant that there was little private investment overall and practically none in industry. Political instability and conflict also caused investors to hold back. When Africa emerged from its long economic hibernation just before the turn of the twenty-first century, African industry was no longer competing with the high-wage industrial "North," as it had in the 1960s and 1970s. It was competing with China. From the point of view of industrial development, the timing of the region's economic recovery was unlucky, to say the least.

Stabilization and fiscal austerity left Africa with very large gaps in infrastructure and human capital relative to emerging Asia. Africa started out in the 1960s with stocks of roads that were generally not very different from those in South or East Asia. The same was true in the 1970s for telephones and in the 1980s for power. By around 2000, Africa trailed in every infrastructure category. The comparison with South Asia is particularly telling. In 1970 sub-Saharan Africa had almost three times the generating capacity per million people as South Asia; in 2000 South Asia had almost twice the generation capacity per million people. In 1970 sub-Saharan Africa had twice the main-line telephone density of South Asia, but by 2000, the two regions were equal.[31] The political and economic turmoil of the 1980s and 1990s also took a toll on the region's institutions. In 2000 sub-Saharan Africa trailed all other developing regions in terms of government effectiveness, regulatory quality, rule of law, and control of corruption, in some cases by wide margins.[32]

31. Foster and Briceño-Garmendia (2010).
32. Kauffman, Kray, and Mastruzzi (2010).

The absence of these "basics," to which we shall return in chapter 7, meant that Africa's initial conditions in 2000 were, if anything, less auspicious than after independence. The World Bank began conducting Enterprise Surveys in Africa in the late 1990s. The legacy of poor infrastructure, low human capital, and dysfunctional institutions emerges clearly in those surveys. Self-reported losses associated with power outages amounted to more than 10 percent of sales in some countries. Bad transport networks emerged as a second infrastructure constraint. Around one-third of firms cited transportation as a major or severe constraint. Firms also reported having to pay bribes to get things done. On average, around 40 percent of African firms in the surveys stated that bribes were common.[33]

Several studies show the adverse impact of these physical and institutional deficiencies on productivity. Eifert and others distinguish between factory-floor productivity and overall productivity. They find that sub-Saharan African firms are substantially less productive, relative to firms in comparator countries, when "indirect costs" such as power, transport, licensing fees, and bribes are included. Kenyan firms, for example, have about the same factory-floor productivity as firms in China but only about half of the overall productivity when indirect costs are taken into account. Harrison and others find that once allowance is made for the quality of infrastructure and institutions, the productivity of African firms is similar to that of firms in other countries.[34]

The failure to industrialize, however, was also due to bad policy. Import substitution sowed the seeds of its own destruction. High protection and heavy import dependency meant that African industry was poorly prepared for international competition. The tendency of many African governments to assign a leading role to the state in creating and operating manufacturing firms simply made the problem worse. Investments were often made with little regard to efficiency, and the managerial capacity of the state was badly overstretched. The reforms of the structural adjustment period

33. Gelb, Meyer, and Ramachandran (2014).
34. See Eifert and others (2008) and Harrison and others (2012).

eventually paid off in terms of better macroeconomic management, but adjustment costs in terms of lost growth were high, and the rapid liberalizations of trade, together with some ill-advised conditions—such as freeing up the import of secondhand clothing for resale—probably caused a more severe contraction of industry than was necessary.

Hindsight is always easy. The key issue today is: Does the current focus on investment climate reform prepare Africa to turn the corner in industrial development? The evidence is not promising. Despite a decade and a half of investment climate reform, most African countries have not reached a turning point in their industrial development. In our view this partly reflects the fact that the investment climate reform agenda was poorly designed and implemented. Although in principle efforts to improve the investment climate were supposed to cover the whole range of issues—from macroeconomic management, to infrastructure and skills, to the policies and institutions that most closely affect private investors—in practice investment climate reform has centered too narrowly on business regulation at the expense of the "basics."[35]

Our country case studies raise a further question: Is investment climate reform alone equal to the task? The two African countries—Mauritius and Tunisia—that went their own way in terms of policies for industrialization have on the whole succeeded in industrializing. The source of their early industrial dynamism came from rapid growth of export manufacturing and only relatively late in the game did they begin to expose domestic firms to greater competition from imports. Both countries also actively supported exporters and industry more generally, developing programs to encourage diversification and increase firm-level productivity. It is fair to say that neither industrialization story is an unqualified success. Both countries have had some difficulty in making the transition from

---

35. It commonplace for scholars in East Asia to point out that countries such as China and Vietnam have sustained high rates of industrial and economywide growth while performing poorly on widely used indicators of regulatory quality and governance (Page, 2015).

low-end manufacturing toward more sophisticated and technology-intensive goods. They are, however, the leading African industrializers, relative to the rest of the Continent. This suggests that in addition to improving institutions, skills, and infrastructure, more active industrial policies may be needed in the rest of Africa.

Summing Up

Africa's industrial stagnation is a consequence of both bad luck and bad policy: bad luck came in the form of a vastly changed global competitive environment, and poor initial conditions. Once the reforms of the adjustment period had begun to pay off at the turn of the twenty-first century, Africa found itself competing with China. The fiscal austerity and political uncertainty of the 1980s and 1990s left the region with deficits in infrastructure, human capital, and institutions that made industrialization more difficult. But part of the responsibility also rests with the design and implementation of public policy.

There is a remarkable similarity in the policies for industrial development followed by sub-Saharan African countries: state-led import substitution, structural adjustment, and reform of the investment climate. In part, this can be ascribed to the similar stages of industrial development of most African economies and to the prevailing thinking among development economists with respect to appropriate policies to promote industrial development. Since the structural adjustment period, it is also partly due to the influence of aid donors. State-led import substituting industrialization led to a short-lived boom but could not be sustained, contributing to the macroeconomic collapses of the 1980s and the arrival of the Washington Consensus. African governments can look back on the structural adjustment period with some degree of relief. Improved macroeconomic management and the opening of the region's economies to international competition were important steps toward building more efficient economies, but they contributed little to industrial development.

Investment climate reform, like the structural adjustment that came before it, reflects the priorities of the international financial institutions and the aid community.[36] As implemented, investment climate reforms have not succeeded in reversing the region's industrial decline. Setting new priorities for the investment climate is certainly possible—and we make some suggestions how to do that in chapter 9—but changes in the investment climate alone are unlikely to be enough to overcome the challenge of industrialization, in much the same way that "getting prices right" was too narrow an approach to ensure a growth turnaround in the 1980s. Mauritius and Tunisia largely emulated the East Asian model of export-led manufacturing growth. Arguably they have succeeded where the rest of the Continent has failed, and their success gives some insight into what needs to be done in order for the rest of Africa to industrialize. Before we return to policy, however, it is important to try to understand the realities of industrial development in the twenty-first century. We begin in the next chapter by taking up the question of whether Africa can break into the global market for industrial goods.

36. Page (2012c).

CHAPTER 3

Can Africa Break In?

We wrapped up chapter 2 by noting that Africa was to some extent the victim of bad luck in its efforts to build industry. By the time the Continent had moved beyond the economic and political turmoil of the 1980s and 1990s, the center of gravity of global manufacturing had moved from the rich industrial countries of the Organization for Economic Cooperation and Development (OECD) to East Asia. Low-income countries trying to compete today are competing with China. This chapter asks: Given its late start, can Africa reasonably aspire to break into the global market for industrial goods?

We believe the answer is yes, for a number of reasons. First, economic changes are taking place in Asia that create a window of opportunity for late-industrializers elsewhere to gain a toehold in world markets. Second, the nature of manufactured exports themselves is changing. A growing share of global trade in industry is made up of stages of vertical value chains—or tasks—rather than finished products. Third, trade in services and agro-industry is growing faster than trade in manufactures. These "industries without smokestacks" broaden the range of products in which Africa can compete, and a number of them are intensive in location-specific factors abundant in Africa. We discuss all these changes in turn.

All of these potential entry points depend at least in part on Africa's assumed low-wage advantage. Over the years there has been a strand in the academic literature suggesting that wages in Africa—or wages relative to productivity—are not really low.[1] This is a critical issue, and so we review and assess several recent contributions to this debate in this chapter as well. We end the chapter by looking at a very real constraint on the region's ability to compete: natural resource abundance.

Competing with Asia

The global economy has experienced major changes over the last quarter of a century. Growth of manufactured exports has greatly exceeded growth of manufacturing output, and developing countries have captured an increasing share of the world market in both simple and complex manufactures. The share of total world manufacturing output produced by developing countries nearly doubled between 1992 and 2012, rising from 18 percent to 35 percent of global production. As manufacturing production has shifted to developing countries, Asia has become the "world's factory." East Asia and the Pacific account for about 58 percent of the manufacturing value added of developing economies, of which over 50 percent is produced by China alone.[2]

Manufactured exports from sub-Saharan Africa grew at 14.5 percent per year on average from 2000 to 2010. Yet, this growth was not enough to keep pace with developing countries as a whole. The region's share of industrializing countries' manufactured exports declined from 3.5 to 2.8 percent over the same period.[3] One measure of the extent of the export challenge is set out in table 3-1,

1. For a recent contribution, see Gelb, Meyer, and Ramachandran (2013).
2. UNIDO (2013).
3. UNIDO (2013).

Table 3-1. *Per Capita Manufactured Exports: Africa, Asia, and Latin America*

Country	Manufactured exports			
	Per capita 2011 (US$)	*Per capita growth 2006–11 (percent)*	*Share in total exports 2011 (percent)*	*Share of medium/high technology 2011 (percent)*
Bangladesh	230	0.0	63.7	21.6
Cambodia	335	9.8	79.6	7.1
Vietnam	764	23.6	70.0	33.7
Costa Rica	1595	6.0	73.8	58.8
El Salvador	701	4.7	82.3	15.4
Guatemala	464	27.3	67.3	19.2
Low-income Africa, leading 5 exporters				
Average	180	22.6	33.2	15.3
Range	118–265	–5.7–43.9	15.6–68.1	5.9–39.68
Africa average	69	9.4	26.0	12.0

Source: UNIDO Industrial Development database. Authors' calculations.
Notes: Low-income Africa leading exporters based on manufactured exports per capita: CDI, GHA, NGA, SEN, ZAM.

which contrasts the manufactured export performance of a number of emerging manufacturing exporters in Asia and Latin America with sub-Saharan Africa's five largest low-income manufacturing exporters in per capita terms in 2011. These countries were Ivory Coast, Ghana, Nigeria, Senegal, and Zambia.

While the leading African exporters compare well with their international competitors in terms of the growth of exports, they are starting from a very small base. The average per capita exports of manufactured goods of the leading African exporters is 55 percent of Cambodia, the lowest of the comparators, and 11 percent of Costa Rica, the highest. The share of manufactured exports in total exports is less than half of the five comparators. These trends are very similar to those observed between 2000 and 2005.[4]

4. See Page (2009).

The emergence of East Asia has shown that it is possible for new entrants to succeed in global markets. However, the East Asian success story also shows what is needed. East Asia only broke into global manufacturing on a massive scale around 1980. By then the gap in per capita incomes and wages between China and the OECD economies had become sufficiently large to offset the productivity advantage of the OECD's incumbent industrial producers. Today, new entrants in global markets must compete with incumbent producers who enjoy both low wages (at least relative to the high-income countries) and high productivity (as a result of the factors we discuss in chapters 4 to 6: exports themselves, rising firm capabilities, and an increasingly dense industrial landscape). Transportation cost differences add to the competitive advantage. Generally they are higher in Africa than in Asia, and high Asian trade volumes reduce costs further.[5]

While the challenges are formidable, we believe there are four reasons to think that Africa may be able to begin to compete with Asia in some products and markets:

—*Rising costs in China.* China is growing so rapidly that it is encountering rising costs in manufacturing production. One source is increasing real wages. Since 2005, real wage growth in China has accelerated significantly. Manufacturing wages rose from just over $150 a month in 2005 to around $350 in 2010.[6] Stiffer enforcement of labor and environmental regulations, gradual expansion of safety net provisions, and the prospect of further increases in the value of the renminbi are likely to erode the low-wage advantage further.[7] Geography will play a role as well. China has only a limited number of coastal cities. As these expand, they are likely to encounter diseconomies of congestion, and although Chinese manufacturers may shift production into the interior, this will increase coordination and transport costs.

5. Hummels (2007).
6. Lin (2011).
7. Dinh and others (2012).

—Domestic demand in Asia. Since the global financial crisis of 2008, Asia's established industrial economies—China included—have introduced domestic policies intended to reduce their dependence on exports. In China, targeted stimulus measures, including higher infrastructure investment, have helped strengthen domestic demand. In the region more broadly, domestic demand has benefited from strong credit growth.[8] Continued growth of domestic demand is likely to cause some reorientation of manufacturing activity toward the local market, creating space for potential competitors in third-country markets.

—Moving up the technological ladder. A number of successful Asian industrializers, including China, Malaysia, and Thailand, are making conscious efforts to move up in terms of the sophistication and technological complexity of their manufacturing.[9] Malaysia and Thailand have shares of medium- and high-technology exports in total exports exceeding 70 percent. China increased its medium- and high-technology share of exports from 45 percent in 2000 to 59 percent in 2010, and Vietnam increased its share of medium- and high-technology exports from about 25 percent to nearly 34 percent over the same period.[10] In part this is a market response to rising real wages. It also reflects the desire to replicate the successful experiences of Japan, Korea, Singapore, and Taiwan in upgrading industry to sustain growth. As countries move up technologically, less sophisticated competitors should be able to enter new sectors and product groups.

—International economic policy in China. There is some evidence that economic policymakers in China have made a decision to "offshore" a portion of low-end manufacturing to Africa. By the end of 2009, China's outward foreign direct investment (FDI) in Africa had reached a stock of US$9.33 billion. A large share (22 percent)—second only to mining—went to manufacturing.[11] More recently,

8. IMF (2014).
9. See Rasiah, Lin, and Sadoi (2013).
10. UNIDO (2009) and UNIDO (2013).
11. Lin (2011).

Chinese investment in African manufacturing has accelerated. From 2009 to 2012 it was estimated at US$1.33 billion. The Chinese government currently offers tariff-free entry to more than 400 products from Africa's low-income countries, and in addition it is backing the construction of six overseas special economic zones in Africa.[12]

These changes in Asia provide a basis for optimism. In contrast to the immediate post–structural adjustment period, there may be increasing room for Africa to break into the market in some low-end, labor-intensive manufacturing activities. To seize the opportunity, however, the region must gain a toehold and begin to master the dominant mode of contemporary international trade—trade in tasks.

Trade in Tasks

There has been a spectacular reduction in transport and communications costs in the global economy over the past twenty years. Freight costs have halved since the mid-1970s, driven by investments in transport infrastructure, better use of capacity, and technological progress. The major cost declines have been in road and air transport; ocean freight rates have declined relatively little since the 1980s. International communication and coordination costs have plummeted.[13] The significance of these changes in transport and communications costs is perhaps nowhere more apparent than in the explosive growth of trade in tasks.

In some manufacturing and service activities, a production process can be decomposed into a series of steps or tasks.[14] As transport and coordination costs have fallen, it has become efficient for

12. Brautigam and Tang (2014).
13. For discussion of these issues, see Hummels (2007) and Fink, Matoo, and Neagu (2002).
14. Grossman and Rossi-Hansberg (2006).

different tasks to be located in different countries. Task-based production has expanded dramatically during the past twenty years. In the period 1986–90, imported intermediates constituted about 12 percent of total global manufacturing output and 26 percent of total intermediate inputs. By 1996–2000, these figures had risen to 18 and 44 percent, respectively.[15] Much of this growth is from intra-firm trade along value chains. The OECD places intra-firm trade by multinational companies based in its members at 8 to 15 percent of total trade.[16] Another recent estimate suggests that as much as 80 percent of global trade is linked to the networks of multinational corporations.[17] Not surprisingly, exports—the core of task-trade—use a substantially higher share of imported intermediate inputs than production for the domestic market: a ratio of about two to one.

For late-industrializers, trade in tasks has great potential. It is easier to master a single stage of the production process than to develop vertically integrated production. Task-based production has been a major driver of rapid industrialization in the new generation of Asian export manufacturers. Exports of assembled garments from Cambodia and Vietnam have grown at double digit rates over the past ten years. Between 1994 and 1999, Cambodia's garment exports more than doubled, from US$495 million to U$1,102 million, with about 90 percent of garment shipments going to the United States. Exports of apparel have continued to increase, reaching nearly US$3 billion in 2008. The textile and garment industry has been among Vietnam's top-five exports since 2001, and despite the 2008–09 global recession, its exports increased at an average annual rate of more than 26 percent during the period 2005–10. Tunisia has enjoyed similar growth in assembly of garments and auto parts for the European market. Manufactured exports to EU countries—mainly France, Italy, Spain, and Germany—have expanded more than 10 percent annually since the 1990s. The Tunisian

---

15. UNIDO (2009).
16. OECD (2010).
17. UNCTAD (2013).

textile industry has gradually evolved from subcontracting to co-contracting and finally to finished goods to become the fifth largest supplier to the European Union.

Success in attracting and retaining trade in tasks is by no means guaranteed. Because end-stage task-based production depends on imported intermediate inputs, the institutions directly related to international trade (e.g., customs) and transport infrastructure are crucial to success. These elements of "trade logistics" must be of a very high standard in order to cut delivery times and avoid delays. Here Africa is currently at a disadvantage, but it is one that can be remedied by giving greater attention to strengthening the institutions and making the investments that directly affect trade costs, a topic to which we return in chapter 7.

Task-trade investors are also highly footloose. The performance of a number of African economies in response to the U.S. African Growth and Opportunity Act (AGOA) shows the speed with which task-based producers can enter and exit in response to changing market conditions and incentives. The relatively liberal rules of origin under AGOA encouraged final assembly operations in clothing manufacturing in countries such as Kenya, Lesotho, and Madagascar in the early 2000s. The exporting firms were almost entirely foreign owned and typically provided assembly, packaging, and shipping services. AGOA not only gave all sub-Saharan African countries extensive duty-free, quota-free access to the United States, its rules of origin allowed "qualified" (as defined in the legislation) countries to use third-country fabrics or yarn and still export clothing under the AGOA preferences, opening the door to their entry into task-trade.

U.S. imports of clothing from AGOA countries more than doubled, from US$730 million in 2000 to US$1,755 million in 2004, but experienced a major setback when the restrictions on their (mainly Asian) competitors were lifted with the expiration of the Multi-Fiber Arrangement (MFA) in 2005. While the industry contracted substantially, it did not disappear; garment exports have remained above 2000 levels since the expiration of the MFA. At the same time, success in the U.S. clothing market has not yet translated into success in other clothing markets—partly as a consequence of much more restrictive rules of origin—or success in exporting other labor-intensive products to the United States.[18]

Industries without Smokestacks

Changes in technology also offer Africa an opportunity that was not available to earlier generations of newly industrializing countries. Falling transport and communications costs have created economic activities in agriculture and services that have high output per worker and are globally traded. Some agricultural value chains and tradable services share a broad range of characteristics with manufacturing. These are "industries without smokestacks," and they are an increasingly important part of global industry.

Tradable Services

Services have historically been viewed by economists as the quintessential "nontraded" activity. For example, eating in a restaurant, getting a haircut, or having a medical checkup all require face-to-face transactions. However, information and communications technology and task-based production have made many other types of services tradable.[19] Services like back-office operations and accounting, which were previously integrated components of enterprises, can now be spun off and subcontracted. Modern tradable services have many features in common with manufacturing. Like manufacturing, they benefit from technological change and productivity growth. Some tradable services exhibit tendencies for scale and agglomeration economies similar to manufacturing, and the relationship between exports and innovation in services is similar to that of manufacturing.[20]

18. Edwards and Lawrence (2011).
19. See, for example, Baumol (1985) and Bhagwati (1984).
20. See Ebling and Janz (1999) and Ghani and Kharas (2010).

Since the 1980s, global trade in services has grown faster than merchandise trade, and developing countries are leaders in many of these offshore services. Service exports from developing countries have almost tripled in the last ten years, growing by 11 percent annually.[21] Modern service exports (e.g., computer and information services, financial services, business services, and communication) are growing much faster than traditional service exports such as travel, tourism, and transport.

The globalization of services will continue for three reasons. First, services account for more than 70 percent of global GDP. Second, communications and information costs will continue to fall. For most developing countries, the average cost of an international telephone call to the United States has fallen by 80 percent or more over the last decade. This is a decline in cost that is much more rapid than the fall in transport costs for goods. Third, the cost differential in the production of services across the world is enormous. Because service providers can now sell services without crossing national borders, the scope for exploiting these cost differentials is much higher.[22]

Although Africa trails other developing regions in the growth of services exports, services exports from Africa have grown at 7.2 percent per year since 1998. This is more than six times faster than merchandise exports. Exports of services are about 11 percent of the total exports of the average sub-Saharan African country, although levels vary widely across countries.[23] Such traditional services exports as transit trade and tourism are important in many countries, but there has also been an uptick in information-related services exports and transborder financial services. Services trade is particularly relevant for Africa's many landlocked countries where transportation costs do not significantly raise export costs, unlike in goods trade. Trade in services accounts for around half of total exports from Rwanda and Ethiopia, and even in diamond-rich Botswana it represents 15 percent of total exports.

21. World Bank (2010).
22. Ghani and Kharas (2010).
23. South Africa is excluded from the average.

As early global service providers transition from low-end to higher-end tradable services, there is growing room for African countries to step into the more standardized segments of the services market. Offshore business services—such as data transcription and call centers—are one example. Unlike East Asia, most African countries use global languages such as English, French, Arabic, and Portuguese. These are great assets for communications-based services.

French investors, for example, established the call center Premium Contact Center International (PCCI) in Dakar, Senegal, in 2002. The company makes prospecting and selling telephone calls to European households for French corporations. Dakar and Paris are in the same time zone. This makes it possible to work within French business hours. Video conferences and the flow of calls travel through a transoceanic cable. PCCI recruited about 1,000 call-center agents, most of them former students at the University of Dakar. The main recruitment criterion was fluency in French with the least local accent. Employees use French names when they are online with clients, and assimilation of French culture is thought to improve productivity. For this reason PCCI staff members take their lunch break while watching French TV.[24]

KenCall is a Kenyan firm that specializes in providing outbound and inbound voice and data services for large OECD companies. The firm began with outbound voice services, such as developing sales leads and doing post-sales calls with customers. Now it has added business in more lucrative data and inbound voice services. The services the firm offers include sales, billing, customer information, administrative, and data management and level 1 tech support. For its tech support business, KenCall's employees are certified by Cisco and Microsoft, among other information and communication technologies (ICT) providers.[25]

Trade in business services has been increasing rapidly in a number of African countries, albeit in all cases except South Africa from

24. Moriset (2004).
25. Dihel and others (2011).

a low base.[26] During the period 2005–10, the average growth of business services of all African countries for which data are available was 36 percent. This is much higher than the average growth in South Korea (9 percent) and China (22 percent) during the same period. A number of countries, including Kenya, Madagascar, Mauritius, Rwanda, and Senegal, have shown revealed comparative advantage in ICT services.[27]

Tourism is a tradable service sector in which Africa has an important resource-based comparative advantage. It receives a growing share of world tourist arrivals for both cultural and wildlife tourism. More than 29 million tourists visited the region in 2007, generating nearly US$22 billion in tourist receipts and contributing an average of 6 percent to GDP. Africa attracts more visitors than the Caribbean and Central America combined. Safari tourism is a key product for East Africa and Southern Africa. The main East Africa safari destinations are Kenya and Tanzania. Resort tourism is important in Mauritius, Seychelles, and Mozambique. West Africa mainly attracts business travelers but has small pockets of resort tourism in Cape Verde, Senegal, and the Gambia. Cultural tourism is perhaps the most underdeveloped area and has considerable potential in the Sahel countries of West Africa. Every country has some cultural heritage attractions, indigenous culture, and craft products.

Agro-Industrial Value Chains

The major agro-industrial activity in which Africa has shown the potential to compete is horticulture. Horticultural production encompasses fresh fruit, vegetables, and flowers. The transport of fresh produce over long distances became possible with the development of refrigeration and "cold chains" linking production and consumption points. The ability to keep products fresh and transfer them quickly from farm to shelf adds value. Value is also added through packaging, preparation, and innovation.

26. World Bank (2010).
27. World Bank (2010).

As transport costs have fallen, an increasing variety of fresh products can be exported profitably. Production of out-of-season crops that can only be grown in northern regions in the summer—citrus, grapes, melons, green beans, peas, asparagus, and cut flowers—has become possible. The most recent trend has been to produce a range of high-value "temperate" exports all year round. Such items as prepared fruit salads, trays of prepared mixed vegetables, and flower bouquets in retail packs can be produced more cheaply in low-income countries due to lower labor costs.[28]

Global market requirements for horticultural products have become more challenging in recent years due to more rigorous formal standards and the product requirements of demanding buyers.[29] The industry is increasingly dominated by lead firms that coordinate vertical supply chains. These lead firms have characteristics associated with modern manufacturing, including product differentiation and innovation, quality assurance based on risk management, and process controls.[30] With fresh fruit and vegetables there is a trend toward growing to order, under contract to major European supermarkets. For European flower imports, the key to success is to produce high-quality, modern, and fashionable varieties at the right time of year. For all varieties of horticultural products, economical and efficient transport as well as cold-storage chains are essential. Half the wholesale cost of African fresh produce in European markets is represented by the cost of transport, storage, and handling.

Our African country case studies point to a number of successes in horticulture. High value added horticulture developed first in Kenya. Starting from almost nothing in the late 1960s, exports of fresh flowers, fresh vegetables, and fresh fruit had reached substantial levels in the European market by 1995. Production spread on a smaller scale to Tanzania and Uganda, and at the end of the 1990s Ethiopia succeeded in breaking into the market for cut flowers and

28. Tyler (2005).
29. World Bank (2008a).
30. Humphrey and Memedovic (2006).

some vegetables. In West Africa, Senegal has had some success with exports of fresh vegetables to European markets.

Is African Labor Too Expensive?

Sub-Saharan Africa's competitive advantage in industry—and in particular its ability to compete in task-based production—hinges in part on low-wage labor. Africa is the world economy's lowest in-come region in per capita terms. Other things being equal, this ought to be reflected in a lower overall level of wages. Not surprisingly, given Africa's sluggish growth of labor-intensive manufacturing, there has been some debate in the academic literature over whether wages and unit labor costs—wages adjusted for productivity—in Africa are too high to compete globally.

Wages and Enclaves

One recent contribution to that debate compares labor costs and productivity in selected African countries with other low-income countries, using data from the World Bank's Enterprise Surveys. It concludes that industrial labor costs are far higher in Africa than one would expect, given its level of GDP per capita.[31] The authors argue that the higher wages to some extent reflect "enclaves" in the industrial sector in Africa. In these enclaves the high-wage outcomes may be the result of rent sharing between labor and incumbent firms protected from external or internal competition, or may reflect other noncompetitive labor market outcomes such as signaling. Control-ling for the enclave effect, however, an "Africa effect" remains with an average wage premium of about 50 percent, relative to income

31. It is important to note that the Enterprise Surveys cover only formal sector firms. Wages in the informal sector are a fraction of formal wages. See Gelb, Meyer, and Ramachandran (2013). Filmer and Fox (2014) reach broadly similar conclusions.

per capita. A wage premium of this magnitude represents a potentially serious barrier to the region's ability to compete.[32]

Case study work sponsored by the World Bank research project on light manufacturing casts some doubt on the high labor cost argument, especially when country and sector specificity are taken into account.[33] The studies compare wages in U.S. dollar terms for skilled and unskilled labor in light manufacturing activities (e.g., polo shirts, leather loafers, wood furniture, and milled wheat) in the formal manufacturing sector in Ethiopia, Tanzania, and Zambia with wages in the same activities in China and Vietnam.

These direct comparisons find that average Ethiopian wages for unskilled labor in light manufacturing are about a fifth of China's and about a third of Vietnam's. In Tanzania, the unskilled wage is 44 percent of China's and equal to Vietnam's. Average wage costs for skilled labor range from 25 to 33 percent of Chinese costs for Ethiopia and 50 to 58 percent of Chinese costs for Tanzania. Skilled wages are 50 to 55 percent of Vietnamese costs in Ethiopia but are double Vietnamese costs in Tanzania. Even in copper-rich Zambia, where average unskilled and skilled wage costs exceed those in Vietnam, average unskilled labor costs a quarter less and skilled labor 10 percent less than in China.

Wage differentials for workers are highly sector specific within individual countries. Wages for skilled workers range from 12 percent

32. One possible explanation of the Africa effect that Gelb, Meyer, and Ramachandran (2013) discuss is that GDP per capita in Africa is underestimated. This has become more relevant as more African economies "rebase" their economic statistics. Revisions along the lines of the 60 percent boost in Ghana's GDP in 2010 and the 75 percent increase in Nigeria's GDP in 2013 would eliminate the distinctive Africa story. A second possibility they explore in some detail is that Africa's high labor costs are partly explained by high purchasing power parity (PPP) price levels. This implies that although labor is more costly in current dollar terms, it is cheaper in purchasing power terms. Higher domestic costs of nontraded goods, especially wage goods, presumably affect wages through the reservation price of labor. The recent revisions of PPP exchange rates released by the International Comparisons Project cast some doubt on this line of reasoning as well.

33. Dinh and others (2012).

of China for making polo shirts in Ethiopia to a wage premium of 42 percent comparing Tanzania with Vietnam in producing leather loafers. Sector specificity matters as well for unskilled workers. Not surprisingly, given its low per capita income, unskilled wages in Ethiopia are uniformly lower than in China and Vietnam across all product groups. In Tanzania, however, the wages of unskilled workers exceed those in Vietnam in such products as polo shirts and leather loafers.

The focus on Africa's small formal manufacturing sector begs the question of the potential supply cost of labor if the current enclave arrangement were broken. Elsewhere in Africa's economies, wages are indisputably low. The current wage premium in large formal firms would presumably fall or disappear under circumstances where enclave enterprises were exposed to greater competitive pressure or labor markets were more competitive. It is also likely that the enclave equilibrium would break down in the face of a massive increase in labor demand, such as occurred during the industrial growth of Bangladesh, Cambodia, and Vietnam. While it is possible that workers in agriculture and informal employment may lack the skills needed to work in large firms, it is difficult to imagine that African workers are any less endowed with the skills needed for end-stage, task-based production than workers elsewhere. The success of several African economies in garment manufacturing under AGOA provides some supporting evidence. It may be that wages are high in Africa because it has too little industry, rather than that Africa has too little industry because wages are high.

Unit Labor Costs

Low wages do not guarantee success in labor-intensive manufacturing. At least two other factors come into play. Productivity is as important as wages in determining competitiveness, and because wages and labor productivity vary across sectors, sector specificity matters. Although Gelb and his colleagues find that unit labor costs are higher in Africa than elsewhere, the difference is smaller than in labor costs; part of the labor cost is offset by higher labor productivity.[34] Other research using the same investment climate surveys comes to a similar conclusion.

One study undertaken by the World Bank finds that, controlling for per capita income, labor productivity in manufacturing does not appear to be consistently lower in sub-Saharan Africa than in other regions. Indeed, more African countries have higher productivity than would be expected at their level of income than do not.[35] A second study using the same survey data finds that, after controlling for the business environment, firms in Africa's formal manufacturing sector perform as well in productivity terms as those in other low-income countries.[36] Surveys of small and medium enterprises (SMEs) in Ethiopia, Tanzania, Zambia, China, and Vietnam indicate that workers in SMEs in sub-Saharan Africa are as productive as those in East Asia.[37]

The case study research on productivity is consistent with the cross-country econometric evidence. Physical labor productivity—the number of items produced by a worker in a day—in the light manufacturing processes studied in Ethiopia, Tanzania, and Zambia is comparable to China and Vietnam, except in the production of wooden chairs. When wages are paired with the number of products a worker can produce in a day, "well managed" firms in Ethiopia and Tanzania—those with physical productivity that falls within the range of the worst and the best practice Chinese and Vietnamese firms studied—show a unit labor cost advantage.

In sum, the body of evidence, both econometric and case study, points to the conclusion that unit labor costs in African industry are

34. Gelb, Meyer, and Ramachandran (2013).
35. Dinh and Clarke (2012).
36. Harrison, Lin, and Xu (2013).
37. Dinh and his colleagues characterize "well managed" firms as those with physical productivity per worker that matches levels typical of their East Asian comparator firms. It is important to note that this is the "right hand tail" of firms in the World Bank African sample. It is not the "representative firm." See Dinh and others (2012).

not out of line with the region's level of income per capita. Wages in some firms and in some countries are higher than those of Asian competitors; in others they are not. Some firms in some industries in Africa are as productive as their Asian competitors and unit labor costs in those firms are not excessive. These are the countries and sectors in which Africa can currently compete. There is, however, considerably more variation in African productivity levels than in East Asia, and the productivity of the "representative firm" is higher in East Asia. The challenge, therefore, is to have more African firms in more industries meet the productivity threshold to break in.

Natural Resources and Industrial Development

Africa is richly endowed with metal and nonmetal minerals, as well as energy resources, and many of its economies are highly resource dependent. Although precise data are not available, principally because much of the Continent is underexplored, it is likely that Africa hosts about 30 percent of the world's mineral reserves. New discoveries of natural resources in previously non-resource-abundant economies such as Ghana, Kenya, Mozambique, Tanzania, and Uganda raise the prospect that an increasing number of African economies will enter the ranks of natural resource exporters. This poses a major challenge to industrialization and, perhaps, to long-run growth as well. Natural resource abundance makes it more difficult to compete internationally in industries unrelated to the natural resource.

Natural Resources and Risk: Price Declines and Shocks

There is extensive cross-country literature linking natural resource dependence to poor economic performance, which is known as the "resource curse."[38] One thread of the resource curse literature

---

38. One thread of this literature runs from Gelb (1988) through Sachs and Warner (1995) to Gylfason, Herbertsson, and Zoega (1999) and Sala-i-Martin and Subramanian (2003). Van der Ploeg (2011) gives a survey.

focuses on risk. High concentration of output and exports in one or two commodities can expose resource-rich economies to long-run declines in commodity prices and price volatility. Both are threats to long-run growth in resource-abundant economies.

Global GDP growth has consistently outpaced the demand for commodities, and despite recent spikes, commodity prices are likely to continue their gradual downward path relative to manufactured goods and knowledge-intensive services. Long-term estimates of the rate of decline range from −0.6 to −2.3 percent per year. The reasons for this secular decline have been widely explored. They include relatively low demand elasticities for primary commodities relative to manufactures and services, growth of substitutes, and rapid technological advances that have reduced the cost of growing or extracting commodities.[39]

A major external change would be required to break the fall in commodity prices, and it is not clear at present what that change might be. One favored scenario—increases in demand due to rapid growth in developing countries that are large net importers of energy, materials, and agricultural commodities—is likely to have two offsetting effects. First, technological advances in both the production and use of commodities in a broad range of developing countries will increase supply and reduce demand. Second, outward investment in the production of commodities by net importers is likely to increase supply. While other commodity prices are expected to decline, oil may be an important exception. The exhaustion of easily accessible reserves may place a floor on oil prices, but some observers are skeptical of this view. They argue that the drive to reduce carbon emissions may begin to make a dent in energy use and oil prices.[40]

Independent of their long-term trend, commodity prices are likely to remain highly volatile, and price spikes such as the ones in the mid-2000s as well as price collapses such as the 2015 crash affecting oil markets will recur. The reasons for high volatility of commodity

39. Dadush (2010).
40. See Collier (2010) and Veit, Lupberger, and Ashraf (2010).

prices have also been widely discussed. They include low short-term income and price elasticities of demand and supply, long lead times before investment and supply respond to changing demand conditions, weather shocks to agricultural commodities, and policy-induced distortions that impede the orderly adjustment of commodity markets. Newer sources of instability include more variable weather because of climate change and increased use of commodities and commodity derivatives for speculation.

Volatility may limit the growth prospects of African economies that are dependent on minerals and other commodities. Historical data suggest that external shocks are especially important determinants of growth in resource-rich countries.[41] While output variability in general is declining among African countries, the relative importance of external shocks as sources of output instability in Africa has actually increased in the past fifteen years. This increase is the result of two factors. One is good news and reflects Africa's marked improvement in economic management—the variance of internal shocks, including conflicts and policy, has declined substantially. The other is not good news: there has been a relative increase in the vulnerability of output to external shocks, such as the global economic recession and price volatility.[42]

Natural Resources and Diversification

One response to the resource curse—and the path chosen by such resource-abundant economies as Chile, Indonesia, and Malaysia—is to diversify the economy away from the resource sector. Industry, with and without smokestacks, is clearly one option for diversification. This is, however, no easy task. Income from resource extraction increases the demand for all goods. In the case of traded goods, the increased demand can be met by imports at fixed international prices. The production of nontradable goods, on the other hand, is usually

41. Collier and Goderis (2007).
42. Raddatz (2008).

characterized by rising marginal costs, and their price will generally rise relative to internationally traded goods. The foreign exchange market will, other things being equal, reflect this in a real exchange rate appreciation. This is the Dutch disease.

While it is appropriate for labor and capital to shift into nontradable goods and services, Dutch disease limits the ability of firms to compete against imports or to export, and it makes the development of manufacturing and tradable services outside of the resource sector more difficult, unless governments take countervailing action through macroeconomic and supply-side policies. The current crop of Africa's resource-rich economies show little evidence of structural change toward higher value added tradable activities outside the natural resources sector. We see this very clearly in table 3-2.

Resource-abundant economies in Africa have structural characteristics that are very different from typical middle-income countries and from their non-resource-rich neighbors. Not surprisingly, the shares of agriculture and manufacturing in GDP are lower in the resource-rich economies than in the middle-income benchmarks. The manufacturing deficit is particularly large. Other industry, mainly extractives, dominates the structure of output but not of employment. Mines and gas fields do not generate many direct jobs. Exports are much more highly concentrated in natural-resource-based products. Three-quarters of exports of resource-rich countries are found in less than three sectors. Resource abundance is likely to constrain the ability of a growing number of African countries to break into other areas of the global economy.

Summing Up

In contrast to circumstances at the turn of the century, some African countries have a real chance to break into global industrial markets. Conditions in Asia are changing, and despite the productivity advantages of Asia's incumbent industrial producers, rising costs and real wages in China and changes in economic policy in Asia's major

Table 3-2. *Structural Characteristics of Africa's Resource-Abundant Economies*

	Value added share				Labor share			
	Agriculture	Other industry	Manufacturing	Services	Agriculture	Other industry	Manufacturing	Services
Upper-middle-income benchmark	7.0	10.3	30.0	52.7	14.0	10.0	19.0	57.0
Lower-middle-income benchmark	21.7	12.2	21.9	44.2	45.2	6.6	11.6	36.6
Africa, resource abundant	17.8	44.3	16.8	21.1	45.4	4.8	6.5	43.4
Africa, low income	27.8	11.8	11.1	49.3	63.1	5.1	6.6	25.2

Sources: World Bank World Development Indicators (WDI) database; de Vries and de Vries (2013). Authors' calculations.

industrial economies offer a window of opportunity. Recent decisions by the Chinese government to offshore some industrial capacity to Africa adds the weight of the world's most successful newly industrializing economy to these possibilities.

Changes in the nature of international trade also open up space. Trade in tasks—the vertical disintegration of the manufacturing production process—offers the prospect for new industrializers like those in Africa to find a foothold along the less demanding stages of the production value chain. Success in trade in tasks is not guaranteed, however. Wages appropriate to low levels of per capita income and good trade-related institutions and infrastructure are all key success factors. Attracting task-based investors and finding ways to keep them are also essential. Cambodia and Vietnam have seized this opportunity, and within Africa Mauritius and Tunisia have done so. There is no reason, apart from misdirected policies, why other African economies cannot do so as well.

Falling transport and communications costs have created a new generation of "industries without smokestacks." These tradable services and agro-industrial exports have more in common with manufacturing than with the sectors to which they are assigned in conventional economic statistics. The good news here is that Africa has many location-specific sources of comparative advantage in these sectors—major languages, a southern hemisphere climate, and exotic wildlife, among them.

Breaking in depends in part on taking advantage of relatively low wages. Because Africa is the world's poorest region, the supply price of industrial labor ought to be low, but the slow pace of industrial development has led some to question whether wages are truly low by global standards. There is some evidence to suggest that wages in Africa's small formal manufacturing sector are high compared to other low-income countries such as Bangladesh, but it is very likely that these wages reflect an arrangement between firms and workers that would break down either in the face of increased competition or a massive increase in labor demand.

Competitive success, of course, depends not only on low wages but on low unit costs of labor as well. These are determined in large part by firm-level productivity. Our reading of the evidence is that the supply price of labor in Africa is not excessive for its level of income and that productivity in some firms and in some sectors is high enough for Africa to compete. The key to success, however, is achieving and sustaining improvements in productivity at the level of the firm. That is the topic to which we turn in part III.

Resource abundance poses a major challenge to industrialization in Africa. It is also a risk to long-term growth if new resource exporters fall victim to the resource curse. At the same time, geology is not destiny. Tradable goods production outside the nonresource economy will expand or contract according to whether it is internationally competitive. This depends not only on the exchange rate, but also on the investments and institutional innovations that governments make to enhance productivity, a subject we take up in chapter 8.

PART III

LEARNING *to* COMPETE

CHAPTER 4

Productivity, Exports, and Competition

In chapter 3 we argued that Africa has a new opportunity to break into global markets in industry, but we were careful to point out that low wages will not be enough to ensure Africa's success. While there is evidence that some African firms have productivity levels that, when combined with low wages, make them competitive with Asian producers, this is not true for all firms. Many firms in Africa are not productive enough to compete globally. Closing the industrial productivity gap between Africa and the rest of the world is therefore essential for any hope of breaking into global manufacturing and staying there. The three chapters in part III deal with firm-level productivity. They present our major findings regarding the role of exports and competition, firm capabilities, and agglomeration economies in productivity at the firm level.

This chapter begins the discussion by presenting the results of our efforts to understand the impact of exports and domestic competition on the productivity of African firms. Because we use the term extensively throughout this book, we begin by defining *productivity* and explaining how it is measured. Next, we present some stylized facts about firm-level productivity and describe some of the factors that cause it to rise or fall. We then turn to one of the central questions of the Learning to Compete project: Do firms in low-income countries learn by exporting? The chapter concludes with a look at the role of competition in raising productivity. Along the way we present evidence obtained from our country and econometric studies.

Measuring Productivity

Before we launch into a discussion of what affects productivity, it is useful to define terms. Simply put, productivity is efficiency in production. It is the amount of output obtained from a given set of inputs. Single-factor productivity measures the units of output produced per unit of a particular input. Labor productivity is the most common measure of this type. In many cases in Africa, it is the only measure of productivity available. The problem with measuring the productivity of a single factor is that, at least in part, it reflects how intensively other factors are used. For example high labor productivity can be the result of using large amounts of capital per worker rather than more efficient use of labor. Unless we can aggregate all of the firm's inputs into a common unit of measurement we cannot reach a definitive judgment.

It is for this reason that most of the empirical microeconomic work on firm-level productivity—and many of the studies to which we refer in the coming chapters—use total factor productivity (TFP). Conceptually TFP is simple. It is the amount of output obtained from all inputs into production: land, labor, materials, and capital combined. Firms with higher TFP produce greater amounts of output with the same set of observable inputs. Measuring TFP is less straightforward. At the heart of the measurement problem is an "adding up" or index number problem. Inputs are measured in different ways—acres of land, hours of labor, tons of steel, or numbers of machines—so we need to find appropriate weights to combine them into a single measure. Ideally the weights should reflect the contribution of each input to output across all firms in an industry.

As a practical solution to this weighting problem, most econo-mists who study productivity assume that the relationship between inputs and outputs can be specified in some way—usually in the form of a production function. Economists then use the production function and some assumptions regarding economic behavior to construct a set of appropriate weights from the data available. The weights are the elasticities of output with respect to each input—the percentage change in output for a 1 percent change in the relevant input, holding other inputs constant.

Output elasticities are normally estimated in one of two ways. One is to invoke the conventional theory of the firm and assume that a cost-minimizing producer uses each input up to the point where the output elasticity equals the product of that input's share of pro-duction costs and the scale elasticity of production. If the input costs can be measured and there is some estimate of the scale elasticity, the output elasticity of each input can be computed from these data. A popular approach is to assume that all firms operate in a world of perfect competition and constant returns to scale. If that is true, the output elasticities equal the share of revenues paid to each input. This approach is often referred to as "growth accounting."

A completely different way to measure TFP is to estimate the production function itself. This approach—while involving fewer strong assumptions about behavior—brings with it a host of chal-lenging econometric problems, which have been extensively discussed elsewhere.[1] In general the new econometric work we carried out under Learning to Compete (L2C) used direct estimates of produc-tion functions to estimate TFP, and the econometric issues are exten-sively discussed in each study. Our country case studies, on the other hand, generally used growth accounting methods that attempted to estimate TFP.

Fortunately, despite the many concerns, the empirical results that we present here, and in chapters 5 and 6, are very robust to how TFP is measured. The variation in firm-level performance is typically so

---

1. An excellent new reference in this area, partly written by one of our team, is Söderbom and others (2014).

large that it swamps measurement-driven differences in productivity estimates. Put simply, high-productivity firms tend to look efficient—and low-productivity firms inefficient—regardless of the specific way their productivity is measured.[2] For this reason we report our insights concerning differences in firm-level productivity without further methodological warnings. However, it is important to keep in mind that if issues of measurement and data are problematic in high-income countries, they are multiplied in economies with lower incomes. This is the reason we do not have a large stock of firm-level productivity studies on Africa.

Firm-Level Productivity

Empirical studies repeatedly find that there are large productivity differences among enterprises in quite narrowly defined industries. Even in rich countries, the magnitudes involved are striking. In U.S. manufacturing, the ratio of total factor productivity between a plant in the 90th percentile in terms of productivity and one in the 10th percentile in the same four-digit economic sector is nearly two to one.[3] This means that, on average, a plant in the 90th percentile of the productivity distribution produces about twice as much output of the same product as a plant in the 10th percentile, using the same measured inputs. In some U.S. industries the dispersion is substantially greater, and these productivity differences persist. Good performers in one year are very likely to remain good performers. Not surprisingly, higher productivity firms are more likely to survive than their less productive competitors.[4]

2. See Syverson (2011) for a comprehensive review of the literature.

3. Syverson (2011). The four-digit International Standard Industrial Classification (ISIC) is quite precise. For example, within food products it distinguishes between processing and preserving of meat and the manufacture of vegetable and animal oils and fats.

4. Syverson (2007).

Firm-Level Productivity in Developing Countries

When we turn to developing countries the differences in plant-level productivity within well-defined industries are even larger. While poorer countries have some firms that achieve world-class productivity levels, they also have a much higher percentage of low-productivity firms. There is a long "left hand tail" of poorly performing firms. In China and India, for example, average 90-10 TFP ratios are more than 5 to 1.[5] In Vietnam, where we have studied firm-level TFP extensively, the 90-10 ratio overall in manufacturing is about 2.8 to 1, and it varies across sectors from 4.4 to 1 in the electronics, electrical equipment, and machinery sectors to 1.5 to 1 in the manufacture of leather and leather products.[6]

In Africa the differences across firms appear to be larger still. Because there is little systematic data on TFP at the firm level in Africa we are forced to fall back on measures of labor productivity drawn from the World Bank Enterprise Surveys. The 90-10 labor productivity ratios for all manufacturing in our eight sub-Saharan case study countries range from 30 to 1 in Senegal to 79 to 1 in Ethiopia. At the broad sector level, the 90-10 ratios in textiles, leather, and garments are lowest in Senegal and Uganda at 10 to 1 and 12 to 1, respectively, and highest in Ghana at 54 to 1 and Ethiopia at 78 to 1. In food products the 90-10 ratio spans the range from 23 to 1 in Senegal to an astonishing 689 to 1 in Mozambique.[7]

These are very large differences in labor productivity and surely reflect major differences in products produced and capital intensity, in addition to efficiency in production across firms. They suggest that TFP differences are likely to be large as well, but substantially less than the differences in output per worker. This conjecture is supported by one set of estimates of firm-level TFP distributions

5. Hsieh and Klenow (2009).
6. Newman and others (2015).
7. The World Bank Enterprise Survey data are presented at a very high level of sector aggregation. We excluded Mozambique in other manufacturing due to an implausible result. See World Bank (2015).

from eighty countries using data drawn from the World Bank Investment Climate Assessments. It finds very high TFP dispersion across firms in sub-Saharan Africa relative to other developing regions.[8] Our TFP estimates for Ethiopia give an overall 90-10 ratio of more than 8 to 1. Clearly, for Africa finding ways to raise firm-level productivity and reduce its dispersion are key objectives.

Of Bathtubs and Churning

Firm-level productivity increases in two ways. The first is through changes that increase the level of productivity within the firm. This could be due to a firm-specific initiative—a change in management, for example—or it could come from a change in the environment in which firms operate. Indeed, one way to look at the investments in infrastructure and education discussed in chapter 2 is that they are public actions designed to help raise the potential productivity of all firms. This or any mechanism that increases the potential productivity of all firms in a sector is sometimes called the "bathtub effect." If the filling tub carries all rubber ducks, it is equivalent to shifting the entire productivity distribution of firms in an industry uniformly to the right.

Not all firms will seize on productivity-changing opportunities when they are available. This is where competition becomes important. It affects the productivity distribution through the exit of less efficient firms and the entry or expansion of their more efficient counterparts. This second, between-firm effect is often referred to as reallocation or "churning." Churning both changes the shape of the productivity distribution, normally shortening the left hand tail, and raises the average level of productivity.

In every economy these within-firm and between-firm changes are taking place all of the time. When they work in tandem they can provide a powerful engine of productivity growth. Two sources of productivity change at the firm level are of particular relevance to contemporary Africa. The first—learning by exporting—corresponds

8. Saliola and Seker (2011).

closely to the idea of within-firm productivity growth. If firms raise their own productivity by exporting, the share of higher productivity firms in the performance distribution increases. In addition, if some of the productivity enhancements spill over to other firms— say, as a result of movement of personnel or of copying new production techniques—the productivity of other firms may increase as well, generating a bathtub effect.

Competition acts primarily through inter-firm reallocations of market shares.[9] If firms with low productivity are driven from the market and higher productivity firms capture their market share, average productivity increases. Similarly, if new market entrants are higher productivity firms they may capture some of the market share of their less productive competitors, even if they do not drive them from the market altogether. Finally, incumbent firms may become more productive in response to increased competitive pressures.

Do Firms Learn by Exporting?

In chapter 2 we pointed out that Mauritius and Tunisia pursued export-oriented industrialization strategies similar to those seen in East Asia. They were also the only African countries to succeed in rapid industrialization. The association between superior export performance and rapid industrial growth in East Asia has been known since the 1960s, but economists continue to differ on the question of whether that growth is (at least partly) a consequence of Asia's export-led growth strategy. Given the striking difference in export orientation between the sub-Saharan countries we studied and Mauritius and Tunisia, as well as our emerging Asian comparators, Cambodia and Vietnam, the role of exports in industrial growth is of considerable interest.

We begin our discussion of the role of exports with a look at the comparative export and productivity performance of the African

9. This dichotomy is not airtight. Firms that learn by exporting may, for example, capture some of the market share of domestic rivals.

and emerging Asian countries in our study. There is an interesting empirical regularity between export performance and industrial productivity growth at the country level. Next, we turn to the relationship between exports and productivity change at the firm level. There has been a long-standing academic debate over whether firms "learn by exporting" and increase their productivity as a result of entering global markets. We summarize the current mainstream thinking on this issue and then present some additional evidence on learning by exporting from L2C.

Exports and Productivity in Africa and Emerging Asia

One of the most striking differences between the eight sub-Saharan countries we studied and Cambodia, Mauritius, Tunisia, and Vietnam was in export performance. Mauritius, Tunisia, and the two emerging Asian economies have all achieved considerable success in manufactured exports (table 4-1). As recently as 2000, manufactured exports per capita in Cambodia were only US$107 and in Vietnam US$87. By 2010 they had reached US$335 and US$764, respectively. Manufactured export growth in Cambodia averaged nearly 10 percent per year between 2005 and 2010, and the 2008–09 global recession notwithstanding, Vietnam's exports increased at an average annual rate of 26.3 percent during the same period. In 2011 the share of manufactured exports in total exports for both countries was above 70 percent. In 2011, Mauritius had manufactured exports per capita of US$1,401. Tunisian manufactured exports to EU countries—mainly France, Italy, Spain, and Germany—have expanded more than 10 percent annually since the 1990s. In 2000, manufactured exports per capita were US$522, and despite the turmoil of the Arab Spring, they more than doubled to US$1,381 in 2010.

Sub-Saharan Africa in contrast entered the twenty-first century with few manufactured exports and a declining share of the growing global market in manufactures. Manufactured exports per capita for the region as a whole (excluding South Africa) in 2000 were US$28 compared with US$291 for all developing economies and

Table 4-1. Indicators of Manufactured Export Performance, 2000–10

	Manufactured exports per capita (constant 2005 U.S. dollars)			Share of manufactured exports in total exports (percent)			Share of medium- and high-technology exports in manufactured exports (percent)		
	2000	2005	2010	2000	2005	2010	2000	2005	2010
Ethiopia	1	1	2	4.8	18.3	12.5	0.5	1.5	4.5
Ghana	56	164	265	66.5	65.1	35.9	2.8	10.4	5.9
Kenya	20	42	62	38.2	52.4	48.9	14.8	11.0	24.9
Mozambique	7	69	35	35.2	76.4	23.4	10.4	4.6	26.7
Nigeria	0	4	121	0.2	2.5	15.6	60.7	74.9	8.9
Senegal	36	88	136	54.0	69.7	68.0	20.9	31.3	12.8
Tanzania	7	22	43	37.0	54.5	42.3	3.9	3.4	16.7
Uganda	5	10	32	29.4	36.6	51.1	12.1	21.4	32.2
Mauritius	774	771	1401	98.3	94.5	96.5	4.9	21.0	23.9
Tunisia	522	889	1381	85.4	85.0	82.0	24.8	31.5	45.8
Cambodia	107	198	335	98.5	97.5	71.5	1.0	0.9	7.1
Vietnam	87	211	764	46.8	54.0	70.0	21.5	21.4	33.7

Sources: UNIDO (2009, 2013).

US$495 for East Asia and the Pacific. In 2000, the manufactured exports per capita of the eight sub-Saharan countries studied in L2C averaged just US$16.50. The share of manufactured exports in total exports for the region (excluding South Africa) was 25 percent compared to 77 percent for developing countries as a whole. In the eight sub-Saharan countries, manufactured exports were on average about a third of total exports.

While it is far from an ideal measure of efficiency, we are limited in most African countries to observing trends in labor productivity. The differences in industrial labor productivity growth between Cambodia, Mauritius, Tunisia, and Vietnam and our set of sub-Saharan countries in Africa are as striking as the differences in export performance. Manufacturing productivity growth in Cambodia averaged 2.5 percent per year during the period 2000–10.[10] Garments were the leading sector in terms of productivity gains, driven by frequent firm turnover, reductions in materials costs and wastage, and improvements in quality. In Mauritius, labor productivity in manufacturing increased by about 60 percent between 2000 and 2010. In Tunisia, growth in value added per worker in manufacturing averaged about 5 percent per year between 1985 and 2005, mainly due to entry of export-oriented foreign firms.[11] Between 2000 and 2010 output per worker in Vietnam's manufacturing sector (in constant 1994 U.S. dollars) increased 5 percent per annum, on average. Much of the gain in productivity was associated with the continuing reform of the state-owned sector. In parallel, rapid entry and growth of exporting firms, especially in new sectors such as wood and wood products, played a major role.

Table 4-2 shows indices of value added per worker in African manufacturing between 1995 and 2010.[12] The trends in output per worker for most of the sub-Saharan countries are worrisome. In

10. APO (2013).
11. Ben Jelili and Goaied (2009).
12. Estimates for Mozambique and Uganda were kindly provided by Margaret McMillan from the extended McMillan-Rodrik database described in McMillan, Rodrik, and Verduzco-Gallo (2014).

Table 4-2. *Manufacturing Value Added per Worker, 1995–2010*

	1995	2000	2005	2010
Ethiopia	100	85	74	64
Ghana	100	123	123	123
Kenya	100	65	53	56
Mauritius		100	128	159
Mozambique			100	36
Nigeria	100	139	192	267
Senegal	100	82	73	66
Tanzania	100	100	101	107
Uganda		100	87	130

Sources: The estimates for countries other than Mauritius, Mozambique, and Uganda are drawn from the Groningen Africa Database in de Vries, Timmer, and de Vries (2013); Macmillan, Rodrik, and Verduzco-Gallo (2014). Mauritius: IMF (2013). Authors' calculations.

Note: Indexed to 100 in first year of series.

Ethiopia, Kenya, and Senegal output per worker declined between 1995 and 2010. In Ghana and Tanzania, productivity growth was near zero. Mozambique suffered a major collapse in manufacturing productivity between 2005 and 2010, although the short time period may mask some important idiosyncratic factors such as the impact of the timing of mega projects. Uganda had a manufacturing productivity growth rate of about 2.7 percent. Only Nigeria registered rapid long-run growth in labor productivity in manufacturing, averaging 6.8 percent per year over the period 1995–2010. Casual empiricism suggests that there may be some relationship between export success and productivity growth in industry. Yet country studies must be interpreted with care, and the idea that firms increase their productivity by exporting is controversial.

The Learning by Exporting Debate

To understand why the idea that firms become more productive by exporting is controversial, we need to take a brief detour into an academic controversy. We noted previously that economists disagree on the causes of the association between extraordinary export performance and superior growth outcomes in East Asia. One group has attributed Asia's high-speed growth partly to productivity gains to firms resulting from the process of exporting itself, in other words to learning by exporting.[13] Others have argued that openness to trade rather than exports per se was central to Asia's success. International trade, in their view, generated competitive pressures on exporters and domestic producers alike, forcing both to improve their productivity. One way of looking at the exports versus openness controversy is that the debate is between whether intra-firm or inter-firm sources of overall productivity change played the dominant role in East Asia's success.

Cross-country econometrics and some early firm-level studies appeared to support the idea of learning by exporting, but by the late 1990s the balance of evidence seemed to move in the direction of openness. A round of firm-level empirical studies using more advanced econometric methods suggested that little, if any, learning from exporting took place. These studies—based on data from Colombia, Spain, Germany, and the United States—found that the most productive firms in a sector or an economy selected into exporting, leading to a strong positive correlation between productivity levels and export status, but the research found no persuasive evidence that once firms had chosen to export they improved their productivity.[14]

A third wave of empirical studies in the 2000s, using data from lower income countries, produced new support for learning by exporting.[15] Notably, several careful studies of African firms found a causal link running from exporting to productivity growth.[16] In weighing the balance of evidence, Harrison and Rodriguez-Clare in a 2010 survey of the literature for the *Handbook of Develop-*

---

13. See, for example, Pack and Page (1993) and World Bank (1993).

14. See Harrison and Rodriguez-Clare (2010) for a survey of the relevant literature.

15. Blalock and Gertler (2004), for example, found strong evidence that Indonesian firms had a jump in productivity of 3 to 5 percent following their entry into export markets.

16. Major contributions to the literature on Africa are Bigsten and others (2004), Van Biesebroeck (2006), and Mengiste and Patillo (2004).

ment Economics argue that despite the ongoing controversy, it is probably safe to conclude that:

—The most productive firms in an economy or a sector are most likely to become exporters.
—While there is selection into exporting, there is also learning through exporting. Productivity in exporting firms rises faster than in nonexporters, at least in some contexts.
—Learning by exporting is most likely to take place in lower income countries and among less productive firms.[17]

Because our interest centers on low-income countries, these conclusions have some powerful policy implications. One of the striking differences between Mauritius and Tunisia and the eight other sub-Saharan countries we studied was in export policies and performance. If learning by exporting is important, one of the causes of Africa's poor industrial development record may lie in the lack of effective policies to promote industrial exports. We would be more confident in our policy judgement, however, if there were a larger body of empirical evidence on the role of exports in raising firm-level productivity, and for that reason we set out to see what we could learn.

Exports and Firm-Level Productivity in Africa and Emerging Asia

Apart from the studies cited, there are very few careful econometric studies of learning by exporting, especially in low-income countries. The reason is simple. It is very difficult to distinguish empirically between the proposition that exports raise productivity and the alternative that higher productivity raises the likelihood that a firm will export. Panel data sets that follow the performance of individual firms over time are required to allow researchers to identify the direction of the causal relationship between exports and productivity.

17. Harrison and Rodriguez-Clare (2010).

It was for this reason that we set out in Learning to Compete to find as many panel data sets as possible that could inform us about the role of exports in firm-level productivity change. In the end, we were able to undertake new research in five of the eleven countries we studied.[18]

The results of our econometric studies provide some additional evidence that firms raise their productivity by exporting, and they also reveal some subtleties regarding how this takes place. For example, in Vietnam, controlling for self-selection, exporting is associated with higher productivity levels in the first years after entry into export markets, but these gains do not persist for all firms. Foreign-owned firms, particularly wholly foreign-owned firms, benefited more from exporting than private domestic firms in the early years following entry into exports, suggesting that their productivity gains may be associated mainly with moving to larger scale in the absence of local market constraints. Domestic firms also raised their productivity by exporting, but in this case the increases, while smaller in magnitude than in foreign firms, persisted longer and were partly due to within-firm improvements in production processes, a result more in line with the learning by exporting model.[19]

In Mozambique we found that most exporting firms were "born global." Firms started out as exporters or nonexporters, and very few firms shifted to exporter status from serving the domestic market. This creates an additional complication in testing the learning by exporting hypothesis. Nevertheless, our results show evidence of a significant export productivity premium of between 15 and 24 percent between exporters and nonexporters, controlling for differences in observable characteristics.[20]

Ethiopia and Cambodia were the two lowest income countries we covered in our econometric studies. In Ethiopia, where less than

18. These papers are available in working paper form (www.brookings .edu/research/papers/2014/11/competition-exports-productivity) and will appear in a forthcoming special issue of the *Journal of African Economies* in early 2016.

19. Newman and others (2014).

20. Cruz and others (2014).

5 percent of formal manufacturing firms export their products, we found that more productive firms self-selected into exporting and this effect was especially strong for the six sectors with the highest proportions of export-oriented firms. Controlling for this process of self-selection, firm-level productivity increased by 8 to 19 percent following entry into the export market, consistent with learning by exporting. We also found that firms with previous exporting experience were much more likely to export subsequently. This may reflect the presence of high entry costs into exporting.[21]

In Cambodia, like in Mozambique, the majority of firms that export are foreign owned and born global. Although the nature of the data we were able to collect did not permit us to identify the causal relationship between exports and firm-level productivity, we found a strong association and an example of institutional learning through exporting. Export-induced improvements in the legal and institutional framework had positive impacts on the productivity of nonexporting firms.[22]

This new evidence strengthens the case that firms in low-income countries can learn from exporting and helps to explain the radically different patterns of export performance and productivity growth observed across the eleven country case studies. The differences in export orientation and in learning by exporting between foreign-owned firms and domestic firms also raise some intriguing questions about what firms learn by exporting, a topic we take up in chapter 5.

Competition and Productivity

Pressure from potential or existing competitors can increase productivity levels within an industry. Usually this happens when more efficient (i.e., lower-cost and generally lower-price) producers enter a sector or expand. Relatively high-cost firms or plants see their

21. Siba and Gebreeyesus (2014).
22. Chhair and Ung (2014).

market shares erode and are sometimes forced to exit the sector altogether. In high-income economies the rate of churning is large. In the United States, for example, more than one in ten jobs is created in a given year through reallocation between firms and more than one in ten jobs is destroyed.[23]

Firm dynamics are hard to trace in low-income countries. To understand the patterns of entry, exit, and growth of firms fully, we also need a panel of data that follows the birth, death, and growth of the same firms across a number of years. Such data are very scarce in Africa, and much of our evidence on the role of competition is anecdotal or, worse still, based on first principles and "international experience." This is important for policy. The focus on regulatory reform that characterizes the investment climate reform agenda (as discussed in chapter 2) is primarily a consequence of the desire to promote a more competitive environment in Africa by reducing the barriers to entry and exit of firms.

Competition and Productivity in Vietnam and Ethiopia

For that reason we set out to look at entry and exit in two of the countries where we had access to panel data of sufficient length to explore firm dynamics: Vietnam and Ethiopia. We found the same reallocation effects that characterize high-income countries at work in emerging Asia and low-income Africa as well. In Vietnam, the General Statistics Office annually surveys the population of all registered firms with thirty employees or more and a representative sample of smaller firms. Based on these data, we were able to study the dynamics of almost 31,000 Vietnamese manufacturing firms. We found high levels of entry and exit across sectors at both the two-digit and four-digit sector level.[24] We also found evidence that firms "switched" sectors, leaving one line of business and

23. Davis and Haltiwanger (1999).
24. The two-digit ISIC sector classification is quite broad—for example, food products, tobacco, wearing apparel. As we noted previously, the four-digit level is considerably more precise.

entering an entirely different one, a topic we will again examine in chapter 5.

Our work revealed that the reallocation of market shares from less productive to more productive firms is an important component of overall productivity growth in Vietnam. Incumbent firms in a sector rank higher in the sector's productivity distribution than firms entering the sector, and exiting firms have the lowest productivity ranking. Firms that switched from one sector to another ranked higher in terms of productivity than newly entering firms. All of this movement adds up: on average, turnover through firm exit, entry, and switching accounted for 40 percent of total manufacturing productivity growth in Vietnam.[25]

There was also evidence of reallocation in Ethiopia. Unlike most other African countries, Ethiopia has collected a lot of data on performance and employment in the manufacturing sector.[26] We were able to use these detailed data—nearly 10,000 firm-year observations—to analyze entry and exit across firms of differing sizes. Our focus was somewhat different from the work in Vietnam. Because the industrial sector in Ethiopia is small—about 1,000 firms—and our interest was the role of small firms as "job creators"—a topic that we address in chapter 9—we chose to study reallocation among firms of different size rather than in individual industrial subsectors.

Our main interest was in survival. Because most firms entered the market before the first survey year, we focused only on the set of 133 new entrants over the ten-year period of the panel. We modeled firm survival on initial size (measured by employment at start-up) and age (years since start-up). Predicted exit rates are shown in figure 4-1. Clearly, there was a great deal of churning going on in Ethiopia, and size mattered for survival.

25. Newman, Rand, and Tarp (2013).

26. Most of the existing data derive from surveys conducted by the Central Statistical Agency (CSA) of Ethiopia. The most comprehensive dataset is based on the Large and Medium Manufacturing Industries Survey (LMMS), which attempts to cover *all* manufacturing establishments in the country that engage ten persons or more and use power-driven machinery. These data were available to us for each year between 1995–96 and 2005–06.

Figure 4-1. *Firm Size, Age, and the Probability of Exit in Ethiopian Manufacturing*

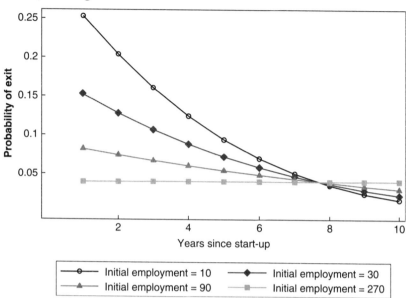

Source: Authors' calculations based on data collected by the Central Statistical Agency of Ethiopia as part of the Large and Medium Manufacturing Industries Survey.
Note: Vertical axis shows the probability of exit. Horizontal axis shows years since start-up.

Half of the firms starting with ten employees (or fewer) were gone after three years, and after eight years two-thirds of the firms starting small had disappeared. Larger firms had a significantly higher probability of surviving than small ones. Firms starting with 270 employees had a higher than 70 percent likelihood of surviving for eight years. At the same time, while young small firms have very high exit rates, conditional on survival for six to seven years, the exit rates were essentially independent of start-up size.[27]

To our surprise we found a remarkable similarity between the results for Ethiopia and the much richer economies in which most of this type of work has been done. In countries in the Organization for Economic Cooperation and Development (OECD) and Latin America, small firms account disproportionately for firm turnover.[28]

27. Page and Söderbom (2014).
28. Haltiwanger, Scarpetta, and Schweiger (2010).

And in the United States and Europe, high productivity is an important predictor of firm survival.[29] In Ethiopia the productivity differences between small firms and large firms are stunning. Value added per worker in firms with 100 employees was more than three times that of firms with five employees; in firms with 200 employees, it was 3.5 times higher.

Concentration and Competition in Africa's Formal Sector

While churning clearly takes place in Ethiopia, there is some evidence to suggest that large, formal manufacturing firms there and elsewhere in Africa face too little competition. The formal manufacturing sectors in all eight of the sub-Saharan countries we studied have highly concentrated product markets. In many industries the top three or four firms account for more than 50 percent of domestic production. World Bank Enterprise Survey data for the formal sector in Kenya shows that the five largest firms account for 58 percent of total value added. In the Mozambique Enterprise Survey, even after excluding the five largest firms, the next five accounted for 47 percent of the remaining value added.[30] In Tanzania the top three or four firms account for more than 50 percent of domestic production in most manufacturing subsectors.[31] Concentration is particularly high in capital-intensive, higher technology sectors such as machinery and equipment, motor vehicles, and electrical machinery and apparatus, but such lower technology sectors as leather and leather products, apparel, textiles, and wood products show high levels of concentration relative to global norms. The Enterprise Maps for Ethiopia, Ghana, Mozambique, Tanzania, and Zambia, to which we refer in chapter 5, consistently find every manufacturing subsector is dominated by a handful of firms.[32]

---

29. Syverson (2011).
30. Gelb, Meyer, and Ramachandran (2014).
31. Yoshino and others (2013).
32. Sutton and Kellow (2010); Sutton and Kpentey (2012); Sutton and Olomi (2012); Sutton and Langmead (2013).

The high level of concentration in formal manufacturing is partly a consequence of the size structure of Africa's manufacturing sector. African manufacturing consists of three distinct segments. At the top are a relatively small number of medium and large-scale firms. These firms generally employ more than fifty workers, are registered with the government, and provide employment contracts that conform to labor legislation. A second segment consists of registered micro and small enterprises (MSEs) in manufacturing; these firms generally employ fewer than fifty employees but are registered with the government. Micro and small firms differ yet again from "household enterprises" that engage in manufacturing. These are tiny firms consisting of a single entrepreneur, perhaps working with unpaid workers who are likely to be family members. Among the manufacturing activities undertaken in the household sector beverages, apparel, and furniture are the most common.

Differences among the three categories in terms of the number of enterprises are stunning. In Tanzania, for example, the 2007 Annual Survey of Industrial Production (ASIP) contained about 540 medium and large-scale enterprises in all sectors. In 2010 the Central Register of Establishments (CRE) listed approximately 6,800 manufacturing enterprises. Of these, approximately 30 percent were micro enterprises and 65 percent were small enterprises.[33] The Tanzania National Panel Survey (NPS) reported that approximately 900,000 household manufacturing enterprises were operating across the country in 2010–11.[34]

Each segment serves the domestic market for manufactured goods, but in general sectors do not compete directly with one another. The products each sector produces and the markets they serve are distinct. Medium and large firms (and some small formal enterprises) sell mainly in the national market and compete most directly with imports. Micro and small enterprises serve more localized urban and rural markets and generally produce lower quality, lower

33. Kweka and Ugarte (2013).
34. Kweka and Fox (2011).

cost goods. Household enterprises serve the poorest and lowest quality market segments. Competition within the micro and small segments and the household enterprise sector can be fierce. In Tanzania, there is significant firm entry and exit among registered firms. About 15 percent of firms exit the market in any given year. Micro and small enterprises account for the vast majority of these exits, around 96 percent of all exiting firms.[35] In Tanzania, as in Ethiopia, there is substantially less churning among large-scale firms.

High concentration need not imply limited competition. In small open economies, imports ought to provide contestability in domestic markets, even those dominated by a small number of large domestic firms. Africa's economies have become much more open to imports over the past twenty years. Yet the World Bank Enterprise Surveys carried out in our eight focus countries often indicate that, imports notwithstanding, many firms do not feel pressed by competition. About 24 percent of large firms in Tanzania, for example, responded to the 2006 Enterprise Survey that there were no new competitors in the markets in which they operated.[36]

Not surprisingly, lack of competition has a negative influence on the incentives for firms to become more productive. The relationship between competition and firm-level performance in Africa has not been extensively studied, but one analysis of firm-level data in Ghana, Kenya, and Tanzania found higher initial profits reduced subsequent productivity growth, which the authors took as evidence of a positive effect of competitive pressure on productivity.[37] In South Africa, other research has found a negative relationship between lagged price-cost margins and productivity growth among firms, which again suggests that there is a positive effect of competition on productivity.[38] The Tanzanian data from 2006 show that firms facing less competition on average made fewer investments in

35. Kweka and Ugarte (2013).
36. Yoshino and others (2013).
37. Harding, Söderbom, and Teal (2004).
38. Aghion, Braun, and Fedderke (2008).

machinery and were less active in introducing new products and new processes in their industrial activities.[39]

One reason that large firms may face too little competition is political influence. Cross-country, firm-level data suggest that companies with strong political connections are able to gain higher market shares, even under circumstances where they underperform in terms of productivity compared to nonconnected companies. The stronger the political links, the higher the market concentration.[40] Our country studies show that larger companies have relatively strong political ties. Early World Bank Enterprise Surveys asked firms to classify themselves as "influential" or "not influential" in terms of their relationships with government. Influential firms reported market shares for their main products at around 40 percent.

This raises the concern that market-dominant firms may have too much leverage in shaping government policies and extracting rents. The evidence on this question is not strong, but it is suggestive. Based on a cross-country sample that included all eight of the African countries we examined in detail, Chong and Gradstein found that the larger the average size of firms and the lower the quality of institutions, the higher the probability that firms will limit government policies designed to create a competitive environment.[41] The negative effects of politically connected firms were found to be greatest when firms operated in countries with high degrees of corruption.

Summing Up

This chapter was the first of three to deal with various sources of firm-level productivity in low-income countries. While measuring productivity presents a number of conceptual and empirical problems, they are not insurmountable. In fact for this chapter and the

39. Yoshino and others (2013).
40. Faccio (2010).
41. Chong and Gradstein (2010).

next two, we were able to undertake a surprisingly large number of studies of the relationship between firm-level productivity and a variety of productivity drivers, despite stiff data requirements.

The empirical literature on the microeconomics of the firm increasingly shows that even within narrowly defined industries differences in firm-level productivity are often large, and they grow as per capita incomes decline. Africa is no exception. There is a long "left hand tail" of inefficient firms in most African industries. Increasing average productivity can be done by raising the productivity of individual firms—a within-firm productivity effect—or by shifting the distribution of firms in the direction of higher average productivity, a between-firm effect. When these two work together, they can be powerful drivers of industrial productivity change.

In this chapter we examined the roles of exports and domestic competition on firm-level productivity growth. Using both country studies and econometrics, we found considerable evidence that learning by exporting takes place. Export success is a within-firm driver of productivity change that does not take place in firms that compete with imports. In chapter 5, we discuss what makes learning by exporting asymmetric in this sense.

Exporting also offers the scope for an important between-firm effect. Firm growth is not limited by the size of the market. Given the small size of most of Africa's economies, the potential productivity gains from reallocation of market shares among firms are limited. Success in exporting, on the other hand, is not limited. More productive exporters can expand without needing to capture market share from local competitors. Moreover, given Africa's tiny presence in global markets, this is possible without any limits to market potential.

Domestic competition matters for productivity as well. We found evidence of reallocation of market shares among firms in some of the countries studied. Indeed, the patterns of birth, death, and growth of firms are not so different from those found in high-income countries. On average, turnover through firm exit, entry, and switching between sectors accounted for 40 percent of total manufacturing productivity growth in Vietnam. In Ethiopia, small firms have much lower prospects of survival than large firms. While churning is clearly present in Africa, our country case studies also suggest that some large-scale firms may be able to shield themselves from competition by exploiting insider privileges. This lack of competitive pressure is reflected in lower rates of firm-level productivity growth.

CHAPTER 5

Firm Capabilities

F irm capabilities are shorthand for the knowledge and practices
used by firms in the course of production and in developing new
products. They are the basic building blocks of productivity and
quality. The term is relatively new, but management experts and
businessmen have known for a long time that firms differ markedly
in the knowledge and working practices of both managers and workers. Globally, firms are competing in capabilities. At some price-
quality combinations they can succeed in entering a market; at others
they will be kept out by higher capability competitors. Part of the
answer to whether African can industrialize hinges on whether its
firms can acquire the capabilities needed to match other producers
in the global market for industrial goods.

This chapter describes what firm capabilities are and management's role in determining productivity and quality. We then discuss
how capabilities shape and are shaped by firms' responses to competition before shifting focus to several ways in which higher capabilities can be brought to low-income countries, including through
foreign direct investment, learning by exporting, and management
training. We finish by describing how capabilities have diffused from

higher capability firms to other firms in Africa and emerging Asia, based on our country case studies and surveys of firm-to-firm knowledge transfers.

What Are Firm Capabilities?

John Sutton—who, as we noted in the preface, has been "mapping" firm capabilities in Africa—writes that "at one level 'capability' is no more than an extension of the traditional notion of productivity to a world in which quality matters."[1] To use his elegant simplification, quality is a "demand shifter." Hence, it is a shorthand expression for anything that moves the demand schedule outward at every price, including such things as technical characteristics, after-sales service or brand image. Used in this way "quality" embraces a much wider range of characteristics than the intrinsic technical excellence of the product itself.[2] For example, for an Ethiopian flower exporter, knowing which varieties of roses will be fashionable at different times of the year may be as important as the appearance of the rose itself. Productivity is a "cost shifter." Modifications in such things as the organization of production, reductions in wastage, or better supervision of the workforce can lower unit production costs at every quantity level.

Productivity and quality in turn rest on the knowledge possessed by the individuals who make up the firm, both managers and workers. In this respect capabilities are fundamentally different from technology. Technology can be written down in a blueprint and purchased, but the skills needed to use it effectively tend to be tied up in firms and the people who work in them. Capabilities are mainly embodied in complex and interrelated working practices, so they are difficult to codify. They reflect the capacity of individuals to work effectively together within some framework of rules, routines,

1. Sutton (2004).
2. See Sutton (2012). This is a broad definition of quality, and not surprisingly it is difficult to measure.

and tacit understandings that have been put in place or have evolved over time.[3] Such tacit knowledge and working practices are used in production and to develop new products, including, as we shall see, the capacity to shift from one type of product into the production of an entirely different one.

Revealed Capabilities

Because capabilities are hard to codify they are difficult to measure. What we can measure are differences in productivity and to some extent quality—revealed capabilities. As we noted in chapter 4, there are large differences in productivity across firms in the same industry, and these differences grow larger as we move from high- to low-income countries. We saw very large differences in productivity across firms in our African country studies; in particular between small and large firms. Large firms were significantly and persistently more productive than smaller enterprises. In Vietnam, the range of productivity levels within narrowly defined product groups was also very large. This is one dimension of the revealed capabilities of firms.

Similar, although less well studied, differences exist in product quality, again even in very narrowly defined product groups. Much of the current literature on quality and trade attempts to measure export quality using unit values. Other things being equal, higher unit values are associated with higher product quality. Globally, higher income per capita is correlated with higher export quality. There are, however, wide variations in average quality among developing countries, even when controlling for income.[4] Vietnam is an example of a country that has achieved considerable quality upgrading, particularly in the miscellaneous manufactures sector, which includes apparel and footwear.[5]

3. See Sutton (2005, 2012).
4. See Hummels and Klenow (2005) and Henn, Papageorgiou, and Spatafora (2013).
5. Henn, Papageorgiou, and Spatafora (2013).

Quality differences are important in domestic markets as well. In one of the econometric studies we undertook for Learning to Compete (L2C), we were able to match the physical characteristics of some standard manufactured products in Ethiopia, such as cement blocks, with their prices in the same market. The variation in prices for the same product was striking and reflected customers' perceptions of quality differences.[6] The "household" manufacturing sector in African economies produces products that are quite different in terms of quality from those produced in the formal sector. They sell at lower prices and serve a distinct, lower quality market.

Capabilities and Competitiveness in Africa

The differences in the contributions of quality and productivity to international competitiveness are subtle yet crucially important. To some extent, shortfalls in productivity can be made up by low wages.[7] Shortfalls in quality, on the other hand, may make it impossible for firms to break into global markets. Recent studies of product quality and trade have made an important discovery. In many sectors higher export volumes go hand in hand with higher export prices.[8] If firms all produced products of the same quality this would not be so. Higher productivity firms would have higher output and exports, not higher prices. The coexistence of high prices and high volumes is what happens when firms compete on quality.

Sutton's Enterprise Maps offer some insight into how current capabilities affect Africa's ability to compete globally. The surveys of five countries—Ethiopia, Ghana, Mozambique, Tanzania, and Zambia—reveal some important common themes. Such industries

6. Siba and others (2012).

7. The low-wage advantage is limited because virtually all manufactured exports require some minimum amount of intermediate inputs sold at fixed international prices. When—as in the case of trade in tasks—intermediate inputs comprise a significant share of total production costs, the low-wage advantage can be significantly eroded.

8. Verhoogen (2008) and Manova and Zhang (2012).

as food and beverages and cement and building materials are fairly highly developed in each country. Metal and mechanical industries, engineering and assembly, and plastics are not. The crucial difference between these types of industries is that food, cement, and building materials all serve the local market and are subject to substantial "natural protection" due to weight, perishability, or bulk. They are also products sold to consumers directly. In each economy firms have evolved that have achieved standards of quality and productivity that allow them to compete with imports successfully.[9]

Metals, engineering and assembly, and plastics are different. While all five countries have some activity in each industry, it is generally limited to the least demanding segments of the market in terms of both quality and productivity. Local steel production from scrap is common, but the range of steel products produced is quite limited. Plastics are mainly confined to injection-molded containers and domestic utensils and a range of plastic pipes and cables. The major internationally traded products in these sectors are not produced in Africa. That is because these are intermediate goods for which the international quality standards are high and the demand on African capabilities is too great.[10]

Management Matters

Intuitively, managers must to a large extent be responsible for productivity and quality differences, either as a consequence of innate differences in their abilities or as a result of differences in management practices. Managers are the "conductors of an input orchestra. They coordinate the application of labor, capital, and intermediate inputs."[11] They must be able to identify and develop new products,

---

9. See, for example, Sutton and Kellow (2010), Sutton and Kpentey (2012), or Sutton and Olomi (2012).
10. Sutton (2012).
11. Syverson (2011, p. 336).

organize production activity, motivate workers, and adapt to changing circumstances. Just as a poor conductor can ruin an orchestra, a poor manager can ruin an enterprise.

Managerial inputs are hard to define and measure. While it is important to know how managers allocate their time, it is equally important to know what managers do with the time allocated; for example, how they motivate workers or deal with suppliers. Some quite recent work at the intersection of management studies and economics helps to take us part way toward understanding the importance of management practices to productivity at the firm level.

Management Practices and Productivity

Nicholas Bloom and John Van Reenen use interviews to score managerial practices from best to worst practice across a wide range of day-to-day operational management activities.[12] They have by now undertaken surveys of nearly 6,000 firms in seventeen countries, including China, India, and Brazil.[13] They find that higher quality management practices (measured by higher scores) are strongly correlated with several measures of productivity and firm performance, including survival.[14] A particularly interesting finding is that China, India, and Brazil all have much lower average management scores than the higher income countries in their sample.[15] This is due mainly to a very large left hand tail of poorly managed (low

12. Bloom and Van Reenen (2007).

13. See Bloom and Van Reenen (2010) and Bloom and others (2010).

14. This approach is not without its problems, which Bloom and Van Reenen acknowledge. Much of what was scored as "best practice" management was based on the recommendations of the management consulting industry. It is possible that these "best practices" are in fact just the latest managerial fads. It is also possible that more productive and profitable firms are better able to hire management consultants, raising the possibility of reverse causation.

15. Bloom and Van Reenen (2010).

scoring) firms in the distribution, a pattern that parallels closely the productivity distributions in these countries relative to higher income countries discussed in chapter 4.

Two factors emerge as important predictors of the quality of management. Greater competition in the firm's market, measured in several ways, is positively correlated with better managerial practice. Family ownership, on the other hand, is associated with poorer managerial practice.[16] Surprisingly, the family tie to poor management is not the result of ownership itself. Controlling for other factors, family ownership is positively associated with good management practice in their surveys. Rather, it is the combination of family ownership with a rigid rule about how the chief executive is selected—usually based on sex and birth order—that is the flaw. This result may be of particular relevance to African industry, where many firms are family owned and the eldest son often succeeds his father.

One problem with the survey approach is that it is difficult to establish the causal direction of the relationship running from better management to higher productivity. This is an area where randomized experiments have something to contribute. Bloom and his associates have provided the first experimental evidence on the importance of management practices in developing country firms.[17]

In a novel experiment they randomly assigned a sample of large, multiplant Indian textile firms to treatment and control groups. The treated firms received a month-long analysis of thirty-eight aspects of operational management followed by four months of intensive follow-up in the plant from a large international consulting firm. The control plants received only one month of diagnostic consulting. Within the first year, productivity increased on average by 17 percent in treated firms. The better-managed firms also grew faster and

---

16. Not surprisingly, this is a somewhat controversial result. It is consistent with evidence from Denmark; see Bennedsen and others (2007). But it is not supported by French stock market data; see Sraer and Thesmar (2007).

17. See Bloom and others (2013).

voluntarily spread the management improvements from their treated plants to other plants they owned.

One of the central questions raised by management training programs is why managerial good practices are not taken up more rapidly if they are a source of sustained productivity improvements. There are at least three answers to this question. First, incumbent managers may have problems of perception—they do not know they are ineffective. Second, managers may have problems of inspiration—they know they are ineffective and don't know what to do about it. Third, managers may have problems of motivation—they know they are not effective; they know what to do; but they fail to act because of lack of competition or lack of incentives.[18]

Interestingly, Bloom and his collaborators observed all three of these problems in the India case. Their evidence, while incomplete, suggests that information constraints were the greatest impediment to better managerial practice. Firms apparently did not believe that such basic practices as measuring quality defects or machine downtime and keeping track of inventory would improve profits. Owners claimed their quality was as good as that of other local firms, and because they were profitable, they felt they did not need to introduce a quality control process. Managers were often simply unaware of such common practices as daily factory meetings, standardized operating procedures, or inventory control norms.

Management and Capabilities in Africa

One of the most important empirical regularities of the Enterprise Maps is that Africa lacks capable medium-size firms. Among registered firms in Africa, large firms (those with more than 100 workers) employ about 50 percent of the labor force. Medium-scale enterprises (those employing from 20 to 99 workers) represent about 27 percent of workers, and small firms a further 23 percent. In the World Bank Enterprise Survey data firms with 30 employees have, on average, twice as much value added per worker as firms with 5 employees.

18. Gibbons and Henderson (2012).

Value added per worker in African firms with 100 employees is more than 50 percent higher than that in firms with 30 employees.[19]

Lack of two major capabilities in smaller firms may drive these numbers. The first is the inability to manage a growing labor force. This is a critical attribute of more capable firms in low-wage economies. The second is the ability to see market opportunities and manage the supply chain. The scarcity of capable medium-scale firms may also help to explain why firms in the formal sector face limited competition. Conventional wisdom has tended to ascribe the limited entry and growth of small and medium firms in manufacturing to lack of access to finance or regulatory barriers to entry. Rather, it may be that the pool of capable entrepreneur-managers is the binding constraint.

Our country study for Tanzania carried out a survey of fifty emerging "sunrise" industrial enterprises. Between 2010 and 2012, the output of these firms grew by an average of 49 percent. About 80 percent of the firms interviewed hired professional managers and cited "quality management" as an important element in the firm's success. Over 90 percent indicated that they had significantly adapted their sales and marketing strategies to changing circumstances in the last three years, and about a third had introduced new products. Half of the firms surveyed reported that they undertook in-house research and development activities.[20]

What about management and quality? Here again, the Enterprise Maps of Ethiopia, Ghana, Mozambique, Tanzania, and Zambia are a useful point of departure. All of these countries have a similar breakdown of the fifty leading industrial companies by origin.[21] About half of the firms originated in the domestic private sector, about a quarter are foreign firms, and about a quarter began as public-sector firms. Of the domestic firms, it turns out that by far

19. Page and Söderbom (2015).
20. Wangwe and others (2014).
21. Sutton's Enterprise Maps are deliberately not representative of the industrial sector as a whole. He identifies and interviews the best-performing firms in the leading industrial sectors of each economy.

the largest group—about half in most countries—had owners and managers who began in trading companies. Many development practitioners, and an even larger number of policymakers, find this result surprising. Seen through a capabilities lens it is less remarkable.

As we pointed out, most successful domestic manufacturing firms in Africa today are found in sectors that use standard technology to meet final demand. The required technical know-how can be obtained from equipment suppliers and by hiring a number of experienced engineers and technical experts. The relevant dimension of "quality" is a detailed understanding of both local and the international markets in order to identify a viable business opportunity and to set up a successful manufacturing enterprise. The trading sector is often where the deepest knowledge of local and international market conditions is found.[22]

Capabilities and Competition

In chapter 4, we described how market pressure can improve firm-level productivity by forcing the exit of inefficient firms and rewarding the entry or expansion of more productive enterprises. Competitive pressure is a major incentive for firms to acquire new capabilities, often revealed in higher productivity. One of the key factors that limited the introduction of new management practices in the training experiments in India was lack of competitive pressure. Competition was heavily restricted by high tariffs in the case of imports and, in the case of new entry, by lack of finance. A surprising result, and one that offers a cautionary tale for Africa, was that competition and reallocation of market shares to better-managed firms were also limited by the number of male family members. Nonfamily members were not trusted by firm owners with any decision-making power, and the inability to delegate decisions outside the family limited the growth of more efficient firms.

22. Sutton (2012).

This raises a red flag. As we pointed out in chapter 4, formal manufacturing firms in the African economies we studied do not feel strongly pressured by competitors. Barriers to entry and the family structure of many African enterprises may act as a disincentive for firms to adopt better management practice. Surveys in Tanzania, for example, found that firms facing less competition were less active in introducing new products and new processes in their industrial activities.[23] In Kenya and Mozambique as well, our country studies found that perceived lack of competitive pressure discouraged firms from introducing new technologies or process innovations.

One of our Learning to Compete studies investigated the different channels through which intermediate imports impact productivity in Vietnam. We found that the most important channel was through competition with domestic suppliers. Domestic firms that supplied inputs to downstream users were forced to match newly liberalized imports in price and quality or lose market share. In short, they improved their capabilities through matching those embodied in the new imports. These competition-induced gains in upstream sectors spilled over to downstream sectors through the supply chain.[24]

Capabilities—in this case mainly those of managers—also partly determine how firms adapt to changes in the competitive environment. Rather than simply close down in the face of increased competition and declining profits, higher capability firms may switch into entirely new lines of activity. In high-income countries the number of firms that switch sectors is impressive. A famous example is Nokia, which began as a gumboot manufacturer. Approximately 8 percent of U.S. manufacturing firms switched sectors (defined at the four-digit level) during five-year periods between 1977 and 1997.[25] It turns out that this capacity for change is also important in

23. Yoshino and others (2013).
24. Newman, Rand, and Tarp (2015).
25. Bernard, Jensen, and Schott (2006).

low-income countries. In Vietnam, our research found that between 1 and 19 percent of firms exited one sector and entered another at the two-digit sector level, and from 12 to 50 percent changed sectors at the four-digit level.[26]

Although we were not able to measure capabilities directly, we found that firms changing sectors ranked higher in terms of productivity than firms entering or exiting the same sector. This suggests they are a separate, more capable group. Switching firms moved into more labor-intensive sectors and were more likely to switch between sectors with a high share of firms that had larger numbers of employees. This is consistent with the idea that a major aspect of capability in low-wage economies is the ability to organize and supervise the firm's labor force. We also found that Vietnamese firms tended to move from sectors with lower levels of foreign ownership into sectors with higher levels of foreign ownership. These were also sectors with higher levels of exports.

Building Capabilities

The first phase of capability building involves the introduction of a higher level of capability into an economy, either as a consequence of the entry of new, more capable firms or as a result of learning by existing firms. Learning involves two closely related elements. The first is the acquisition of technical know-how or engineering expertise. This "mastery of technology" is the element that has been most studied by economists interested in economic development.[27] The second is the improvement of "working practices," which has traditionally been the domain of management studies. While working practices are always critical to achieving high quality, the relative importance of technological know-how shifts as countries move up the technological ladder. Engineering good practice is far more

26. Newman, Rand, and Tarp (2013).
27. UNIDO in particular has had a long tradition of studying the role of technological knowledge in development. See UNIDO (2003) for an example.

important in manufacturing pharmaceuticals or machine tools than in making T-shirts. Foreign direct investment, learning through exporting, and management information and training are all ways in which capabilities have been built in low-income countries.

Foreign Direct Investment

Foreign direct investment (FDI) is one way of introducing higher capability firms into a lower capability environment—and some would argue that for countries at low levels of industrial development, it is the most important means. The foreign investor brings the technology, managerial knowledge, and working practices it has developed elsewhere. A majority of researchers find that firms with foreign equity participation in developing countries typically have higher output per worker or higher levels of total factor productivity (TFP) than similar domestically owned firms.[28] Most of the literature on FDI has focused on its role as a source of technology transfer, but because of the way in which productivity is measured, these econometric results may equally be capturing the transfer of working practices or managerial good practice.

FDI has played an important role in the industrialization and export performance of Cambodia, Mauritius, Tunisia, and Vietnam. Asian-based FDI has largely driven Cambodia's manufactured exports. Forty-seven percent of foreign-owned establishments are owned by Chinese investors and another 12.5 percent by Koreans and other Asian nationalities. During the period 1990–2013, FDI represented 34.4 percent of total investment. FDI inflows to Mauritius have increased rapidly in the past several years, mainly into tourism, property and real estate, banking and finance, information technology, and health and education services, reflecting the economy's stage

---

28. For a survey of the relevant literature, see Harrison and Rodriguez-Clare (2010). When we launched Learning to Compete we hoped to be able to replicate the kind of econometric work referred to previously for some of our sub-Saharan Africa countries. What we found was that there were too few foreign and joint venture firms in the data—and more importantly in the countries—to give accurate statistical results.

of structural transformation.[29] In Tunisia, the "offshore" policy regime was specifically designed to attract foreign investors to a task-based export platform near Europe. Tunisia's offshore sector was an early magnet for European investors, particularly in textiles and garments. Vietnam has been a target for relocation of labor-intensive industries from other countries in Asia. Foreign direct investment as a share of total investment in Vietnam averaged 23.2 percent between 1990 and 2013. Manufacturing has been the largest and fastest-growing FDI sector, taking up over 60 percent of all FDI.

Our country case studies highlighted some of the ways in which the introduction of new capabilities takes place through FDI. A number of large multinationals, including Nike and Adidas, have strengthened their contract manufacturing activities in Vietnam. As a result, the Vietnamese-made share of Nike's footwear production increased from 25 percent in 2005 to 41 percent in 2012. In the software industry IBM has developed a program called PartnerWorld to integrate its Vietnamese suppliers into its global value chain. There have been some signs that regional investors in Vietnam are moving into more sophisticated products. In the steel industry, Formosa Plastics Corporation has started to invest in a US$8 billion plant. In the electronics industry, leading companies such as Foxconn and Samsung are also investing in several multibillion-dollar projects.

Foreign investors, including from countries such as Brazil, China, India, and Turkey, are starting to make inroads into African manufacturing and services. Ghana and Mozambique, for example, have received some market-seeking FDI fueled by the relatively strong growth of their economies in recent years. Vodafone Group (United Kingdom) acquired a 70 percent stake in Ghana Telecommunications Company Ltd. for US$900 million. Privatization attracted considerable FDI into Mozambique and Ghana, drawing international firms such as Coca-Cola and SABMiller. Uganda has also attracted substantial foreign direct investment. Between 1991 and 2009, one-third of Uganda's FDI, close to US$2.9 billion, went into manu-

29. Zafar (2011).

facturing. More than half of the firms in Uganda's manufacturing sector are foreign owned. There are a growing number of success stories of export-oriented FDI in manufacturing not directly related to extractive industries—for example, shoe manufacturing in Ethiopia, bicycles and motor bikes in Tanzania, and pharmaceuticals in East Africa.

Our surveys of foreign and domestic firms revealed an important way in which multinationals help introduce new capabilities related to working practices and managerial good practices into Africa. The surveys show that transfers of capabilities are often manifested in terms of spin-offs by former employees of FDI firms and in labor movements from foreign to domestic companies. One-third of multinationals interviewed for the L2C project reported employees leaving their company to set up local enterprises directly connected to the multinational. These linked domestic entrepreneurs often became either customers of or suppliers to the multinational. Moreover, over one-fourth of these linked domestic firms reported that they hired employees initially trained by multinational companies.[30]

Learning Capabilities by Exporting

As we saw in chapter 4, manufactured exports are an important driver of productivity change in Africa and emerging Asia. Here, as in the case of FDI, the focus of most economists interested in these issues has been on the role of exports in the acquisition of technology.[31] The more recent empirical literature on learning by exporting, including the result of the new studies done under the Learning to Compete project, provides a different perspective. It strongly suggests that "learning by exporting" helps to strengthen firm capabilities through improvements in working practices and management. Two of the key mechanisms by which higher capabilities are introduced to firms are:

30. Newman and others (2015).
31. See, for example, Pack and Page (1993).

—*Demanding Buyers.* In some industries—apparel and agro-based industry, for example—exchanges of information between suppliers and buyers with a reputation for high quality are well developed and add to the capabilities of supplying firms.

—*Repeated Relationships.* In many industries there is a close and continuing contractual relationship between buyer and supplier that often involves a two-way movement of technical and engineering personnel between their respective plants.[32]

Demanding buyers and repeated relationships are characteristic of global markets, spanning the range of industries from traditional manufacturing to tradable services and agro-industry. These inter-firm relationships are often the means by which tacit knowledge is exchanged between supplier and purchaser.

Ethiopia's cut flower industry illustrates how demanding buyers help to develop capabilities. Floriculture is the newest of Ethiopia's export industries, having grown very rapidly over the past five years to become the country's fourth largest export industry. The industry began in 2005 when a number of foreign firms (mostly flower producers from Kenya) and local businesses started production. There are today about a hundred flower producers and exporters, and the industry directly employs more than 50,000 workers.

The main market for Ethiopian flowers is the Netherlands (which accounts for 80 percent of revenue). The main product is roses. The international wholesale market is characterized by demanding buyers with respect to quality, timeliness, and fashion. Flower retailers in high-income markets are increasingly entering into direct marketing agreements with producers to control product selection, quality, and delivery. Different types of roses are demanded at different times of year, and selection of particular varieties to plant is a critical element of quality.

The most successful Ethiopian firms—mainly foreign or expatriate owned—are linked to direct sales channels, allowing them to produce and export more varieties and benefit from the expert

32. Sutton (2005).

advice of buyers. One of Ethiopia's largest exporters has its own sales and distribution company in the Netherlands. Another has distribution networks in the international market, and an international production quality expert visits the firm at least once a month to oversee production and ensure that quality is maintained. A third leading exporter has become a "Fair Trade Certified" company, based on its environmental and social track record. The firm believes that this certification will enable it to win niche markets with the potential to earn premium prices.[33]

Our econometric results on learning by exporting also suggest that much of the productivity enhancement observed in exporting firms, especially domestically owned exporters, comes as a result of increases in capabilities. In Vietnam, for example, we found that the sources of productivity improvements differed between foreign and domestic firms. Foreign firms experienced an early surge of productivity growth upon entering export markets, but it was short-lived and attributable to increases in scale. Domestic firms, on the other hand, had longer durations of productivity improvements, mainly from introducing process innovations. This pattern of learning by exporting is consistent with the initial presence of higher capabilities in foreign firms and the greater opportunities for learning by domestic enterprises.

In Mozambique we found that exporting firms were largely foreign owned and "born global," established to serve the export market primarily. The foreign firms presumably began with higher levels of capabilities than local firms, developed on the basis of their operations elsewhere. Nevertheless, we found that these firms further increased their productivity in the process of exporting, largely through supplier-purchaser relationships.

In Ethiopia, fewer than 5 percent of industrial firms export, but those that do reap significant benefits in terms of productivity gains. These firms are concentrated in a small number of sectors, and a prior history of exporting is a good predictor of whether an Ethiopian firm will export again. For Ethiopia, a relatively isolated and

---

33. Gebreeyesus and Iizuka (2010); Sutton and Kellow (2010).

landlocked country, key elements of the fixed costs of entering new export markets are the ability to identify a viable market opportunity and mastery of the logistics of getting to distant markets. These capabilities are learned in the process of exporting.

Management Information and Training

The association between better management and higher firm capabilities suggests that organized efforts to acquire and spread good management practices can play a role in capability building. These efforts could take the form of collective actions by firms or a public-private partnership to seek out and make available information on managerial good practices. In India, for example, the Confederation of Indian Industries, which is almost wholly funded by the private sector, provides services of this kind at fees that are within the reach of India's smaller manufacturing companies. The Fundación Chile is another example of a public-private partnership for building capabilities. Its success in helping to establish Chile's world-class wine and salmon export industries has been widely documented.

Management training of the type offered to large firms in India by Bloom and his associates is another means of improving capabilities. The expertise of the international consultants certainly proved highly valuable to the firms trained. In addition to increasing productivity, the intensive training led to significant improvements in quality and inventory control. Management training is not a panacea for capability building, however. Business training is one of the most common forms of support to micro, small, and medium enterprises (MSMEs) in Africa and around the world. There are a large number of programs offered by governments, aid donors, microfinance organizations, and nongovernmental organizations (NGOs). This is a very different target group for training than medium- to large-scale Indian textile plants, and the results of most training programs have been disappointing.

A recent review of what we are learning from evaluations of the impact of MSME training programs makes for unhappy reading. Although almost all of the impact evaluations found that participating firms started implementing some of the business practices taught, the extent of change in behavior was in most cases small. Because virtually all of the evaluations suffered from a combination of small changes in business practices and low statistical power, few studies found training to have any significant impact on sales, profitability, or growth. Ironically and disturbingly, training was found to have no or a slightly negative impact on the survival of female-owned businesses. These results suggest that major rethinking of the design of MSME training programs is needed.[34]

Diffusion of Capabilities

Once a higher level of capability has been introduced—say, through a new foreign direct investment or through a newly successful export activity—its potential benefit to the host economy at large will depend in part on the extent to which the technical knowledge and working practices held by the firm are transmitted to other firms. Most of what we know about how capabilities are transferred comes from case studies or from econometric analyses of "spillovers" from FDI. Both types of evidence point in the same direction: buyer-seller relationships along the value chain are effective ways to transfer both technological knowledge and better working practices.

Productivity Spillovers

A cottage industry in the analysis of FDI spillovers has developed in the economics literature in the last ten years. Once again the attention of most economists has been on technological spillovers, and the empirical indicator used has been some measure of firm-level productivity. It broadly points to a consistent set of findings. There is evidence of positive productivity spillovers from foreign firms to domestic suppliers (backward linkages) and from foreign suppliers to domestic firms (forward linkages), although in the case of forward

---

34. McKenzie and Woodruff (2012).

linkages the evidence is much sparser. These are "vertical" spillovers. The same studies generally find insignificant "horizontal" spillovers to firms within the same industry.[35] This is not altogether surprising. Firms have little incentive to transfer capabilities to competing enterprises while they may benefit from improvements in the capabilities of suppliers or customers.

Our work in Vietnam finds that a large part of vertical spillovers from FDI, particularly forward spillovers, accrues to firms that are directly linked to foreign-owned firms, highlighting the importance of firm-to-firm interactions in the knowledge transfer process.[36] Case study evidence supports the view that these productivity spillovers may have very little or nothing to do with technological or engineering knowledge. They often reflect the impact of better management practice or production routines. In industries where business practices or production routines have become standardized—such as clothing or horticultural exports—the transfer of knowledge of business practices through firm-to-firm interactions has become highly efficient.

Equipment and input suppliers can also play a key role in capability transfer. Recently some empirical evidence of the links between increased imported intermediates and firm-level productivity has emerged, mainly drawn from middle-income countries. In Indonesia one study found that the productivity gains from tariff reductions that allowed cheaper intermediate inputs were at least as high as the gains associated with lower output tariffs.[37] Similar evidence for imported inputs as a channel of productivity growth has been found for Columbia and for Chile.[38]

These productivity gains reflect both within-firm changes and competition. Firms that directly import intermediates gain productivity from new, more advanced input technologies.[39] Domestic

---

35. Harrison and Rodriguez-Clare (2010).
36. Newman and others (2015).
37. Amiti and Konings (2007).
38. Fernandes (2007) and Kasahara and Rodrigue (2008).
39. Grossman and Helpman (1991).

producers of intermediates that compete with new imports may also learn from the imported goods, in particular if they are more technologically advanced, are of higher quality, or are a new variety. In Indonesia, for example, opening the economy to imports of intermediates appears to have pushed domestic suppliers along the supply chain to innovate, improve quality, and reduce costs and prices.[40]

Firm-to-Firm Interactions in Practice

What can we say about the transmission of capabilities in the African and the emerging Asian countries we have been studying? As we noted earlier, there are so few foreign-owned manufacturing firms in sub-Saharan Africa that the statistical power of any attempt to test for the presence of inter-firm productivity spillovers would be minimal. Instead of taking that route we have spoken directly with firms. Drawing on information from investment promotion agencies, we conducted interviews with over 100 multinational enterprises (MNEs) and over 200 domestic firms linked to these MNEs as suppliers, customers, or competitors in seven countries (Cambodia, Ethiopia, Ghana, Kenya, Mozambique, Uganda, and Vietnam).

We studied whether and how direct relations between MNEs and domestic firms led to recognized transfers of knowledge (capabilities) and technology. As noted previously, we generally observed fewer direct linkages between MNEs and domestic firms in sub-Saharan Africa than in Asia. But, where these business-related linkages existed, upstream and downstream connections in Africa were more likely to involve explicit transfers of capabilities from MNEs to domestic firms.

Our interviews suggest that multinational enterprises are an important source of capabilities for domestic firms in Africa, and that the transfer of capabilities takes place mainly through structured firm-to-firm transmission of good practices.[41] Most of these transfers were directly stipulated in contracts between the foreign-owned

40. Blalock and Veloso (2007).
41. Newman and others (2015).

firms and their domestic customers and suppliers.[42] These contractual exchanges of knowledge were a "repeated relationship," and the knowledge transferred appeared to have more to do with working practices than technological know-how. Most domestic firms acquired their technology (equipment and machinery) through direct imports. While equipment suppliers were one source of production knowledge, the contractual knowledge transfers occurred more frequently through FDI.[43]

Summing Up

Firm capabilities are the knowledge and working practices possessed by the people who make up a firm. They are the basic determinants of productivity and quality. In chapter 3 we focused on productivity's role in breaking into world markets. The new empirical literature on international trade tells us that quality matters a great deal in global markets for industrial goods as well. Thus, firms are actually competing in capabilities. One of the reasons Africa has so little industry is that it lacks a range of capabilities needed to be internationally competitive. This makes the questions of how higher capabilities are acquired and how they are diffused of central interest.

Intuitively, firm capabilities must be closely related to management. Historically, economists have neglected management, preferring instead to focus, as we did in chapter 4, on factors external to the firm, such as exporting or competition. Recent work at the intersection of economics and management studies very strongly points to the conclusion that management matters a great deal. Differences in management practice between firms and countries are responsible for much of the difference in measured productivity. Management also matters for the ability of firms to adapt to competitive pressure.

42. This is consistent with the findings of other case studies. See Moran (2001).
43. A point made long ago by Kenneth Arrow (1969).

Building firm capabilities is a complex process, driven mainly through firm-to-firm interactions. The capability transfer itself consists of both "hardware"—technological knowledge and engineering practice—and "software"—the working practices that are crucial to master the technology and achieve higher quality. The relative importance of these two factors changes as countries move toward more complex, technologically sophisticated products. Our interviews of foreign and domestic firms suggest that in low-income countries, such as those in Africa and emerging Asia, for the time being working practices are likely to be more important.

Foreign direct investment and learning by exporting are two well-known ways in which higher capabilities are acquired. Management information and training is another. Capability spillovers can take place when firms interact along the value chain. Our empirical work indicates that these firm-to-firm interactions are important, especially in Africa. Geography can also play a role. It is often easier to serve customers or monitor competitors and learn from these interactions if they are located close by. This is one of the reasons that firms tend to cluster, which is the subject of chapter 6.

CHAPTER 6

Industrial Clusters

Firms tend to concentrate in clusters and cities, drawn by the markets they serve, the products and services they produce, and the skills they require. In France, the United Kingdom, and the United States, 75 to 95 percent of industry is clustered or concentrated relative to overall economic activity.[1] Firms in low- and middle-income countries show similar tendencies toward geographical concentration. More than half of the large-scale industrial firms in Tunisia are located in only two geographical areas. In Vietnam, villages in ancient times concentrated on producing individual products such as wooden furniture or ceramics, and today large firms are surrounded by literally tens of thousands of small enterprises in two major industrial clusters near Hanoi and Ho Chi Minh City. In Cambodia, manufacturing and service firms cluster near major cities. In Africa, the Suame Magazine near Kumasi, Ghana, is home to thousands of small metalworking firms, such as lathe turners, welders, and casting foundries.

1. World Bank (2009b).

Agglomeration economies are the productivity benefits that come when firms locate near one another. The motivations for and the benefits of agglomeration have been recognized and studied at least since the time of Alfred Marshall.[2] Recent theoretical and empirical research has helped us to understand better the nature of agglomerations and their role in the industrialization process. In this chapter we are mainly interested in understanding how industrial agglomeration impacts firm-level productivity in poor countries. This is important because virtually all of the evidence we have on agglomeration comes from countries with middle and higher incomes. Thus, in Learning to Compete (L2C) we attempted to undertake a number of careful econometric studies of the relationship between geographical concentration and firm-level productivity.

We begin by defining what agglomeration economies are. Then we turn our attention to some of the ways the spatial concentration of industry has evolved in our sample of African and emerging Asian countries. The chapter briefly describes how the urbanization of industry is taking place in Africa, based on our country case studies. Following that, we present new evidence—to our knowledge the first of its kind—on the relationship between spatial concentration and the productivity of firms in low-income countries. We wrap up by discussing how agglomerations, capabilities, and competition are interrelated.

Understanding Agglomeration

Broadly speaking, agglomeration economies come from two sources: localization (i.e., proximity to producers of the same commodity or service) and urbanization (i.e., proximity to producers of a wide range of commodities and services). At the risk of simplification, localization economies are the forces that drive the formation of industrial clusters, while urbanization economies are the forces that

2. Marshall (1920).

help drive the formation of cities. The Suame Magazine and the Arusha furniture cluster are examples of agglomerations driven by localization economies. The world's megacities are the extreme expression of urbanization economies.

Localization Economies and Industrial Clusters

Beginning with Marshall, economic geographers have argued that the proximity of firms in similar or related activities can lead to a number of localized external economies. Geographic concentration helps to broaden the market for input suppliers, allowing them to exploit economies of scale in production. A large localized market permits suppliers to provide specialized goods and services tailored to the needs of their buyers. Proximity may also help to ensure timely delivery, lower inventory costs, and enhanced quality. The result is higher profits for upstream firms accompanied by easier access to a broader range of inputs for their customers.

"Thick" labor markets expand the range of skills available to employers and facilitate better matching to their distinctive needs. Workers with skills specialized in a sector will be attracted to areas where employment in the sector is high, relative to the total labor force. The density of employment reduces search costs and provides a measure of insurance against unemployment. Similarly, firms will be attracted to areas where there are a large number of workers (or managers) with skills relevant to their industry. Location in a large labor market also makes it easier to find specialized labor, such as designers, engineers, and consultants.

Concentration makes it more likely that workers and entrepreneurs will learn from each other. When firms in the same industry are located close to one another, it is easier to monitor what the neighbors do and learn from their successes and mistakes. Workers and managers may move across firms, facilitating knowledge spillovers. Closeness to competitors in the same sector also allows firms to stay abreast of market information. Collective action through intra-cluster cooperation between firms can help overcome common constraints such as information failures or weak contract enforcement, leading to efficiency gains for all firms within clusters.[3] Industrial concentrations in low-income countries attract specialized trading firms, including those engaged in international trade, that benefit small and medium firms trying to break into new markets.[4]

Case studies provide evidence that when upstream and downstream firms in a particular industry and the institutions associated with them—for example, universities and trade associations—cluster together, competitive pressures force firms to innovate or fail.[5] Since a firm's competitors are by definition within its own industry, this is a localization effect. This is clearly the story of Silicon Valley, centered on Stanford University and close to the University of California at Berkeley. The province of Penang in Malaysia provides a middle-income country illustration. The electronics cluster in Penang has evolved from simple assembly operations to integrated electronics manufacturing and product innovation. In part, this evolution was due to the active role played by universities and public-private partnerships aimed at upgrading the industry.[6]

Evidence suggests that spatial concentration varies with the level of sophistication of the industry. It is more pronounced in high-skill and high-technology industries—electronics, computing machinery, process control instruments, semiconductors, and pharmaceuticals—than light industries such as footwear and textiles. In the United States, for example, electrical and electronic equipment and transport equipment tend to be more concentrated than metal products, machinery, and equipment manufacturing.[7] In Korea, heavy and transport industries (e.g., metals, chemicals, and transport equipment) tend to be found in a few highly specialized cities, while traditional or light industries (e.g., food and textiles) are more spatially dispersed.[8]

3. Schmitz (1995).
4. Sonobe and Otsuka (2006).
5. Porter (1990).
6. Rasiah (2007).
7. Henderson (1997).
8. Henderson, Shalizi, and Venables (2001).

Localization effects can be powerful, even for simple products. The Nnewi automotive parts cluster in Nigeria is home to some eighty-five firms that manufacture and export automotive parts, primarily to West Africa. Nnewi became a hub for local traders in automotive parts in the 1970s. When the traders began importing machinery, mainly from Taiwan, a vibrant cluster of manufacturers of automotive parts emerged. The key to its success was the transfer of technology through the training of Nigerian technicians in the new technologies acquired from Taiwan and a focus on learning by doing and on-the-job training. A successful apprenticeship program and a long history of cooperation among traders in the community assisted in this flow of knowledge. Of particular note is the fact that the Nnewi cluster thrived despite major infrastructure and credit constraints and little by way of government support.[9] Electricity and water, for example, were provided through private generators and boreholes paid for by the firms themselves. Business associations such as the Nnewi Chamber of Commerce, Industry, Mines, and Agriculture and the Nigerian Association of Small Scale Industries played an important role in the organization of enterprises within the cluster.[10]

In Arusha, Tanzania, 234 furniture manufacturing firms are found in four subclusters surrounding the city. The industry has been growing rapidly since about 2000, serving mainly local demand from residential housing and from the hotel and construction industries. Proximity to the heavy traffic along the Nairobi-Moshi international road brings a large number of potential customers into the area. The cluster consists of small furniture workshops and specialist woodcutting, planing, and shaping firms that work on contract to the furniture makers. The furniture workshops purchase raw lumber and consign it to the specialist subcontractors for cutting and shaping to specifications. The components are then brought back to the workshops for assembly and finishing. Once the furniture is made, it is usually the customer who picks it up and transports it.

9. Chete and others (2014).
10. Oluyomi-Abiola (2008).

The division of production between the workshops and the specialist subcontractors is an outcome of the downstream firms' efforts to avoid the large (to them) and indivisible investments associated with purchasing woodworking machinery and to mitigate the production risks associated with variable electrical power. Two vocational and technical institutions, Arusha Technical College (ATC) and the Vocational Training and Service Centre (VTSC), are located in the Arusha area. Both institutions train carpenters for the industry in the area, providing a thicker labor market for workers with the relevant skills.[11]

Originating in the 1930s (at the site of an old colonial army depot called the "Magazine"), the Suame Magazine is an example of successful spontaneous agglomeration of smaller enterprises. Its location near the most important junction of the artery roads connecting the major cities in Ghana proved a natural magnet for auto repair shops and their parts suppliers. In the early 1980s, the government realized the potential of the industrial cluster and established a training institution (the Intermediate Technology Transfer Unit) to facilitate technology upgrades by the most promising entrepreneurs. Today, Suame Magazine is the largest artisan engineering cluster in sub-Saharan Africa. It is possibly the largest light manufacturing cluster in Africa, covering over 900,000 square meters with approximately 10,000 smaller enterprises and employing more than 100,000 workers with higher technical skills than any other industrial cluster in West Africa. Most of these firms are engaged in automobile repair services (i.e., garages), automobile parts production, retail sales of autos, and different types of metal processing.[12]

Urbanization Economies and Cities

In economies at all levels of income, cities contain a high proportion of manufacturing and services firms. In Vietnam the major industrial clusters are located in and near the two main urban cen-

11. Muto and others (2011).
12. Iddrisu, Mano, and Sonobe (2012).

ters, Hanoi and Ho Chi Minh City. In Ghana and Uganda, the majority of firms are found in and near the capital. Cities often are the hosts to several different industrial clusters, as in Tunisia.

Urbanization economies come mainly from between-industry interactions. Unrelated firms in the same city can become more productive for a number of reasons. Urban diversity fosters the exchange of ideas and technology. Firms in different industries can share indivisible facilities—such as infrastructure—or public goods. Cities offer a wider variety of intermediate input suppliers and a larger pool of narrowly specialized workers. Co-location stimulates the growth of specialist services, such as legal, software, data processing, advertising, and management consulting firms. These firms provide a thicker labor market for highly educated individuals.

As local market scale increases, firms are more likely to outsource their service functions to local suppliers. This outsourcing further encourages competition and diversity in the local business services market. Firms also gain from the generation and diffusion of knowledge that is not specific to their industry, often through universities and research organizations. These urbanization effects appear to become more important in more sophisticated industries. There is some evidence from Korea that greater diversity of firms in an agglomeration raises productivity in high-technology industries. This is not the case for more standardized, light industries such as food, textiles, and apparel.[13]

Evidence of the importance of urbanization economies for productivity comes primarily from developed countries. A consensus view is that doubling city size is associated with a productivity increase of some 4 to 8 percent. This is a large effect. Moving from a city of 100,000 workers to one of 3 million would increase productivity by about a third.[14] These urbanization effects may be even more powerful in poorer countries. China is one of few developing countries for which we have evidence on urbanization effects. Au and Henderson estimate that moving from a Chinese city of 100,000

13. Henderson, Lee, and Lee (2001).
14. See Rosenthal and Strange (2004)

workers to one of 1.3 million workers raises productivity by 80 percent.[15]

The limited evidence available suggests that the relative importance of localization and urbanization economies changes as countries grow richer. Localization economies predominate at low levels of development, as firms related along a value chain learn from each other. As incomes grow, urbanization economies seem to become more important. Of course, both localization and urbanization economies can be present at the same time in the same place. The Suame Magazine and the furniture cluster in Arusha are industrial clusters of micro, small, and medium-scale firms within cities. It appears, however, that firms in the cluster benefit primarily from localization economies.

Industrial Clustering in Africa and Emerging Asia

Our studies of agglomeration in four countries (Cambodia, Ethiopia, Tunisia, and Vietnam) offer some richer details of the way in which markets, transportation costs, and agglomeration effects shape the spatial distribution of firms in low-income countries. Ethiopia is the poorest country among those we studied. Its large size, combined with the poor state of infrastructure, make transport costs high. For this reason firms tend to concentrate in population centers, mainly market towns.

The Ethiopian Industrial Survey data, to which we referred in chapter 4, gives a detailed picture of the distribution of industry across space in Ethiopia. Manufacturing firms are present in all the large urban centers of the country, and there is a relatively high concentration of manufacturing production in the capital city, Addis Ababa, and its neighboring areas. Because Ethiopia is landlocked, exporting firms tend to be located near to access corridors such as the airport at Addis Ababa and the Djibouti rail corridor. Firms producing for final consumption are more spatially diversified. These

15. Au and Henderson (2006).

firms operate in highly localized markets, which bring with them substantial competitive pressures.[16]

Cambodia is also a poor country in which infrastructure remains poorly developed and transport costs are high, leading—as in Ethiopia—to a significant amount of clustering of economic activity. We used firm-level data for Cambodia covering over 500,000 enterprises in both manufacturing and services in the formal and informal economy to get a picture of the spatial pattern of economic activity.[17] The highest density of firms is in provinces along Tonle Sap Lake and in Phnom Penh and its surrounding province, as well as in the southern provinces where the population density is also highest. There are very few firms located in the northeast, northern, and southwestern regions of Cambodia. The spatial distribution of employment closely matches the spatial distribution of firms. The largest establishments, however, are mostly located in the urban centers.

Although the main purpose of our research in Cambodia was to try to understand the impact of agglomeration on firm-level productivity (which we shall discuss later in this chapter), we were also able to tease out some interesting spatial patterns. Most firms in Cambodia are informal and in the service sector. For this reason we thought it important to see if clustering appeared to affect formal and informal firms differently and if manufacturing and services firms responded in the same way to spatial concentration. We found that, in general, the effects of clustering were the same in formal (registered) and informal (unregistered) firms. We also found that while all firms were more productive in more populated clusters, manufacturing firms appeared to derive less benefit than service firms from more populous agglomerations. This may be due to the fact that most service firms need to locate close to their customers, and there are naturally more potential customers in areas of high population and economic activity.

Manufacturing firms in Vietnam are highly clustered. There are two main industrial agglomerations anchored by large firms, one

16. Siba and others (2012).
17. Chhair and Newman (2014).

located in the north near Hanoi and another in the south near Ho Chi Minh City. Over the past decade new and smaller clusters have begun to appear along the coast in eastern south-central Vietnam. These new clusters appear to be the result of smaller firms clustering around individual large firms. Very few small manufacturing firms in Vietnam are located away from clusters. In contrast, while most medium firms are located in clusters, some are also in seemingly random locations around the country.

Most research on agglomerations takes clustering as a given and makes no attempt to measure its extent, so one question we asked in Vietnam was to what extent industrial concentration was significant. To do this we used the tools of network analysis to measure the extent of clustering.[18] We found that manufacturing enterprises were in fact highly spatially concentrated and that this clustering was not driven by institutional factors such as zoning or location restrictions on firms. Our results further revealed that there was significant clustering outside of Vietnam's well-known Special Economic Zones. When we attempted to determine the effect of population density on the locational choice of firms, we got a result that is consistent with the view that localization economies matter more than urbanization for a country at Vietnam's per capita income and level of industrial sophistication. We found that population density alone was not driving the high degree of clustering we see in Vietnam.

Industry in Tunisia—the highest income economy among the countries studied—is also highly spatially concentrated. Historically, the coastal regions have been the center of economic activity and the western interior has lagged. The degree of industrial concentration grew dramatically between 1995 and 2010. In 2010, two governorates—Tunis, the capital, and Sfax on the northeast coast—held 16.1 percent and 19.4 percent of the total number of manufacturing firms, respectively. In contrast, sixteen governorates out of a total of twenty-four had less than 3 percent of the total number of firms. Tunisia's spatial distribution by type of manufacturing supports the notion that even for middle-income countries, localization

18. Howard, Newman, and Thijssen (2011).

economies predominate. More than 30 percent of textile firms are concentrated in Monastir governorate and more a third of chemical firms are in Tunis. Agro-food firms are mainly located in Sfax. Exporting sectors (electronic, textile, and chemical) are concentrated in the littoral regions. Only products associated with local markets are more diversified spatially.[19]

Urbanization and Industry in Africa

Our country studies of Ghana, Mozambique, Senegal, and Uganda provide a snapshot of how urbanization of industry is evolving across Africa. Mozambique and Senegal are characterized by high spatial concentration. Industrial production in Senegal is mainly concentrated in Dakar, with nearly nine out of ten firms and three-quarters of permanent jobs and revenue in 1995. The great majority of industrial enterprises and employment are similarly concentrated in and around Maputo in Mozambique.

Ghana's industrial firms are primarily concentrated in its two major urban centers: Accra, the capital, and Kumasi, the capital of the interior Ashanti region. Together these two regions account for half of the total number of industrial firms. The high degree of concentration in Greater Accra and the Ashanti region is mainly driven by firms producing similar products or working in the same value chain. Larger scale manufacturing activity is mainly concentrated in the Greater Accra-Tema corridor, where it benefits from urbanization.[20]

During the 1960s and early 1970s, Uganda's eastern region was the main industrial hub of the country. This has since changed and Kampala, the capital, has emerged as the major industrial center. The central region around Kampala accounts for 61 percent of manufacturing firms with 42 percent located in Kampala alone. Kampala has the largest share of firms in all manufacturing subsectors except for coffee processing, grain milling, and tea processing, for

19. Ayadi and Mattoussi (2014).
20. Ackah, Adjasi, and Turkson (2014).

which proximity to supplying agricultural producers drives location choices.[21]

Africa's urban population has increased more than tenfold since 1950, from 21 million to 235 million, doubling every twenty-two years. Most African countries have a single large urban area, but several countries (South Africa, Algeria, Cameroon, Egypt, Ghana, Nigeria, and Democratic Republic of the Congo) are seeing the rapid growth of secondary urban areas. Despite the challenges posed by rapid urbanization, Paul Collier and Tony Venables raise a stunning possibility: Africa's cities may be too small. Because big cities generate powerful scale economies, they believe that to be competitive globally in manufacturing and services, Africa will need cities that are much larger than those that exist today. Citing the rule of thumb described previously, they argue that a firm operating in a city of 10 million people has unit costs around 40 percent lower than a firm operating in a city of only 100,000. Collier and Venables argue that because Africa is a continent of small countries, there is a serious risk that its cities will prove too small to be competitive industrial locations.

City size is overwhelmingly correlated with country size. If two identical countries are merged, the size of their largest city increases by 75 percent.[22] A comparison with India brings home the point. India is a single country whereas Africa is divided into fifty-four independent political units. India has two cities of over 20 million people. Africa's biggest city is Lagos, with 10 million people, and it is located in Africa's most populous country. The more typical African capital city such as Nairobi has a population of only around 3 million.

If Africa's political fragmentation has inhibited the emergence of large cities with their attendant productivity-enhancing effects, what can be done without redrawing national boundaries? One possible solution to the problem is to pursue deeper regional integration, including freeing up intra-regional migration. The free movement of

21. Obwona, Shinyekwa, and Kiiza (2014).
22. Collier and Venables (2008).

people across borders in regional economic communities would permit migration from interior countries to a number of coastal locations with the potential for urban growth.

Agglomeration and Firm-Level Productivity

A large and growing volume of empirical literature documents the significant productivity gains to firms from industrial agglomeration in middle- and high-income countries.[23] However, we know little about the impact of spatial concentration on firm-level productivity in low-income countries. Isolating productivity gains to firms as a result of locating in a cluster is notoriously difficult. In addition to the usual problems of finding a suitable estimate of productivity using firm-level data, identification of the impact of clustering on productivity is confounded by the possibility of self-selection and the "reflection problem." It may be that the most productive firms choose to locate in areas that are attractive, due to the presence of better infrastructure or a thicker labor market, for example. Because they are more productive, they are able to afford the higher costs associated with these more desirable locations. If this is the case, an association between agglomeration and firm-level productivity may simply reflect self-selection rather than the impact of proximity on productivity. As was true of learning by exporting and firm dynamics, we need a panel of data to identify the relationship between a measure of geographical concentration and total factor productivity. In the case of agglomeration, the demands on the data are even more exacting: we need to know where firms are located in space.

Because we are particularly interested in the impact of agglomeration in low-income countries, our focus is mainly on localization rather than urbanization economies and on the impact of clustering in low-technology industries. These industrial clusters may be (and often are) in cities, but we are mainly interested in the benefits of concentration that come from within-industry interactions. Later we

23. See UNIDO (2009) and World Bank (2009b) for surveys.

discuss inter-industry interactions and their role in knowledge diffusion.

Despite the demanding data requirements and identification challenges, we were able to undertake econometric studies in four of our countries: Cambodia, Ethiopia, Tunisia, and Vietnam. In three of the four studies we found evidence of urbanization economies: the more firms that are clustered together, regardless of what they produce, the better they perform. While this is interesting in itself, it is not that surprising, given that firms tend to cluster in areas where there are natural advantages, such as urban centers, coastal areas, or other areas of strategic importance. We would expect firms to be more productive where infrastructure is better, markets are larger, and transport costs are lower. What is interesting about our country-level econometric studies is that even when we control for urbanization economies we find evidence of productivity spillovers associated with the clustering of similar firms (i.e., localization effects).

The strongest evidence for localization effects comes from Vietnam, where we found significant productivity gains associated with the clustering of firms. The evidence points in the direction of localization economies. Firms located in smaller clusters experienced increases in productivity to a much greater extent than those in larger clusters. One result, which raises some intriguing questions about the sources of these localization effects, was that the productivity gains varied with firm ownership. We found strong evidence that foreign-owned firms enjoyed the greatest productivity benefits from clustering. Privately owned domestic firms also experienced agglomeration economies, but not to the same extent as foreign-owned firms.[24] In Tunisia, which is the highest income economy in our sample, we found evidence of localization economies as well. These productivity effects appear to result from the transmission of production knowledge between closely related firms located in proximity to one another.[25]

24. Howard and others (2014).
25. Ayadi and Mattoussi (2014).

In Cambodia and Ethiopia, economies at significantly lower levels of per capita income, we found similar evidence of productivity gains from agglomeration. In Cambodia, we were able to look at the impact of clustering on both formal and informal firms in both manufacturing and services. We found the strongest evidence of productivity gains from clustering in informal enterprises and in manufacturing firms.[26]

These results are consistent with the view that clustering is one source of capability building. Transfers of knowledge between firms may be more beneficial to informal firms, because they are likely to have more to learn from formal firms than the other way around.[27] It is also not surprising that manufacturing firms experienced productivity gains from clustering to a greater extent than service providers. They have greater potential to benefit from knowledge transfers than firms engaged in such market services as wholesale and retail trade.

Firms in Ethiopia had higher productivity when they were located in the same geographical area, but only if they produced products similar to other firms in the cluster.[28] Clusters of unrelated firms did not appear to offer any significant productivity gains from agglomeration. This is quite strong evidence of the importance of localization economies in countries at lower levels of development. The vast majority of firms in Ethiopia are engaged in quite simple manufacturing processes. These results are consistent with the other evidence we have—mainly from case studies—that localization economies are the main source of productivity gains in unsophisticated industries.

Clusters, Competition, and Capabilities

In chapters 4 and 5 we described how competition and firm capabilities help to determine firm-level productivity. We pointed out that the distribution of firms across space plays a role in the degree of

26. Chhair and Newman (2014).
27. See, for example, Overman and Venables (2005).
28. Siba and others (2012).

competitive pressure faced by firms, and we also noted that co-location of firms may be an important element in capability building. As promised, we return to these topics, using our quantitative studies of agglomeration and our firm-level surveys to provide some insights into how agglomeration affects competition and the diffusion of capabilities in low-income settings.

Clusters and Competition

The econometric studies of agglomeration we carried out for Ethiopia and Cambodia both provide important insights into the ways in which transport costs and localized markets in low-income countries set up an important trade-off between the productivity-enhancing effect of localization economies and the competitive pressures generated when a large number of firms in the same industry locate in a limited geographical area. Increased competitive pressure in localized markets is likely to drive down the price of goods and services.[29] Because of heterogeneity in the production costs of firms within clusters, competition for a limited local market will lead to a weeding out of higher cost producers, and survivors will experience an erosion of markups.

A novel contribution of the study on Ethiopia is that it distinguishes between the effect of agglomeration on productivity and prices. Although clustering raises firm-level productivity, clustering of firms producing similar products also has a negative effect on prices.[30] While this is good for consumers, it impacts negatively on the revenue of firms. Taken together with the positive productivity gains associated with agglomeration, the net benefit to firms in Ethiopia of locating close to firms engaged in the same industry is close to zero. The consequence of the productivity-price trade-off for firms in Ethiopia is a spatial distribution of industry characterized by small localized concentrations of firms producing essentially similar products.

29. Syverson (2007).
30. Siba and others (2012).

We also found that competitive pressures from clustering placed strong downward pressure on firm revenues in Cambodia.[31] Competition had a strong negative effect on the price-cost margins of formal enterprises in particular. This may have been due, in part, to the higher and less flexible cost base associated with formality. Formal enterprises in Cambodia face more stringent legal and institutional requirements than informal firms.[32] Faced with these constraints, formal firms may have found it more difficult to adjust their costs in the face of increased competition than informal firms. We also found that competition effects were more pronounced for firms in the manufacturing sector than those in the service sector.

Our results from Cambodia, Ethiopia, and Vietnam suggest that we should take a closer look at firms' incentives to form clusters, taking into account that they may weigh productivity gains against the adverse effects of stronger competition on prices and revenues. In both Cambodia and Ethiopia, the negative effects on prices and markups of more intensive competition due to restricted local markets often outweighed the productivity gains to the firm of localization. In contrast, the positive productivity spillovers associated with clustering found in Vietnam do not seem to have been affected by negative competition effects.[33]

Market structure plays an important role in this context. If markets are localized so that local rents may be available, the incentives to agglomerate are weak. It is better for a firm to forgo the increase in productivity in the hope of gaining a market protected from potential competitors. In contrast, if markets are competitive and integrated, firms cannot avoid competition by strategic location. In such a case, the firm's incentives to agglomerate will be stronger, since the gains from doing so will be larger. One notable difference between Cambodia and Ethiopia and Vietnam was the degree to which internal markets were better integrated. This meant that firms in Vietnam

31. Chhair and Newman (2014).
32. World Bank (2009d).
33. Howard and others (2014).

could exploit a larger domestic market, reducing the productivity-profitability trade-off.

The productivity-profitability trade-off introduced by low market integration has some important implications for policy. Investments in infrastructure that increase connectivity and reduce transport costs to larger geographical markets can have an important role in increasing the incentives for and benefits to firms of agglomeration, especially in low-income countries where the primary source of externalities comes from location near firms engaged in the same industry. This also raises another important point: exporting firms, because they face fixed international prices, do not face a price-productivity trade-off.

Clusters and Capabilities

Seen from a capabilities perspective, many of the benefits to the firm of locating close to other firms come from the process of building capabilities. Because the transfer of capabilities is most often the outcome of firm-to-firm interactions, the tendency toward geographical concentration is understandable. Firms in the same industry can see what their nearby rivals or counterparts do and seek to emulate them. Workers may leave one firm and join another, carrying their tacit knowledge with them. Common customers or service providers may transfer knowledge along the supply chain. Looked at in this way, localization effects are a source of the transfer of capabilities, and localization economies are revealed capabilities. Similarly, urbanization economies reflect the tendency for technological know-how and innovation to become more important as economies grow richer and industries become more technologically sophisticated. Cities and the knowledge institutions they house are a rich seedbed of new ideas and innovations.

As part of the study of agglomeration in Vietnam, we investigated the driving forces behind the tendency of firms to co-locate.[34] We explored the relative importance of natural advantages, trans-

---

34. Howard, Newman, and Thijssen (2011).

port costs, knowledge transfers, and thick labor markets and found that formal (intentional) and informal (unintentional) knowledge transfers were the most important agglomerative force. We also found that sectors at higher technology levels agglomerated to benefit from a pool of skilled workers. These results suggest that in lower income economies such as Vietnam, formation of clusters of related industries facilitates the transfer of knowledge through the supply chain and the movement of skilled labor.

Our qualitative surveys of supply chain relationships between foreign and domestic firms in seven countries also give us some insight into how geography has shaped the transfer of capabilities in Africa and emerging Asia.[35] Most of the multinational firms that we interviewed were centrally located in industrial clusters and their interactions with purchasers and suppliers tended to be within the agglomeration. As we pointed out in chapter 5, the density of relationships between firms along the supply chain was substantially greater in Cambodia and Vietnam than in the countries we studied in sub-Saharan Africa. There were few links between multinational enterprises and domestic firms observed in Africa, even within established clusters.

Because the transfer of capabilities from foreign firms to domestic firms most often required direct and close interaction between the parties involved, our results suggest that industrial clusters in Africa have not reached their full potential for the transfer of capabilities. This is primarily because Africa's industrial clusters, anchored on foreign firms, are much less densely populated with domestic firms than those in Cambodia and Vietnam. This limits the potential for firm-to-firm interactions.

Summing Up

Economic geographers and business people have long recognized that firms tend to cluster together, often in cities. Mainstream economics

---

35. Newman and others (2015).

appears to be finally catching up. The New Economic Geography has raised our awareness of the importance of agglomeration economies as a source of firm-level productivity. At the risk of simplification, the productivity-enhancing role of agglomeration can be divided into two sources. The first arises when firms producing similar products and their purchasers and suppliers congregate in the same geographical area, forming an industrial cluster, and the benefits conferred by such clusters are often referred to as localization economies. The second occurs when firms in diverse sectors locate in a city. The benefits conferred by these agglomerations are often referred to as urbanization economies.

Like many of the patterns we have described throughout this book, the relative importance of localization and urbanization seems to vary with the level of development and the level of sophistication of the industry. At low levels of per capita income, localization economies appear to be the most important. This is true not only for manufacturing. Case studies suggest it applies to industries without smokestacks as well, such as information technology–based services and agro-industrial exports, including horticulture. As income rises, cities grow and urbanization economies become increasingly relevant. There is also some evidence—almost wholly drawn from middle- and high-income countries—that as the level of technological sophistication of industry increases, urbanization effects begin to outweigh localization effects.

While there has been a substantial amount of quantitative research into the nature and extent of agglomeration economies in middle- and high-income countries, virtually all of what we know about agglomeration in low-income countries comes from case studies.[36] For this reason we tried in Learning to Compete to understand the quantitative impacts of agglomeration on firm productivity in low-income countries. Our most significant finding was that, as in higher income countries, agglomerations raise firm-level productivity.

We found that in a number of important ways agglomeration effects in low-income countries differ from those found in higher

36. See, for example, UNIDO (2009) and Sonobe and Otsuka (2006).

income settings. To the extent that we are able to distinguish between them, localization economies appear to be more important than urbanization to the firms in our sample of countries. Our results also point to an important countervailing factor: competition. In poor economies with limited infrastructure, markets are highly localized. Entry of new firms into the same industrial cluster increases competitive pressure on all firms and may result in reductions in price. Firms face a price-productivity trade-off, which becomes more acute the less well integrated product markets are nationally. This trade-off is not present when the firms in a cluster are exporters, a theme to which we return in chapter 7.

PART IV

How Africa Can Industrialize

CHAPTER 7

A Strategy for Industrial Development

Conventional wisdom has it that Africa's failure to industrialize is primarily due to its poor investment climate, and notwithstanding our concerns with how the investment climate agenda has been implemented, conventional wisdom is still relevant. Africa entered the twenty-first century with large gaps in infrastructure, human capital, and institutions compared with other parts of the developing world. If Africa is to compete, it must get these basics right, but efforts to strengthen the investment climate on their own have not succeeded in helping Africa to reverse its industrial decline. We believe some unconventional wisdom is needed as well. In this chapter we outline a four-part strategy for industrial growth in Africa that combines conventional with some unconventional wisdom.

Two considerations led us to the conclusion that a new strategy is needed for African industrialization. The first is the need to be selective. Implementing an investment climate agenda that truly attempts to close the region's infrastructure and skills gaps is likely to exceed the fiscal capacity of most African governments, even with the support of their development partners. For example, by one set of estimates, if efficiency gains are fully achieved through reforms, at existing rates of expenditure Africa's low-income countries will only meet modest targets for infrastructure development after twenty years. If the efficiency gains are not fully realized, it could take thirty years.[1] This means that where and when infrastructure investments are made is critically important to short-run success in industrial development.

As the preceding chapters show, the drivers of firm-level productivity in low-income countries are interdependent and mutually reinforcing. Investments in infrastructure and skills, for example, raise the potential productivity of all firms, making some of them more likely to succeed in external markets. New industrial exports help to build firm capabilities, which are then transferred through agglomerations. Foreign direct investment is an important source of higher capabilities, but it is unlikely to seek out destinations that lack a critical mass of other firms. This leads to our second consideration: public actions to raise the productivity of firms need to take place across a broad front and recognize the interdependence of the sources of firm-level productivity.

We begin with the basics. More and better investments in infrastructure and skills are essential, especially those that enhance international competitiveness. Better-designed efforts at regulatory reform have a role to play as well. We suggest some new priorities for investment climate reform. We then draw on the results of our research to set out the three additional elements of the strategy—mounting an export push, building capabilities, and creating clusters. We conclude by turning to the question of how governments can set priorities in these four areas through closer engagement with the private sector.

Getting the Basics Right

Over the last fifteen years, African governments have attempted to reform their investment climate. Clearly, these reforms have not given

1. Foster and Briceño-Garmendia (2010).

the decisive boost to African industry that their proponents fore-saw. Yet the basics are important. Our country studies all highlight the productivity penalty that African firms pay as a result of poor infrastructure and skills, and regulatory burdens and poorly func-tioning institutions in many countries inhibit competition, increase the cost of doing business, and reduce competitiveness. More infra-structure and better skills have a bathtub effect on firm-level pro-ductivity. Better and more reliable electrical power, lower costs of transport, and workers who are better able to perform their jobs raise the potential productivity of all firms in an economy. Reform of regulations can promote competition. So, we begin with the ba-sics. If it is to have any hope of industrializing, Africa needs to turn around its growing infrastructure and skills gaps with the rest of the world, and it needs to focus on appropriate regulatory and institu-tional reforms.

Closing the Infrastructure Gap

African countries lag behind their peers in the developing world on almost every measure of infrastructure coverage.[2] The differences are particularly large for paved roads, telephone main lines, and power generation. Only about 30 percent of the population has access to ground transport, while the average for the developing world is 50 percent. Internet penetration is about 4 percent, compared to the average for the developing world of about 40 percent. Thirty coun-tries face regular power shortages, and many pay high prices for emergency power.[3] By one estimate the current infrastructure deficits in Africa contribute to a loss of about 2 percentage points per year in GDP growth.[4]

Infrastructure deficiencies are a significant barrier to greater competitiveness. Africa's infrastructure services are twice as expen-sive as elsewhere, and poor infrastructure is strongly correlated with

2. Yepes, Pierce, and Foster (2008).
3. Foster and Briceño-Garmendia (2010).
4. See NEPAD, AU, and AfDB (2011).

lower firm-level productivity.[5] Africa has been expanding its infrastructure much more slowly than other developing regions, and unless
something changes, the gap will continue to widen. Governments
interested in industrializing will need to increase public investments
in infrastructure substantially, particularly those that impact the
ability of firms to compete.

Reliable electrical power may be Africa's greatest single infrastructure constraint. The quality of electricity service is ranked as
a major problem by more than half of the firms in more than half
of the African countries in the World Bank's Investment Climate
Assessments. The average number of power outages in a typical
month in sub-Saharan Africa is 7.8. This is lower than in South Asia
(17.2) but higher than in East Asia (3.5). However, the duration of
outages is often longer, resulting in relatively high estimated costs (as
a percent of sales) of unreliable electricity. The production loss in
percent of sales among firms experiencing outages is 7.7 percent,
more than double that of East Asia (3.0 percent).[6] Lack of electrical
power disproportionally impacts the region's most successful economies. In countries that are growing faster than Africa as a whole,
poor-quality electricity reduces the total factor productivity of firms
more than in other countries on the African continent.[7]

Infrastructure directly affecting the competitiveness of exports
has been particularly neglected. Road infrastructure has received
little attention, and although concessions have been awarded to operate and rehabilitate many African ports and railways, financial commitments by the concessionaire companies are often small. Productivity losses from transport interruptions particularly affect countries
such as Kenya, Tanzania, and Senegal. Access to communications
services has increased dramatically, thanks to the cellular revolution,
but high-speed data transmission, which is critical to exporting and
especially to information technology-intensive exports, lags badly.[8]

5. Escribano, Guasch, and Pena (2010).
6. See World Bank (www.enterprisesurveys.org).
7. Escribano, Guasch, and Pena (2010).
8. World Bank (2009c).

Our country case studies give an idea of the magnitude of the challenge faced by individual countries and point to some directions for change. Not surprisingly, power emerges as a major constraint in every country. Uganda has one of the lowest per capita electricity consumption levels in the world.[9] Manufacturing firms surveyed reported, on average, 39 power outages in the previous year. Large firms reported 54 outages. Firms estimated the resulting production losses in the range of 4 to 7 percent of output.[10] In Uganda, 35 percent of exporters cited energy as a major or severe constraint. Manufacturing firms in Tanzania experienced on average almost 9 power outages per month, costing about 15.1 percent of total sales for the firms affected by the outages.[11] The median manufacturing firm in Mozambique faced an average of 1.6 power cuts per month, costing about 1.2 percent of total sales.[12]

Transport finishes a close second. Ugandan firms on average lost 1.8 percent of domestic sales and 1.1 percent of exports due to delays in transportation services. Even more important, transport costs are high, in some cases half the value of goods, depending on bulkiness and weight. Almost one-quarter of the enterprises surveyed in Mozambique considered transportation to be a major obstacle to investment. Currently, it is more expensive to transport cargo within Mozambique than to ship it to a different continent.

Increasing public investments in power, transport, and other infrastructure will confront the reality that most African governments do not have the fiscal space to deal with all of their pressing needs. In part this can be addressed by increases in domestic revenue effort and efficiency, but the size of the gap is sufficiently large that it will also need the active support of the aid community and the private sector. For that reason we return to the subject when we set out our agenda for aid in chapter 9. Even with the support of donors, governments will need to sequence infrastructure investments to

9. Wiebelt and others (2011).
10. World Bank (2004).
11. World Bank (2007b).
12. World Bank (2009a).

achieve maximum impact. Priority should be given to trade-related infrastructure and to addressing the spatial requirements for industrialization. Focusing infrastructure investments in limited geographical areas designed to attract export-oriented investors is an effective way to boost competitiveness when fiscal resources for infrastructure investments are constrained.

Closing the Skills Gap

Africa's skills gap with the rest of the world is large and growing. At the most basic level, educational attainment across the region still lags relative to other parts of the world. Although Africa's young people have more schooling today than any previous generation, they still have little overall. Nearly 60 percent of those age fifteen to twenty-four have completed primary school only. About 35 percent have continued beyond primary school, and only 19 percent have gone beyond lower-secondary school.[13]

At the postprimary level the gap grows wider still. Between 1990 and 2005, as East Asia increased secondary enrollment rates by 21 percentage points and tertiary enrollment rates by 13 percentage points, Africa (starting from a lower base) managed to raise secondary enrollments by 7 percentage points and tertiary enrollments by only 1 percentage point. Real expenditure on tertiary education in Africa fell by about 28 percent between 1990 and 2002, and expenditure per pupil declined.[14]

Educational quality is a problem at all levels. Learning assessments in Africa show that most primary students still lack basic proficiency in reading at the end of second or third grade. In Tanzania, for example, a 2011 assessment of children's abilities revealed that 70 percent of students complete elementary level Standard Two without meeting the numeracy standards of that level. Assessments in Kenya and Uganda revealed similar shortfalls in students' cogni-

13. Filmer and Fox (2014).
14. World Bank (2007a).

tive skills.[15] Employer surveys report that African tertiary graduates are weak in problem solving, business understanding, computer use, and communication skills.[16]

The skills gap poses a major constraint to industrial development and exports. Among firms owned by indigenous entrepreneurs, those with university-educated owners tend to have higher growth rates.[17] In Mozambique we found that firms with better-educated managers were more likely to survive and expand in terms of employment. Cross-country research indicates that there is a strong link between export sophistication and the percentage of the labor force that has completed postprimary schooling.[18] There is also evidence to suggest that enterprises managed by university graduates in Africa have a higher propensity to export.[19]

What is lacking most are skills related to production. A survey of country experts from forty-five countries for the *African Economic Outlook 2013* found that over 50 percent of respondents cited lack of specialized skills as a major obstacle keeping African firms from becoming competitive.[20] Growing firms in Uganda import skilled labor, and the Ugandan Labor Force Survey reports that a significantly higher share of secondary graduates are underemployed than those with more specific vocational training. In Mozambique there is a significant shortage of technical and higher level skills, especially in math and science, and firms see lack of employee skills as a serious constraint to growth.[21] In Ghana, managerial education plays a strong and positive role in driving firm productivity and growth.[22]

Major increases in postprimary and vocational/technical education are needed to address the skills gap, and quality must improve

15. Filmer and Fox (2014).
16. World Bank (2007a).
17. Ramachandran and Shah (2007).
18. World Bank (2007a).
19. Wood and Jordan (2000); Clarke (2005).
20. AEO (2013).
21. World Bank (2007b); DNEAP (2013).
22. Ackah and others (2014).

at all levels. As we show in chapter 9, closing the skills gap is at least as daunting a fiscal task as closing the infrastructure gap, in part because there is less certainty about how educational expenditures translate into educational outcomes. Secondary and tertiary education is a long-term investment; the payoff in terms of a more highly skilled labor force will only begin to appear after the first cohorts have finished secondary school or university.

These considerations again call for sequencing of the public actions to increase skills. In view of the identified shortage of skills in production, vocational and technical training is a logical place to begin. The lack of managerial capabilities and the success of management training programs (discussed in chapter 5) suggest that improving management education at the postsecondary level and specialized management training courses of shorter duration have the potential to boost firm-level productivity. As in the case of infrastructure, focusing specialized skills training in a limited geographic area, such as a special economic zone (SEZ), has proved an effective use of limited resources in China, Malaysia, and Vietnam.

Much of this training will have to be done by the public sector. Yet, education budgets across the Continent are limited. African governments have generally been reluctant to encourage private provision of educational services, especially in technical, vocational, and tertiary education. These activities do, however, have high private returns and are very suitable for private provision. In technical and vocational training, private-sector providers are often more attuned to the needs of the marketplace and more agile. Involving the private sector in skills development is an essential element of becoming competitive.

Reforming Regulations and Institutions

Our country case studies point to the many ways in which regulations and regulatory discretion affect firms. In Uganda, inadequate regulatory capacity, an unclear regulatory framework, and inconsistent interpretation of policies and regulations have increased the regulatory burden on firms. Senior managers of manufacturing firms spend more than thirteen days a year on average dealing with government officials, and 40 percent of the manufacturing firms surveyed complained that regulations were not interpreted consistently.[23] In Mozambique business regulations—and the opportunities for corruption engendered by the regulatory regime—increase firms' costs and reduce competitiveness.[24]

There is, however, a serious question about whether regulatory burdens are the binding constraint to industrial development in Africa. Better regulations raise productivity by promoting churning through the entry and growth of more efficient firms and the exit of less productive ones. The previous discussion of infrastructure and skills and the research described in chapters 4 through 6 make a strong case that bathtub sources of productivity growth are likely to be more relevant to Africa's competitiveness at its current stage of industrial development.

The most widely used measure of regulatory burden is the World Bank *Doing Business* ranking, and it has become the centerpiece of the agenda for regulatory reform in most African countries. As we show in chapter 9, *Doing Business* is a flawed diagnostic tool, and it should be abandoned as an agenda-setting framework for regulatory reform. Instead, African governments will need to develop homegrown mechanisms to identify the problems that most constrain industrial development. At the end of this chapter we offer some suggestions for how that can be done.

Pushing Exports

Although learning by exporting offers the potential to improve firm capabilities and raise productivity, there are often high costs of entering export markets that may not be recovered by an individual firm. This makes a strong case for public actions to promote industrial exports. Most of Africa has had little success in developing

23. World Bank (2004).
24. World Bank (2009a).

industrial exports. Cambodia, Mauritius, Tunisia, and Vietnam, in contrast, have had significant export growth. A major part of the difference in performance can be put down to differences in policy. The four export successes each employed a concerted set of public investments, policy reforms, and institutional changes focused on increasing the share of industrial exports in GDP. In short, they created an "export push." Here, we set out some of the policy instruments we believe are appropriate—and World Trade Organization (WTO) friendly—to create an export push in Africa's new industrializers.

Policy and Institutional Reforms

Because task-based exports depend on imported inputs, Cambodia, Mauritius, Tunisia, and Vietnam all established a "free trade regime for exporters" through various mechanisms to eliminate or rebate tariffs on intermediate and capital inputs used in export production. Tariff exemptions, duty drawbacks, and rebates of indirect taxes were well administered and timely, reducing the regulatory burden on exporters. This is not the case in most of Africa. While duty drawback, tariff exemption, and value added tax (VAT) reimbursement schemes exist, they are often complex and poorly administered, resulting in substantial delays. Port transit times are long, and customs delays on both imported inputs and exports are significantly longer for African economies than for their Asian competitors. Export procedures—including certificates of origin, quality and sanitary certification, and permits—can be burdensome.[25] These institutional and regulatory barriers must be removed if Africa is to succeed in trade in tasks. One approach that has succeeded elsewhere is to streamline the regulatory regime first in special economic zones.

Trade-related institutions are also important for industries without smokestacks. The regulatory regime in telecommunications is vital to remote tradable services, and tourism is sensitive to the behavior of public officials ranging from immigration inspectors to the

---

25. Clarke (2005); Yoshino (2008); Farole (2011).

police. Horticultural exports are perishable and particularly vulnerable to delays in shipping caused by inefficient or corrupt inspection procedures at airports. Officials have the power to use delaying tactics to cause the loss of an entire consignment. The relatively slow growth of airfreighted fresh produce exports from West Africa is in part due to corruption at airports.

Improving Trade Logistics

Trade in tasks has greatly increased the importance of trade logistics. Because new entrants to task-based production tend to specialize in the final stages of the value chain, poor trade logistics can make it impossible for firms to break into task trade. For this reason investments and institutional reforms to improve trade logistics are essential to export success. African countries have an average ranking of 120 out of 160 countries in the World Bank 2014 Trade Logistics Index.[26] The region has an especially bad ranking in terms of trade-related infrastructure, and poorly functioning institutions and noncompetitive logistics markets further increase costs. Value chain analysis identifies several choke points: high costs of import and export logistics, lack of timely delivery of inputs, and low speed to market.[27]

Poor logistics constrain the region's ability to compete in tradable services and agro-industry as well. There is a strong correlation between the number of long-haul flights per week and the performance of a tourist destination. Africa's top three countries for tourist arrivals, South Africa, Nigeria, and Kenya, are also the top three countries for long-haul flights per week. Africa is underserved by major airlines. Sixty-six percent of countries have either no major carrier connections or are dependent on just one airline. The aviation industry is heavily protected, generating a plethora of small and uneconomic national airlines. While adopting an open skies policy might endanger some national airlines, it would introduce greater

26. World Bank (2014b).
27. Subramanian and Matthijs (2007); Dinh and others (2013).

competition and reduce the cost of airfreight through the development of competing, specialized, private charter airfreight companies.

Strengthening Regional Infrastructure and Institutions

The small size of Africa's economies and the fact that many countries are landlocked make regional approaches to infrastructure, customs administration, and regulation of transport in trade corridors imperative. Africa is the continent with the highest concentration of landlocked developing countries. For exporters in landlocked countries, poor infrastructure in neighboring coastal economies, incoherent customs and transport regulations, as well as inefficient customs procedures and "informal" taxes in transportation corridors slow transit times to the coast and raise costs. The median landlocked country's transport costs for a standard twenty-foot container are 46 percent higher than the equivalent costs for the median coastal economy. Distance explains only about 10 percent of the difference. Poor road infrastructure explains three-fifths.[28] Regional approaches to building and, equally important, maintaining transborder infrastructure are critical.

Institutional reforms at the regional level to improve trade logistics in transnational corridors—such as common standards, regulations, and one-stop border facilities—have moved slowly. Africa's busiest regional transport corridor is the North–South Corridor, which is the most efficient in Africa. It links Kolwezi in the Democratic Republic of the Congo to the ports of Durban in South Africa (more than 3,500 kilometers away) and Dar es Salaam. The journey from Kolwezi to City Deep, an inland container depot in Johannesburg, takes on average fifteen to twenty days, 70 percent of which is spent as downtime at border crossings.[29] Clearly, more extensive harmonization at the regional level is needed.

28. Limão and Venables (2001).
29. AfDB (2010).

Building Capabilities

As we pointed out in chapter 5, one of the most important ways in which some newly industrializing countries have built capabilities has been through mounting an export push. Learning by exporting is a major source of the knowledge needed to raise capabilities. The relationship between exporting and capability building is a good example of how the drivers of firm-level productivity are mutually reinforcing. In addition to the export push, policies and institutions to attract foreign direct investment, deepen value chains, and provide management information and training have been used effectively in capability building by a range of countries and could be more effectively implemented in Africa.

Attracting Foreign Direct Investment

We saw in chapter 5 that foreign direct investment (FDI) is an important source of higher capabilities. Policies and institutions for attracting FDI are therefore potentially a key tool in capability building, and there is some evidence to suggest that they are most effective where they are most needed. One study uses data from 124 countries to study the effect of investment promotion on inflows of U.S. FDI. It tests whether sectors explicitly targeted by investment promotion agencies in their efforts to attract FDI received more investment relative to the period before targeting began and to nontargeted sectors. Controlling for other factors, the research finds that investment promotion leads to higher FDI flows to countries where red tape is likely to be severe and information asymmetries between potential investors and governments are large.[30] Put differently, the results suggest that an FDI agency can help to overcome some of the negative aspects of the investment climate and is likely to be most effective where the institutional and regulatory regime functions least well.

Ireland's Industrial Development Authority of the 1960s provided an institutional model for attracting and keeping FDI that has become

30. Harding and Javorcik (2011).

international best practice. A small, elite agency under the office of the president or prime minister is set up to manage the country relationship with potential and existing foreign investors. Four features of this agency play a crucial role—high-level political support, high-quality personnel, independence, and focus.[31] Best practice FDI agencies excel at three phases of the foreign investment cycle: recruitment and screening, embedding, and aftercare.

Recruitment is for the most part a matter of responding to potential investors. Active recruitment, on the other hand, requires more—including selling the country. This is one reason the formal link to and the active participation of the national chief executive is critical. Inquiries from interested firms need to be screened to establish their credibility. In screening it is important to have personnel with sufficient breadth of private-sector experience to know what questions to ask, what issues to probe, and what characteristics to look for. This is why there must be a priority on selective hiring and adequate compensation in FDI agencies.

Screening should be an important part of the overall industrialization strategy. Ireland, Malaysia, and Singapore are good examples of how, after some initial success, FDI agencies sought specific types of foreign investors believed to offer more in terms of firm capabilities. At the start, FDI agencies in Africa must demonstrate that they can attract and retain foreign investors across a wide range of activities. Once they have achieved a track record, screening and recruitment should focus on two objectives: attracting a critical number of firms producing (and exporting) similar products or in related value chains in order to promote localization economies, and identifying and recruiting firms willing to engage local suppliers and purchasers in order to build domestic capabilities.

Domestic regulatory and administrative requirements may be complex, and the job of embedding is to minimize their costs to the new foreign investor. This is a task that requires active coordination across the government, independence, and a pragmatic focus on problem solving. It is also another area in which the active support

31. Barry (2004); Sutton (2005).

of the head of government is essential. Aftercare is concerned with removing unnecessary obstacles to the operation and growth of the foreign enterprise and reducing the barriers to the formation of linkages with domestic firms.

Although this approach to FDI promotion has been introduced into Africa over the past decade, implementation has not always yielded the results expected. Often FDI agencies lacked the active support of the chief executive. Personnel practices and compensation policies were frequently not sufficiently attractive to make it possible to recruit the high-caliber staff needed, and the agencies were frequently burdened with multiple objectives, diluting their focus. Embedding and aftercare have been largely neglected. Today, the vast majority of Africa's foreign investment promotion agencies fall short of international best practice.[32] Reform of the region's FDI agencies must begin at the top. Africa's national chief executives need to signal that attracting foreign investors is a national priority by placing the agencies in the office of the presidency or the prime minister and taking an active interest in their operations.

Deepening the Value Chain

Because transmission of capabilities most often takes place through firm-to-firm relationships, it largely depends on the existence of competitive local value chains. A striking finding of our country studies is how few linkages exist in most African countries between foreign and domestic investors. To deepen these vertical linkages, serious barriers up and down value chains need to be addressed. This is where capability building intersects with spatial policies. In many countries, current policies and regulations, especially in export processing zones (EPZs), place serious obstacles in the way of linkages between foreign and local firms.

The architecture of most African EPZs is "closed" in the sense that excessive concern with evasion of tariffs and other taxes by local investors has led to rules that choke off purchaser-supplier

32. Page (2012c).

relationships between firms in the zone and domestic firms outside. In addition, in many countries regulations restrict the movement of managers and workers between EPZs and the rest of the economy. A key area for government action is to remove these obstacles.

Outside of the EPZs, governments need to reduce administrative and legal obstacles to the formation of value chain relationships. Some of these barriers are as simple as immigration policies that inhibit the temporary entry of the engineering and managerial personnel critical to the transfer of capabilities by equipment suppliers. Other obstacles operate through tariff and nontariff barriers to the import of capital equipment and intermediate goods that limit supplier-purchaser knowledge transfers.

Management Information and Training

There is very little incentive for firms to invest in the productivity and quality of their rivals. This raises a collective action problem. In most economies, and certainly in poor economies, firms will underinvest in capabilities if they are not able to appropriate their benefits fully. Establishing an institutional framework, perhaps in the form of a public-private partnership, within which domestic companies can have access to information on international best practice is one approach to solving this problem. As we noted in chapter 5, one initiative that has shown promise is supporting the formation of knowledge networks among firms. These networks "import" global best practices in a sector and make them available as public goods to their members. Governments in Africa can work with the private sector to form such public-private networks.

The management experiments in India highlight another potential channel of capability building: management training at the firm level. Should African governments, perhaps funded by their development partners, seek to replicate the Indian experience among larger domestically owned firms? Clearly, if firms do not adopt good management practices out of ignorance, then training programs in basic operations management, like inventory and quality control, offer a potentially substantial payoff in terms of increased productivity.

India also offers a cautionary tale. Unless the incentives are right in terms of competitive pressure and customs and attitudes adapt to allow firms to grow beyond the limits of the family, training may not achieve its full potential. African industry shares some important characteristics with its Indian counterparts. As we have seen, competitive pressures on large firms serving the domestic market are less than they might be, and many firms are family owned. Nevertheless, management training for larger firms is an area with enough upside potential to warrant further experimentation.

Creating Clusters

In Cambodia, Tunisia, and Vietnam the export push was accompanied by policies designed to promote the formation of industrial clusters. Government commitment to spatial industrial policies in these countries was not accidental. The productivity boost that agglomerations provide sets up another collective action problem. Because a critical mass of firms is needed in a new industrial location before they will realize productivity gains, no single firm has the incentive to locate in a new area in the absence of others. One of the key success factors in the industrialization experiences of Cambodia and Vietnam was the ability to attract a critical mass of Asian regional investors to relocate task-based export production from higher cost economies in East Asia to both countries. A similar mass movement of European investors took place in Tunisia. Africa in contrast has few large-scale, modern industrial agglomerations. For this reason it is both more difficult for existing African firms to compete and more difficult to attract new industry.

Spatial Industrial Policy

Governments can foster industrial clusters by concentrating investments in high-quality institutions, social services, and infrastructure in a limited geographical area, such as a special economic zone.[33] Public policies to bring a critical mass of investors into such areas are a prerequisite to breaking into global markets in manufacturing. Spatial industrial policies are also important in industries without smokestacks. In countries with unreliable public infrastructure, services export companies look for customized facilities such as information technology (IT) parks with modern office space, high-speed broadband links, reliable power supply (including backup supply), security services, and ancillary infrastructure including banks, travel desks, restaurants, transportation systems, and hotel accommodations for visiting executives. The Software Technology Parks of India (STPI) initiative was launched by the Indian government in 1991 to provide data communication facilities, office space, and "single window" government services to potential IT investors. The technology parks proved essential to the growth of the software industry in a broader environment of deficient infrastructure and bureaucratic red tape.[34]

To date, Africa's experience with spatial industrial policy has been largely disappointing. A review of the performance of SEZs—most of which are export processing zones—in Ghana, Kenya, Lesotho, Nigeria, Senegal, and Tanzania concluded that most African SEZ programs are underperforming. The African zones have low levels of investment and exports, and their job creation impact is limited. They have few links with the domestic economy, and from the perspective of agglomeration it is notable that African SEZs have a much lower density of enterprises within the geographical boundaries of the SEZ than zones in Asia or Latin America. Most African SEZs are disconnected from domestic value chains, limiting their utility in the transfer of capabilities. Business support services, training, and skills upgrading are also often ignored.[35]

33. See UNIDO (2009) and Farole (2011).
34. Dongier and Sudan (2009).
35. Farole (2011).

Infrastructure, Attitudes, and Institutions

Most African SEZs have failed to reach the levels of physical, institutional, and human capital needed to attract global investors. For example, in the World Bank study cited previously, non-African SEZs had an average downtime from electricity outages of only four hours per month, compared with an average downtime of forty-four hours per month in African SEZs. A similar pattern was observed in customs clearance, where clearance times in African zones are about double that of their non-African counterparts. Much of the problem derives from a lack of coordination between SEZs and the local and national organizations that control public services and institutions outside the zones. Power, roads, and the public administration outside the SEZ often work at cross-purposes in the attempt to lower the costs of international transactions.[36]

A major stumbling block to better SEZ performance has been the management of the zones themselves. Often senior SEZ managers lack an understanding of the private investors they are attempting to support. Many of the SEZs in the countries we studied were managed by political appointees or former civil servants. Management was often unavailable to existing occupants of the zone and to potential new investors. During three visits to the flagship Benjamin Mkapa EPZ in Tanzania by one of our colleagues, no senior member of the zone's management team was ever present.

Institutional coordination is essential. Ideally, both the FDI agency and the SEZ authority should be located in the office of the presidency or the prime minister and should coordinate closely. There is a major disconnect in most countries between the institutions designed to attract FDI and the SEZs. For example, currently about 300 enterprises operate in Ghana's export processing zones. EPZ manufacturing firms are involved in food processing, wood and veneer processing, processing of shea nuts and oil seeds, lubricants and biofuels, garments, and the manufacture of food processing machines and spare parts. The zones also host such tradable

36. Farole (2011).

services as data processing, telecommunications, and software development. The sheer variety of firms in the zones raises a red flag. In an economy like Ghana, clusters of firms connected along a value chain are more likely to realize significant firm-level productivity gains than geographical concentrations of unrelated firms.[37] One reason for the heterogeneity of firms is that neither the FDI agency nor the SEZ management had a strategy for attempting to attract firms in the same or closely related value chains into the zones.

Setting the Agenda

To implement this new agenda for industrial development, African governments will need to do something that they have so far shown themselves not to be very good at doing: developing a productive engagement with the private sector in order to identify the binding constraints to industrial development.[38] Consulting the private sector can be done in at least two ways. The first is through the use of firm surveys, such as those underpinning the World Bank Investment Climate Assessments.

These surveys have generated some important insights into the perceived obstacles to investment and growth by firms in Africa. Figure 7-1 provides a snapshot of the obstacles to the operation of small and large firms drawn from the World Bank Enterprise Survey database for the countries we have studied in sub-Saharan Africa.[39]

The constraints are somewhat different depending on firm size. The differences, however, are less striking than one might expect. It

---

37. As we pointed out in chapter 6, the nature and sources of agglomeration economies change with the level of per capita income. For countries in Africa, localization economies are likely to be most relevant during early industrialization, which calls for a strategic approach designed to promote linkages between domestic and foreign firms along a value chain.

38. A set of WIDER-sponsored case studies of business-government coordination in Africa are available (www.wider.unu.edu/research/TIS -programme/transformation/en_GB/jobs-poverty-structural-change-africa/).

39. World Bank (2015).

Figure 7-1. *Perceived Obstacles to the Operation of Small and Large Firms*

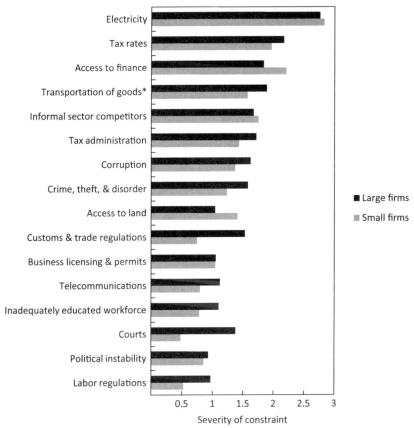

Source: Authors' calculations based on firm-level data from Ethiopia (year 2002), Ghana (2007), Kenya (2007), Mozambique (2007), Nigeria (2007), Rwanda (2006), Senegal (2007), Tanzania (2006), and Uganda (2006), collected as part of the World Bank's Enterprise Surveys.
Notes: Firms are classified as large if they employ fifty or more workers. * Including inputs and supplies. Horizontal axis gives respondent's assessment of degree of severity of constraint.

is informative that regulatory constraints do not figure among the top-five constraints identified by either small or large firms. Tax administration and corruption rank sixth and seventh. Access to land and customs and trade regulations are in the middle of the list, below crime, theft, and disorder. This does not mean they are unimportant; it simply indicates that in the view of the business community, other constraints, notably those associated with inadequate infrastructure, are more binding. Surveys of this type can be used to set priories for public investment and policy reform and to check on progress in implementation.

A second way to engage with the private sector is to conduct a structured dialogue to identify reform priorities. Economists have termed this structured dialogue, close coordination, and many argue it is essential both for the design of appropriate public actions and for feedback on their implementation.[40] While close coordination between public decision makers and private investors is needed, it is a risky business. The massive literature on rent seeking and government failures suggests that in many cases a close relationship between business and government can lead to inappropriate policies.[41] Managing the tension between close coordination and capture is critical to the success of this approach to agenda setting.

Africa has some experience—both positive and negative—with efforts to design institutions to foster business-government communication and problem solving. A number of these were in the countries we studied intensively. Ethiopia provides the best example of success. Its head of government, the late prime minister Meles Zenawi, led a close coordination process in the cut-flower industry that identified the binding constraints to exports and resolved them through public-private action. An experiment in coordination, sponsored by the World Bank and the International Monetary Fund (IMF), may provide the best example of failure.

In 2001, the heads of the IMF and World Bank made a joint visit to Africa. Shortly after, Presidential Investors' Advisory Councils (PIACs) were created by the presidents of Ghana, Tanzania, and Senegal in 2002, and by Uganda's president in 2004. Ethiopia launched a Public-Private Consultative Forum, loosely modeled on the PIAC, in 2010. The councils were expected to enable the presidents to hear the views of experienced and successful business leaders and to identify constraints to foreign and domestic investment

40. Rodrik (2007); Harrison and Rodriguez-Claire (2010).
41. See, for example, Krueger (1974). A balanced review of the relevance of this literature is contained in the report of the Commission on Growth and Development (2008).

and generate recommendations for concrete action. In short, they were public-private coordination mechanisms.

Over slightly more than a decade, Ghana's council disappeared, while Uganda's has been judged something of a success. The councils in Senegal and Tanzania have had some impact, but fall between Ghana at one extreme and Uganda at the other in terms of their performance. Ethiopia's council is still very new, but early signals are not encouraging. The councils suffered from a number of deficiencies as coordination mechanisms, including capture of the agenda-setting process by the international financial institutions (IFIs), but perhaps the single most important factor in the performance of these councils was the level of commitment of the head of government or head of state.

Uganda is the only country in which the president has found time to hold more than one council meeting a year, and in which he has a reputation for following up on council deliberations. Ghana and Ethiopia represent the other extreme. In Ghana, the president quickly lost interest and the council lost momentum. In Ethiopia, the late prime minister, who had a track record of close engagement with private investors at the sector and industry level, failed to call for a national meeting of the newly created council.[42] Put bluntly, the region and its heads of state will need to raise their game in close coordination.

Summing Up

For most African countries investment climate reforms alone are unlikely to be enough to overcome the advantages of the world's existing industrial locations. A strategy that recognizes and deals with the drivers of firm-level productivity is urgently needed. This chapter outlines such a strategy. It combines a refocused investment climate reform agenda with three new strategic objectives identified by our Learning to Compete research. It begins with the basics. Closing

42. Page (2014a).

the region's growing infrastructure and skills gaps with the rest of the world can lower costs and boost firm-level productivity. Better approaches to the reform of regulations and institutions affecting the private sector are also needed. Because fiscal resources are constrained, early public actions to improve the investment climate should focus on supporting the specific strategic interventions needed to raise firm-level productivity.

The second component of the strategy is an export push—a coordinated set of public investments, public policies, and institutional reforms to boost the share of industrial exports in GDP. With the exception of Mauritius and Tunisia, African governments have largely failed to pursue effective, systematic efforts to promote nontraditional exports. Regulatory and institutional reforms to create an effective "free trade environment" for exporters are needed. Infrastructure focused on trade logistics and more strenuous efforts to build and maintain regional infrastructure are also important.

The last two components address building capabilities and agglomerations. Foreign direct investment is a key source of capabilities, and policies and institutions for attracting FDI are essential. Regulations that restrict the transfer of capabilities should be changed. Public policies to promote the dissemination of management information and to provide management training offer considerable promise. African governments can promote industrial agglomerations by concentrating investments in high-quality institutions, social services, and infrastructure in special economic zones. Until now, African SEZs have failed to attract global investors. Thus, a first order of business is to upgrade their performance to international standards. For upgrading to succeed, governments will need to take a very hard look at how they select and reward their SEZ managers. FDI agencies need to work in tandem with SEZ administrations to attract a critical mass of firms in industries related along the value chain into the zones.

The strategy for industrial development that we have outlined will not succeed if it is implemented in a piecemeal or haphazard way. Because the drivers of firm-level productivity are so closely interrelated, progress in one area—say, promotion of industrial exports—will not achieve its desired effect in the absence of actions in the others. This calls for a level of coordination across government and a degree of engagement with the private sector that is far more demanding than that implied by the investment climate reform agenda. The industrial success of Mauritius, Tunisia, Cambodia, and Vietnam has been largely a result of their ability to undertake such a coordinated effort. It is surely not beyond the capability of some African governments to emulate them.

Earlier in this book we criticized one-size-fits-all approaches to industrial development, and we do not want to make the same error here. The extent to which our strategic recommendations fit each individual country's circumstances will vary. For example, landlocked countries will undoubtedly face tougher headwinds in exporting manufactured goods than those with coastal locations. Nevertheless, because tradable services and agro-industry share many characteristics with manufacturing, we believe that the strategy we have outlined is applicable to industrial development—broadly defined—across a wide range of countries in Africa.

CHAPTER 8

Dealing with Resource Abundance

Africa is richly endowed with natural resources, and new discoveries in such previously non-resource-abundant economies as Ghana, Kenya, Mozambique, Tanzania, and Uganda raise the prospect that an increasing number of African countries will become resource exporters in the future. The exploitation of natural resources is a huge opportunity. It is also one that, as we pointed out in chapter 3, carries considerable risks. Relative prices in resource-rich economies tend, all else being equal, to push them toward economic structures where a high share of output is concentrated in the resource sector and in nontraded services.

If African resource exporters were able to sustain high levels of income based on rents to resources and returns on foreign financial assets indefinitely (like some countries in the Arab Gulf), this structure might not matter too much. This is, however, not the case for most resource-abundant economies in Africa. The resource is finite, so economic structure matters a great deal. The long-run success of Africa's newly resource-abundant economies will therefore depend on the choices they make as to how resource revenues are used to support future growth. For most of Africa, natural resources are best seen as a medium-term source of public income that can help countries put in place the institutions, policies, and diverse public investments that will underpin the changes needed to sustain growth once the resource is depleted.

This chapter begins with a look at the savings and investment questions raised by a resource boom. Because governments have the option of using resource revenues to increase the productivity of private investment in industries beyond the resource sector, we also examine how public actions can be used to deal with Dutch disease. This is followed by a discussion of the opportunities the presence of a resource discovery may open up for spatial industrial policies. The chapter concludes with a discussion of two options for diversification in newly resource-abundant economies: investing in new production knowledge and linking industry to the resource.

Understanding the Boom

Although our central concern is how resource revenues can support diversification into industry, it is important to begin with the larger questions posed by a natural resource discovery. These are mostly questions of public financial management. There is by now a great deal of writing on the issues of transparency and accountability in the management of resource revenues. We certainly do not need to repeat the lessons here.[1] Our focus is further upstream and downstream. Understanding the size and timing of the boom and putting in place the policies and institutional structures needed to manage resource revenues and public investments are essential first steps toward diversification. They set the boundaries on what will be saved and invested and can improve the efficiency and effectiveness of public investment out of resource revenues.

---

1. A survey of good practices in transparency and accountability is available at the Natural Resource Charter (www.naturalresourcecharter .org).

How Much Revenue and When?

The first questions are: How big is the revenue boom likely to be, and when will revenue come online? These are often the questions that are least well understood by politicians and the public. The experiences of Ghana, Kenya, Mozambique, Tanzania, and Uganda show that, in general, the size of the boom is overestimated and the delay in receiving revenues is underestimated. In addition, lack of transparency regarding the terms of extraction agreements between the foreign investor and the government has frequently led to a great deal of confusion and, at times, suspicion.

In Uganda, for example, we found that there are not going to be any significant oil revenues any time soon. With production starting at modest levels as early as 2015, it will take until the second half of the next decade—about 2026—before revenue climbs toward 5 percent of GDP, or just over one-third of nonoil taxation. Even at its height, the size of the boom is modest. A relatively narrow range for the oil price—given the history of the last ten years—of US$75 to $105 per barrel could put revenue per person at US$20 to nearly US$80 in 2030. This is as low as 3 percent of GDP (smaller than aid inflows today) or as much as 9 percent of GDP.[2]

The Uganda case points to a common thread among the five emerging African resource exporters we have studied. In all of these countries the resource boom most probably will not be large enough to be transformative—none of the oil exporting countries is likely to become another Kuwait—but it could well be large enough to be potentially disruptive, if not well managed. Gas in Mozambique and perhaps Tanzania could bring a larger windfall, but even in these cases the timing and magnitudes are uncertain, and neither is likely to end up as Qatar.

Ironically, the long lead time before revenues begin to flow is on the side of the resource exporters. Prudent revenue management requires establishing how much public spending should increase and how much to save before resource revenues begin to accrue to

---

2. Henstridge and Page (2012).

the treasury. Countries with new discoveries have a window of opportunity to make these decisions and lock them in before pressures to spend become irresistible.

Save or Spend?

Sustainable development depends on the rents from resource extraction being converted into other sources of income. This inevitably leads to the conclusion that some of the revenues must be saved and invested. In a low-income country it also raises the question of where to invest. The rules governing saving from nonrenewable resources—such as those implied by the permanent income hypothesis or the bird-in-hand rule—tend to place substantial, perhaps excessive, weight on the welfare of future generations and in practice encourage the accumulation of foreign assets.

In a poor, capital-scarce economy, this is inappropriate for two reasons. First, it is likely that future generations will be richer than those today, making it reasonable for government to use a portion of the windfall to increase the consumption of today's poor. Second, the returns to domestic investment in a capital-scarce economy should exceed those offered by foreign assets.[3] Put another way, while it may make sense for rich, capital-abundant Norway to invest in U.S. Treasuries, it doesn't make much sense for most African countries—provided, of course, that the funds are invested and spent well.

This raises the question of how to assess how much spending is too much. Regardless of whether spending is in the form of consumption or public investment, there is an absorption constraint. Getting feedback from the economy as the public investment program is executed will show whether the limits of absorptive capacity have been reached. The most direct signals are in inflation and the market exchange rate. When inflation is going up and the exchange rate is appreciating, spending needs to be scaled back. Once the overall volume of spending consistent with prudent macroeconomic man-

---

3. Collier and others (2010).

agement is set, whatever part of revenue should not be spent—
either on consumption or domestic investment—should be parked
in sensible investments overseas, allowing plenty of room for flexibility in case of unexpected events and shocks to the domestic
economy.

The Quality of Public Spending

One frequently neglected determinant of the appropriate quantity
of public spending is the quality of that spending. The experience
with public expenditure management in the emerging resource exporters we studied suggests that two critical measures are needed to
increase the quality of spending: improving the quality of project
appraisal and budgeting of recurrent costs of maintenance. One of
the major contributors to Botswana's success in translating diamond
revenues into rapid economic growth was a firm insistence on good
quality appraisal of every public investment project. Chile, another
resource-rich economy, followed similar rules.

To replicate this in other resource-exporting countries would en-
tail building a cadre of economists with training in project appraisal
and making them responsible for project preparation across each
spending ministry. It would also require designing incentives for the
use of project appraisals through the budget process and personnel policies. In Botswana and Chile, writing sound appraisals and
identifying and rejecting weak or inadequate appraisals were skills
required for officials to advance their careers in the Ministry of
Finance.[4]

Frequently public investments are made without adequate provision in the budget for recurrent costs of maintenance. This is especially
dangerous in the case of spending out of resource revenues. Lack of
maintenance can seriously degrade the returns to the investments
made, and the spending rule is that investments in the domestic
economy should only be made when they offer higher returns than
foreign assets.

4. Henstridge and Page (2012).

Dealing with Dutch Disease

Because of the relative price changes that tend to occur in a resource-abundant economy, diversification into tradable goods production outside the oil sector is difficult, even with prudent management of overall spending. While Dutch disease reduces the range of internationally competitive industries available, competitiveness does not depend on the exchange rate alone. Governments can use public policies and investments to enhance the productivity of investments outside the natural resource sector.

In resource-rich economies there is an important role for policies and investments directed at improving the investment climate. While we have been critical of the way in which investment climate reforms have been implemented, if properly designed to embrace infrastructure and skills development in addition to regulatory reform, investment climate reforms have the potential to boost the productivity of a wide range of firms outside the resource sector.

Regulatory Reform

Regulatory reforms are an attractive place to begin. They have low fiscal costs and potentially high payoffs. Surveys of manufacturing firms in resource-abundant countries highlight a wide range of areas in which regulatory or administrative burdens raise costs and reduce competitiveness. While the same concerns we raised in chapter 7 apply to the design of the regulatory reform agenda, reforms that encourage the entry and exit of firms and reduce administrative burdens can have a positive impact on firm-level productivity. Well-designed institutional and regulatory reforms should be undertaken sooner rather than later in newly resource-rich countries in order to exploit the opportunity offered by the waiting period before resource revenues begin to flow. This is because institutional and regulatory reforms may prove more difficult to initiate and sustain in resource-abundant economies.[5]

5. Collier (2010).

The institutions that create and enforce regulation can limit competition and create rents. Incumbent workers and firms benefit from lack of competition and have little incentive to support improvements in the regulatory regime. Normally, pressures for regulatory reform would come from other interest groups in the society, but in resource-exporting countries there is some evidence that resource rents gradually weaken the checks and balances that provide scrutiny over the government, making these competing interests less successful in changing policy.[6]

Infrastructure and Skills

The new revenues that will flow from natural resources open up fiscal space for governments of resource-abundant economies to address two of the fundamental constraints to competitiveness we highlighted in chapter 7: lack of infrastructure and skills. Investments in trade-related infrastructure can make an important contribution to diversification. The nine currently resource-rich African countries have an average trade-related infrastructure (ports, rail, road, and telecommunications) ranking of 122 out of 160 countries in the World Bank 2014 Trade Logistics Index. Africa's best-performing resource-rich economy in terms of trade-related infrastructure was Nigeria, ranked at 83. Seven of the remaining eight are in the bottom third of the global distribution and four are in the bottom quintile.[7]

Increasing investments in infrastructure, particularly in the area of trade logistics, can help lower costs and offset the worst effects of Dutch disease. The increase in public revenues made possible by the resource can be partly directed to priority investments in trade-related infrastructure. At the same time, not all infrastructure projects will have the same impact. Careful cost-benefit analysis of proposed infrastructure investments is needed, and governments should have a prioritized list of vetted projects ready for funding.

6. Collier and Hoeffler (2008).
7. World Bank (2014b).

The skills gap poses another major constraint to diversification. For example, in Uganda and Mozambique, two emerging resource exporters, lack of skills is emerging as a significant constraint on firm-level performance. Forty-seven percent of Ugandan companies reported lack of skills as a moderate, major, or very severe constraint to business.[8] One-third of the large firms surveyed in the World Bank Mozambique Investment Climate Assessment reported the educational attainment of the workforce as a major constraint to growth.[9] As we saw in chapter 7, the main skills that are lacking are those related to production. These are largely the product of postprimary education, although investments in quality to raise cognitive skills at all levels are also important.

Public spending on improving quality and expanding postprimary education have been heavily limited by the influence of the donors and their pursuit of the primary education Millennium Development Goal (MDG). Newly resource-rich economies should devote some of the incremental funding made possible by resource revenues to secondary, technical-vocational, and university education and to improving quality at all levels. This will not be an easy task. Pressures may still come from the donors to place priority on expanding primary enrollment, and the links between educational spending and educational outcomes are still not well understood. While cost-benefit analysis of projects to develop human capital are difficult, there is no excuse for not demanding rigorous attempts to assess the cost-effectiveness of various proposed skill development programs as an input to sensible policymaking.

Debt management is important. Because the needs in infrastructure and skills are large and the timing of revenues is uncertain, governments face strong pressures to borrow on international capital markets in anticipation of the arrival of resource revenues. In the case of Ghana, for example, the government ramped up infrastructure spending before resource revenues were in place, raising the public debt burden through sovereign borrowing. This means that raising

8. World Bank (2007b).
9. World Bank (2009a).

revenues from general taxation will be needed to service the debt during the waiting period for revenues to come onstream, which may affect the country's ability to borrow in the future. While it is difficult to resist pressures to spend, prudent debt management is essential.

"Investing to Invest"

Investing resource revenues to expand infrastructure and education will to some extent require transforming public expenditures into physical assets. The construction sector largely determines the ability of an economy to transform investment effort into investment outcomes. In infrastructure, for example, there is evidence from a large sample of countries that higher construction costs are significantly associated with poorer roads. A 10 percent increase in unit road construction costs is associated with a country-level reduction of 0.7 percent in the kilometers of paved roads per person and a 0.4 point reduction in the quality of the trade and transport-related infrastructure index component of the World Bank Logistics Performance Index.[10] Similar considerations apply to public investments in structures, including those needed to improve education.

If construction faces bottlenecks in production and is unable to increase supply, any surge in demand will force up costs and prices, reducing the physical output for a given amount of nominal investment. Paul Collier has emphasized the need for policies to reduce the marginal cost of physical investment, which he terms "investing to invest." It is potentially an important part of dealing with the challenges of Dutch disease.[11]

Evidence is mixed among the countries we studied with respect to construction costs. In Uganda, construction cost increases have outpaced overall inflation significantly over the past several years and appear to be accelerating. Prices for the construction sector rose by 35.3 percent from September 2010 to September 2011. Reflecting the attempt to boost public investment, the increase in prices was

10. Collier, Kirchberger, and Söderbom (2013).
11. Collier (2011b).

greatest for nonresidential buildings.[12] In Tanzania, on the other hand, most large-scale construction is carried out by foreign contractors. While this poses problems from the point of view of capability building in the domestic construction sector, it means that the supply price of construction services on major public investment projects is less sensitive to domestic supply constraints.

One reason construction prices tend to rise sharply in response to increases in demand is that the construction sector encounters bottlenecks. The first step in investing to invest is therefore for the government to learn from the construction sector about the bottlenecks it faces. Because the speed with which construction can be expanded without severely driving up prices determines the pace at which public investment can be increased, the government also needs a rapid flow of information to determine the pace of public investment.

Botswana provides a good example of how this can be done. When it realized that construction costs were rising rapidly as a result of the increase in public investment from diamond revenues, the government created a separate annual plan for the construction sector within its overall five-year development plan. Each year construction firms were called in, the feasibility of government construction plans was discussed, bottlenecks were identified and addressed, and the rate of implementation of the overall plan was adjusted.

Public policies can address some bottlenecks. Construction requires land, material inputs, skills, organization, and finance. Each can potentially constrain the expansion of output. Sometimes urban land rights are confused, which can delay construction projects. Similarly, planning permission might be slow. Clearly, these are stages in construction that government can prevent from becoming constraints. Policy restrictions on imports, poorly performing institutions such as customs, or the poor performance of the port may become a bottleneck and should be addressed head-on. For nontradable inputs a combination of economizing on their use and stimulating local production may be needed.

12. Uganda Bureau of Statistics (2011).

Construction will not be able to expand if there are few skilled construction workers. Bricklayers, welders, electricians, and plumbers are complementary to unskilled labor and capital, and the cost of importing them can be high. With planning, construction skills can be developed locally. Therefore, the government should allocate resources to technical and vocational training in construction skills before the flow of resource revenues begins. Immigration policies that encourage the temporary location of service providers can also be liberalized to reduce the cost of importing skilled labor. For East Africa's emerging resource exporters this could be done within the context of deeper regional integration of the East African Community.

Corruption and collusive behavior among firms are more difficult areas to deal with. Corruption lowers the efficiency of capital investment generally.[13] It seems to have a particularly strong impact on construction. The study we previously referred to found that unit costs in countries with a level of corruption above the median, as measured by the Worldwide Governance Indicator's corruption measure, have on average 12 percent higher road construction costs, even after controlling for the business environment and public investment capacity.[14]

We have a very imperfect understanding of the mechanisms by which corruption flows through into higher costs. One obvious channel is "leakage" of funds. The use of inferior materials and the failure to meet specifications are other likely suspects. Inferior inputs are a serious concern. They raise the cost of construction, but they also increase subsequent maintenance costs for the government. Some suggested mechanisms for dealing with corruption include strengthening the role and integrity of the project engineer and checking the wealth of key procurement agency officials.[15] Countries could also experiment with different incentive contracts for engineers to encourage reporting of corruption and fraud.

13. O'Toole and Tarp (2014).
14. Collier, Kirchberger, and Söderbom (2013).
15. World Bank (2011a).

Collusive behavior by construction firms raises costs in both developed and developing countries. By one estimate overcharges due to cartels lead to about 40 percent higher construction prices on average in developing countries. Given the magnitude of these effects, limiting collusion is a major concern. Collusion, however, has been difficult to detect in advanced economies, making it a daunting task for the average African country. Building up and publicizing databases of unit costs of comparable construction activities can assist governments in ensuring that they are not overpaying, but publishing the data carries a downside risk. There is some evidence that new bids closely track the publicly available data, suggesting that higher transparency has helped companies collude.[16]

Resources and Geography

We have shown that agglomeration economies are important, even in countries at quite low levels of development, and in chapter 7 we outlined some spatial industrial policies we feel are appropriate for those African countries trying to break into the global market for manufactured goods. The relative price structure of the region's resource-abundant economies is likely to make rapid expansion of manufactured exports significantly more difficult. On the other hand, the presence of natural resources and the revenues and foreign investors they bring can open up new areas for spatial industrial policy.

Resource-Based SEZs

Resource-rich economies will need to develop spatial policies in line with their resource endowments and factor costs. Rather than focus on developing export processing zones (EPZs) to attract trade in tasks, a more promising approach might be to use special economic zones (SEZs) to promote industrial activities in sectors linked to the resource. One example in Ghana is the Shama EPZ, an industrial

16. World Bank (2011a).

park targeted to the petroleum-petrochemical sector, situated in the Western Region. The zone provides investment support to a downstream refinery, distribution, transit, and supply chain businesses and resource-based products (plastics and jellies) intended for export. It also offers development and capacity-building services for employers and employees. The zone provides land for tank farms, storage yards for logistics and haulage contractors, and manufacturing of chemical inputs and accessories for the petroleum industry.

The presence of new natural resources can have knock-on impacts on the communities surrounding the extractive activity through job creation and, as in the case of manufacturing, unanticipated effects on women's lives and household welfare. Some new research, based on a large sample of mining projects, finds that mining in sub-Saharan Africa creates substantial numbers of jobs that are not directly connected with the mining sector itself, and it has the potential to draw women into work outside the household. The presence of a mine has a positive and statistically significant effect on the likelihood that a female will secure a job in the service sector. Indicators of infant health are also higher in areas near mining projects.[17] Resource-based SEZs can become a focal point for programs designed to increase the benefits to local communities and in particular to women living near an extractive activity.

The challenges surrounding the development of resource-based SEZs are very similar to those for export-oriented zones. Infrastructure, institutions, and attitudes continue to matter. Unless infrastructure and institutions are world class, it may prove impossible to draw a critical mass of firms into the zone. Managers with business experience and a business outlook are critical to success. One important difference is that the zones are designed to foster value chain relationships between the extractive industry and mainly domestic firms, upstream and downstream. This implies that the design of institutions intended to foster value-chain relationships is critical to the success of the SEZ. This is an important topic to which we shall turn later in this chapter.

17. Tolonen (2015).

Growth Corridors

A number of governments are experimenting with the development of regional special economic zones, often called "growth corridors." Regional SEZs can be developed around key trade infrastructure (ports, roads, power projects) and natural resource discoveries. Both Mozambique and Tanzania are working to design regional SEZs around their newly discovered natural gas deposits. These regional economic zones are intended to play a catalytic role in integrated regional growth initiatives by attracting investors to locations from which specialized regional inputs can be tapped and production scaled up.

Regional SEZs are attractive for two reasons. First, they emphasize the complementarities between transport infrastructure and resource- or agriculture-based projects within the region. The SEZ approach can help to solve coordination problems between investments in related projects, and it raises the prospect of rapid private-sector response to infrastructure improvements. Second, it is possible that in resource-centered zones the bulk of capital spending on infrastructure for both transport and power can be financed by the resource projects themselves. Growth corridors also highlight the possible complementarities between investment projects.

A successful corridor-based approach requires the implementation of a much broader set of policies than those found within an EPZ. These interventions include (i) promoting skills development, training, and knowledge sharing; (ii) developing industry clusters and targeting links with zone-based firms at the cluster level; (iii) supporting the integration of regional value chains; (iv) strengthening public-private institutions; and (v) ensuring that labor markets facilitate the movement of labor across firms. Throughout the process, links with the wider domestic economy must be developed and deepened.

The experience of some countries, including Malaysia and China, suggests that growth corridors hold some promise, but a realistic assessment of the potential of different zones and a rigorous analysis of the costs and benefits of public spending on alternative projects is needed. This is a difficult area. Narrow cost-benefit analyses of infrastructure projects often miss the role of infrastructure in triggering private investment. Wider analyses run the risk of wishful thinking.

Transnational Transport Corridors

One intriguing possibility is to attempt to use natural resource discoveries and the major infrastructure investments that often accompany them to break the logjam currently inhibiting the development of transnational transport corridors. Oil in Uganda provides an example of the potential and the pitfalls of this approach. Uganda is a landlocked country that cannot solve its connectivity problem by itself. Regional approaches to infrastructure, customs administration, competition policy, regulation of transport, and trade-related services are essential for Uganda's ability to compete.

During the postindependence period the governments in the East African Community have failed to sustain the necessary levels of political cooperation needed to make transnational roads, railways, and institutions operate effectively. Oil is a potential game changer. If the rail transport option for Uganda's petroleum exports proves to be attractive, an opportunity will arise to develop and operate a rehabilitated rail corridor, either through Kenya or Tanzania. Such a rail line should not be the monopoly of the oil industry. A third-party commercial operator with core competence in infrastructure is the most credible option to carry out rehabilitation and operation of the railway.[18]

For the new transnational rail line to be commercially viable, the risks to investors and customers would need to be addressed at the start of negotiations. The rail contracts would need to include agreements with the governments and commercial users on access and tariffs, enforced by reference to a dispute settlement mechanism. In effect, the governments involved would have to agree in advance to a limited, clearly specified degree of pooled sovereignty. To achieve this, an intergovernmental rail authority that has sufficient power

18. Collier (2011a).

to negotiate credibly with a rail company and its commercial users—including the oil companies—would need to be established. The high stakes to all parties of the resource discovery increase the incentives for sharing of sovereignty. Having established a precedent, a similar approach could be used to establish intergovernmental road authorities.

Some Options for Diversification

Although the discoveries of natural resources in Africa in many ways make the process of industrial development more challenging, they also offer new opportunities. We want to explore two of them. The first is using resource revenues to develop specialized knowledge, either linked to the resource itself or in unrelated areas in which a resource-abundant economy may have geographical or other country-specific sources of comparative advantage. The second is to use the presence of the resource to acquire firm capabilities from foreign investors.

Investing in Knowledge

In addition to investments in the skills needed for production, a strong case can be made for efforts to build specialist knowledge and skills linked to the extractive industries themselves. Resource extraction is idiosyncratic. Particular problems are associated with technology and location-specific geology. This creates scope for specialist knowledge of these localized features, giving local firms a comparative advantage.[19] Norway is a well-known case. When petroleum was discovered Norway had no local expertise in deepwater exploration and production of oil and gas. Through a deliberate policy of building up such expertise through universities and the state oil company, today Norway is a major player in deepwater oil and gas technology, including off the East Coast of Africa. Qatar provides a different ex-

19. UNIDO (2009).

ample; its expertise is in dealing with the environmental consequences of oil spills. Qatari companies have developed a global reputation that has involved them is such high-profile containment and cleanup operations as the BP spill in the Gulf of Mexico.

One appropriate investment for Africa's newly resource-abundant economies might be to build up the geology and engineering departments of universities with the intention of developing a services export industry related to resource extraction. A public-private partnership between the Jubilee Partners and Takoradi Polytechnic in Ghana, the Jubilee Technical Training Center (JTTC), is an example. The first batch of petroleum engineering trainees (thirty-two in total) graduated in April 2014. While it is neither efficient nor feasible for each African resource-rich country to develop such expertise individually, it should be possible to develop regionwide centers of excellence in mining and petroleum engineering and geology. Makerere University in Uganda, for example, has a long tradition of serving as a regional hub for Eastern Africa and is close to a wide range of new natural resource discoveries.

Knowledge-intensive industries, such as some information technology–based services, and those that exploit localized sources of competitive advantage, such as tourism, may be less sensitive to Dutch disease than final stage task-based manufacturing. Chile provides a good illustration. In Chile, resource revenues made it possible to develop a wholly new line of business—horticulture and agro-industry—in which local geography played a significant role. Chile's abundant lakes and rivers are ideal for the cultivation of salmon, and its climate is highly suited to the production of wine. The main drivers of productivity improvements in both industries were investments in the generation and diffusion of production knowledge across firms. The initiative was led by an innovative public-private partnership, the Fundacion Chile, and eventually involved private firms, government at all levels, universities, and specialist research institutes.

Many new African resource exporters—Kenya, Mozambique, Tanzania, and Uganda, among them—may, like Chile, find opportunities to invest in knowledge relevant to new exports in agriculture or services, such as tourism, where geography or other endowments provide a comparative advantage. One approach might be to develop three-way partnerships with the private sector and universities and specialist research institutions: the private firms carry the commercial risks of investments, the research organizations focus on knowledge generation, while the state provides new knowledge as a public good. In this area, as in education and skills development more generally, accurate estimates of the costs and benefits of public investments are difficult but critical.

Linking Industry to the Resource

Natural resources change the balance of power between governments and foreign firms. In countries that are not resource-abundant governments are engaged in a global beauty contest to attract foreign direct investment (FDI). For this reason the types of FDI institutions outlined in chapter 7 are essential to attract and retain high-capability foreign investors. In natural resource–rich countries it is the foreign investors who are engaged in the beauty contest, often competing to gain access to the resource. This provides a unique opportunity for African governments to broaden the country's industrial capabilities by integrating domestic companies into the supply chains of multinational resource extraction firms.

This is an area where governments will need to exercise great care. Simple rules of thumb, like domestic content legislation, that specify a minimum percentage of domestic inputs that need to be sourced locally are usually ineffective. The multinational corporations (MNCs) that dominate extractive industries have long experience complying with the letter of such legislation without meeting its spirit. In general, governments come to the bargaining table with inflated expectations of how many domestic firms can be integrated into the resource-related value chains and the foreign firms come with the expectation that few, if any, domestic companies have the capabilities to become reliable suppliers.

A major pitfall to be avoided is the temptation to take an overly narrow view of what kinds of firms can benefit from the resource boom. There is a tendency for policymakers to focus on two areas.

Upstream the focus is usually on opportunities for local engineering, fabrication, assembly, and construction firms to participate in the construction phase of the new extractive investments. Downstream the emphasis tends to be on further processing of the resource. Ghana's industrial development strategy, for example, calls for the establishment of new industries such as petrochemicals, fertilizer, and liquefied petroleum gas (LPG) cylinder production linked to its oil and gas industry. This is too narrow a view of the potential for engagement with the natural resources sector and runs the risk of focusing attention on capital-intensive sectors that require high levels of firm capabilities and generate little employment. It also diverts attention from other opportunities, some as mundane as catering, cleaning, and security services.

One way to move forward is for the government to develop programs in partnership with the foreign investors to identify domestic firms with the capabilities to participate in their value chains in the short run. A first step is to open an active dialogue with the foreign investors to determine their view of the opportunities to source goods and services locally. In many cases capabilities are adequate to permit some degree of integration of local companies into the resource sector's value chain.

Initially a very small number of local firms may be able to play a leading role in any area of activity. This raises the need to put in place training programs for potential supplying firms that cover both technical and business management subjects. Programs to improve the capabilities of potential supplying firms through training and contacts with the resource sector's foreign subcontractors can be developed. The success of this approach rests on a willingness, on the part of the foreign investor, to engage in the process and the effectiveness of the government agency charged with implementing the program.[20]

One of the most important considerations in attempting to bring local firms into the multinationals' supply chains is finding a way to achieve both transparency and effectiveness in an environment where the number of suitably qualified local firms is initially low. In

20. Sutton (2012).

Ghana and Tanzania, the number of well-functioning firms in steel fabrication can be counted on the fingers of one hand.[21] This is where access to training becomes important. Effective training can raise the capabilities of firms to the minimum level needed to enter the MNC value chains, but if any firm can apply, substantial resources may be wasted on firms that are unable to meet the productivity and quality standards needed, even after training.

Selecting those who are likely to be able to meet the minimum standards of the MNCs or benefit most from training in the early phases of a resource boom is a process fraught with risks, both economic and political. Because some selectivity is essential and the number of domestic firms hoping to benefit from the resource boom is likely to be large, selectivity opens up the door for rent seeking. A solution is to set up a process that allows any local firm to apply, but specifies in advance a set of criteria that will be used in selecting applicants.

For example, one criterion to identify local firms with the potential to enter the business of supplying tank farms might be "proven commercial success in large-scale metal fabrication." In Ghana, Mozambique, or Tanzania, this requirement alone would restrict eligible applicants to quite a small number of local firms.[22] Oversight of the program, ideally by an independent watchdog organization composed of public sector, private sector, and civil society representatives with a reputation for probity and public disclosure of their findings, can help to diminish concerns that selectivity is being abused.

Summing Up

The expansion of new discoveries of oil, gas, and minerals represents an unparalleled opportunity for Africa's newly resource-abundant economies, but one accompanied by substantial risks. Success or

21. See the Enterprise Maps for Ghana and Tanzania: Sutton and Kpentey (2012); Sutton and Olomi (2012).
22. Sutton (2012).

failure will largely depend on how the rents from natural resource extraction are invested. Current trends in economic thinking suggest that for poor and resource-abundant countries some, though not all, of the resource windfall should be saved and invested in their own economies, provided the proposed investments are sound. This places a particular burden on public financial management and public investment planning. Two important steps can help to ensure that the public investments selected are in fact sound. The first is to subject every proposed public project to rigorous cost-benefit analysis. The second is to ensure that recurrent costs of maintaining the asset are reflected in the budget.

For the typical resource-rich economy in Africa, natural resources are not sufficiently abundant to ignore economic structure, and diversification is important. It helps to establish the basis for further sustained growth once the resource has been depleted. The relative price changes that occur in a resource-exporting economy— symptoms of Dutch disease—place Africa's resource-rich countries at a disadvantage with respect to industrial development.

Policy reforms and public investments can mitigate the worst consequences of Dutch disease. Some of these incorporate conventional wisdom. Investment climate reforms, if properly designed and implemented, can help to raise the productivity of firms outside of the resource sector. This will require a redesign of the regulatory reform agenda to make it address the regulatory constraints to entry, exit, and firm growth. It will also mean making productive investments in infrastructure and skills most relevant to international competitiveness. Investing to invest should play an important role in transforming investment effort in these areas into investment outcomes.

Beyond investments in institutions, infrastructure, and skills, natural resources offer African governments a range of options for diversification. Using spatial policies is one. Growth corridors and regional transit corridors are a potentially powerful way to leverage the investments made by multinational resource extraction firms for regional development. These initiatives need to be carefully designed and rigorously evaluated to ensure that regional rather than narrow corridor growth takes place during implementation.

Investing in knowledge related to the resource itself or promising high value added activities outside the resource sector is one path toward diversification. Agro-industry, tourism, and tradable services may prove to be less affected by appreciation of the real exchange rate than task-based manufactured exports. It makes sense for resource-rich economies in Africa to look for market niches in these industries without smokestacks.

Finally, governments can carefully promote supply chain relationships between domestic firms and the extractive industry. Because they control access to the resource, governments can seek an understanding with multinational resource extraction companies regarding the integration of local suppliers into the resource value chain. Here the challenge for policymakers is to be realistic and patient. Creating a viable public-private partnership to integrate domestic firms into a resource sector's value chain is not a trivial task. It requires a deep understanding of the current capabilities of domestic firms and a strong commitment to develop the institutional framework needed to expand them.

CHAPTER 9

An Agenda for Aid

Chapters 7 and 8 addressed what African governments need to do to bring industry to Africa. This chapter focuses on Africa's "development partners," the international donor community. Official development assistance—foreign aid—exercises significant influence over public policymaking in Africa. The aid industry has pretty much set the agenda for industrial development policies since the 1980s. In doing so, it has given little scope to African governments to develop their own industrialization strategies along the lines we have outlined. The results in terms of industrial development speak for themselves.

We propose a new agenda for aid. We begin by suggesting some sweeping changes to the investment climate reform agenda. As noted in chapter 2, the original concept of the investment climate encompassed macroeconomic management, investments in infrastructure and skills, and institutional and regulatory reform. In practice, investment climate reform has centered on business regulation. While regulatory reform is important, the focus on regulation has diverted attention from infrastructure and skills. It is imperative that a rebalancing take place, and so we begin the chapter with some new priorities for the investment climate.

We have argued throughout this book that reform of the investment climate alone will not be sufficient to address Africa's industrialization challenge, and in chapter 7 we presented a new strategy for industrialization. Many of the existing instruments of aid and trade policy—such as "Aid for Trade" and preferences—can be used to support that strategy, if they are redesigned and refocused. This chapter makes some suggestions. Donors also have an important role to play in helping the region's resource-rich economies to diversify, and we describe ways to support this diversification. Finally, some very hard thinking is needed regarding the donor community's support to micro, small, and medium enterprises (MSMEs). The reasons are set out at the end of the chapter.

Aid and the Investment Climate: A Missed Opportunity

Since about 2000, the industrial development efforts of donors in Africa, including both multilateral and bilateral agencies, have focused on improving the investment climate. According to the Development Assistance Committee (DAC) of the Organization for Economic Cooperation and Development (OECD), around one-quarter of official development assistance (some US$21 billion per year) currently supports investment climate reforms.[1] As originally conceived, the investment climate reform agenda was intended to balance reducing the physical constraints to industrialization, mainly infrastructure and skills, with reforms to the regulatory and institutional environment.[2] As implemented by the donors, however, the focus of investment climate operations has been on a narrow set of regulatory reforms defined in Washington.

1. OECD-DAC CRS (2013). The OECD-DAC is the club of the traditional aid donors. China, notably, is not a member.
2. Stern (2002; 2003).

Easy Answers: Institutional and Regulatory Reform Agenda

Much too often the centerpiece of the donor approach to the investment climate has been the World Bank/International Finance Corporation (IFC) *Doing Business* surveys.[3] *Doing Business* measures select business regulations in nearly 190 countries and ranks the countries on nine dimensions, ranging from ease of opening and closing a business to investor protection. It is supported by a highly efficient and well-funded public affairs machine. A defining characteristic of the *Doing Business* indicators is that they primarily measure laws and regulations as they are written or interpreted by local experts, rather than attempt to measure the impact of the regulations on firms. The philosophical underpinnings of *Doing Business* are unambiguous: seven of its nine indicators "presume that lessening regulation is always desirable."[4] Table 9-1 lists the indicators and their components.[5]

In 2014 the average rank of African countries on the *Doing Business* indicators (moving from 1 as the best to 189 as the worst) was 136. Clearly, Africa can do better at *Doing Business*. At the same time, the key issue in setting reform priorities is whether the binding regulatory constraints have been correctly identified by the surveys. The answer to that question is very likely to be no for a number of reasons. First, *Doing Business* was not designed to be used as a country-level diagnostic tool. It is a "league table" or cross-country benchmarking exercise, and the indicators were developed to support

3. The Independent Evaluation Group assessment of the *Doing Business* program notes that in 2008 the budget for "dissemination" by *Doing Business* management alone exceeded US$1 million. This figure did not include the costs of the World Bank's public affairs staff assigned to the program, nor the time of its country-based staff. See World Bank (2008a). For the most recent publication, see World Bank (2014a).

4. World Bank (2008a, p. xv).

5. In 2011 the World Bank removed the controversial ease of hiring and firing indicator from the rankings, although it continues to report the results of the annual data collected.

Table 9-1. *The* Doing Business *Indicators*

Starting a business Procedures, time, cost, and paid-in minimum capital to open a new business	***Paying taxes*** Number of tax payments, time to prepare and file tax returns and to pay taxes, total taxes as a share of profit before all taxes borne
Dealing with construction permits Procedures, time, and cost to obtain construction permits, inspections, and utility connections	***Trading across borders*** Documents, time, and cost to export and import
Registering property Procedures, time, and cost to transfer commercial real estate	***Enforcing contracts*** Procedures, time, and cost to resolve a commercial dispute
Getting credit Strength of legal rights index, depth of credit information index	***Closing a business*** Recovery rate in bankruptcy
Protecting investors Strength of investor protection index: extent of disclosure index, extent of director liability index, and ease of shareholder suits index	

Source: World Bank (2014a).

cross-country comparisons. Second, the indicators all have uniform weight, even if it is clear that not all reforms will have equal impact at the country level. Is a trade reform, for example, more or less urgent than reducing the number of days to open a business? Without country context it is impossible to say. *Doing Business* rewards the quantity of rankings changes, not the quality.

Because the indicators neither prioritize among the nine dimensions of regulation nor provide detailed country-level analysis, they are not suited to the evaluation of specific country regulatory reform programs. In view of these limitations, changes in the *Doing Business* ranking ought properly to be viewed as an outcome, not an objective, of a well-designed regulatory reform program, and yet the annual *Doing Business* reports strongly convey the message that lack of progress in reforming the institutions and regulations covered by the survey constrains private investment and growth.

If *Doing Business* were used by the international community in Africa in a way that recognized its limitations, it could be dismissed as an innocuous, if glitzy, means of calling the attention of African policymakers to regulatory reform. Unfortunately, it has often proved fatally tempting for donors to argue that African governments should target rapid progress in moving up the *Doing Business* rankings as the primary objective of investment climate reform. As a result, *Doing Business* may have contributed to an atmosphere of "teaching to the test," encouraging efforts to improve country rankings at the expense of deeper analysis of investment climate constraints.[6] In countries where the World Bank or its affiliate the IFC have established business-government coordination mechanisms in Africa, *Doing Business* has been used as the principal agenda-setting instrument.[7]

Equally worrisome, despite their inherent limitations, the *Doing Business* indicators are being used to guide resource allocation by donors. The days required and cost of starting a business feature as "guideposts" under the World Bank's Country Performance and Institutional Assessment (CPIA) component on the "business regulatory environment." The CPIA is a critical factor in determining the volume of concessional assistance provided to countries by the World Bank Group under the International Development Association (IDA). The time and cost to start a business are used as two of the fourteen "outcome" indicators in the "IDA results framework."

The indicators have also entered the country-level policy dialogue of bilateral donors. Since 2005 the same two indicators have been used by the United States' Millennium Challenge Corporation (MCC) in its formula for determining countries' eligibility for grants. In Nigeria, the United Kingdom's Department for International Development (DFID) is supporting the collection of *Doing Business* indicators for every state. The data will be used for diagnostic analysis and for benchmarking by the government and donors. The multidonor Business Enterprise Strengthening in Tanzania

6. Page (2012c).
7. Page (2014b).

(BEST) program, based on *Doing Business*, has now become a key "deliverable" for release of budget support.

Not surprisingly, the World Bank has been sensitive to criticism, and its 2014 *Doing Business* report takes a step back from the triumphalism of earlier reports. In reviewing the academic literature on regulations and economic performance, *Doing Business 2014* concedes that "although empirical research provides ample evidence for positive links between better business regulations and economic performance, more rigorous research is needed to better understand whether and to what extent the former causes the latter."[8] The report also tells us that "while *Doing Business* indicators are actionable this does not necessarily mean that they are all 'action-worthy' in a particular context. Business regulatory reforms are one element of a strategy aimed at improving competitiveness and establishing a solid foundation for sustainable economic growth. . . . Governments have to decide what set of priorities best fits the needs they face."[9]

Unfortunately, in the end the World Bank cannot admit that the way in which its own operational staff and collaborating donors have used the surveys in their dialogue with governments may have crowded out more serious efforts to identify the binding constraints to industrial development. Rather, it writes: "Over several years of engaging with authorities in a large number of economies, the *Doing Business* team has never seen a case where the binding constraint to say, improvements in tax administration or contract enforcement was the feverish pace of reforms in other policy areas."[10] This is getting things the wrong way around. Tax administration and contract enforcement are *Doing Business* indicators. It is precisely because of excessive attention to *Doing Business* that a "feverish pace of reforms in other policy areas" was missing.

8. World Bank (2014a, p. 39).
9. World Bank (2014a, p. 25).
10. World Bank (2014a, p. 26).

Neglected Priorities: Infrastructure and Skills

At the same time that regulatory reform has dominated the discussion of the investment climate, donor attention to Africa's growing infrastructure and skills deficits has waned. In the case of infrastructure a naive belief in the ability of the private sector and non-OECD donors to finance the region's growing infrastructure deficit may have led to complacency. In the case of skills, the pursuit of the primary education Millennium Development Goal (MDG) has crowded expenditures on postprimary education out of development budgets.

Closing Africa's infrastructure gap will require around US$93 billion a year, about 15 percent of the region's GDP. Forty percent of the total spending needs are for power alone.[11] Existing spending on infrastructure in Africa amounts to about US$45 billion a year. About US$15 billion of this amount comes from external sources, including the private sector, official development assistance (ODA), and nontraditional development partners, mainly China. Even if potential efficiency gains could be fully realized, a funding gap of about $31 billion a year would remain, about 60 percent of which is in power.

Despite the magnitude of the infrastructure gap, infrastructure financing by the members of the OECD-DAC has been falling as a share of ODA since the early 1970s (figure 9-1). For most of the 1990s and early 2000s, ODA to infrastructure in sub-Saharan Africa remained steady at US$2 billion a year, mainly financing public goods such as roads and water supply that were seen as aligned to the MDGs. DAC donors have neglected power for two decades, and any increase in donor financing should focus first on the power sector.

Although the private sector can contribute to funding power generation, donors will still need to scale up substantially to address the current crisis in the sector. Greater cooperation and coordination between DAC donors and nontraditional donors, perhaps

11. World Bank (2009c).

Figure 9-1. *Share of Aid to Africa for Infrastructure, 1973–2010*

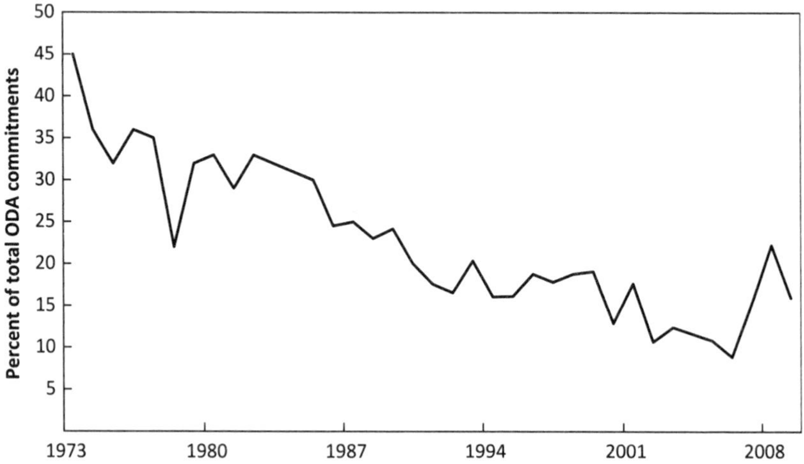

Source: OECD-DAC CRS (2013) online database.

through the international financial institutions to which they both belong, could improve the focus and efficiency of resource use.[12] There is also an urgent need to think creatively about how aid can be used to crowd in more private investment in African infrastructure. The international financial institutions (IFIs) will need to develop better guarantee mechanisms for investors and use the headroom in their capital structures to assist governments to avoid excessive sovereign borrowing.

Financing an expansion of postprimary education presents at least as daunting a challenge as closing the infrastructure gap. A 2010 report by the World Bank undertakes a number of education policy and financing simulations for thirty-three African countries. In the most ambitious scenario the aggregate gap in recurrent funding for postprimary education in 2020 amounts to US$29.1 billion a year. Even in the most restrictive scenarios—those reflecting highly

---

12. Climate change financing—whether on concessional terms or not— is likely to further complicate the infrastructure financing picture, in particular for energy generation. For a survey of the issues on aid and climate change, see Arndt and Bach (2011).

selective policies for coverage in upper secondary and tertiary education and low unit costs—the recurrent funding gap is projected at US$3.4 billion a year for postprimary education.[13]

The likelihood that these funding gaps will be addressed adequately is small. DAC donor commitments to all levels of education in Africa only approach US$4 billion. African governments are confronted with rising unit costs in primary education, increasing pressures on lower secondary education as a result of higher primary completion rates and limited prospects of external finance. They have little choice but to open a dialogue with their development partners on the desirability and realism of the primary education MDG, and 2015 is the time to do so.[14] If a broader target were to be used, governments would have greater flexibility to reallocate expenditures from primary to postprimary education while still making and reporting measurable progress in building human capital.

In addition to allowing greater budget flexibility and providing additional funding, donors can support two additional ways of expanding educational services. Because many of the returns to higher level education are appropriable by the individual, encouraging private provision of educational services, especially in technical, vocational, and tertiary education, represents a significant financing and service provision option. Private provision of technical and tertiary education raises important equity issues. Lack of financial depth in many African countries is likely to constrain poorer students from privately financing their education. Donors can strengthen equality of opportunity by supporting grants and low-cost loans.

Donor countries with significant African immigrant populations can help to develop new ways of engaging the diaspora to build skills in their countries of origin. Africa is the region of the developing

13. Mingat, Ledoux, and Rakotomalala (2010).

14. Some African governments have already begun this dialogue in the context of moving from first-generation to second-generation Poverty Reduction Strategy Papers (PRSPs). Early PRSPs, which were mainly expressions of donor objectives, largely excluded reference to expanding postprimary education. More recent PRSPs have introduced the topic, most often without specific goals.

world in which the highly skilled form the largest share of all migrants. This "brain drain" offers the possibility of becoming a "brain bank" from which migrants are recruited to support skills development through virtual, temporary, or permanent return.[15] Aid and migration policies can work together to build skills.

Aiding Industrialization

In chapter 7 we set out the elements of a strategy for African industrial development. The international community has a major role to play in supporting each of the three new pillars of that strategy: creating an export push, building firm capabilities, and supporting industrial clusters. Donors also have a role to play in helping Africa's regional economic communities develop the institutions and infrastructure needed to support industrial development.

Supporting the Export Push

International support for an export push should act on two fronts—aid to improve trade logistics and policies to increase preferential market access. Since the 2005 Hong Kong World Trade Organization (WTO) Ministerial Conference, "Aid for Trade" has attracted considerable donor attention. Based on a generous definition, written by the donors themselves, it comprises about 25 percent of total development assistance and about 30 percent of aid that governments allocate to individual sectors.[16] Although Aid for Trade commitments have increased since the launch of the initiative, donors are not fulfilling the promise made at Hong Kong to make Aid for Trade additional to existing aid budgets. In fact, Aid for Trade's share in total development assistance has fallen steadily since 1996.[17]

15. See Page and Plaza (2006).
16. This "sectoral allocable aid" excludes funding for debt relief, administrative costs, and budget support.
17. Gamberoni and Newfarmer (2009).

Given the very broad definition of Aid for Trade, it is perhaps unsurprising that little is known about its impact.[18] There have been few attempts at impact evaluations of individual projects under the Aid for Trade umbrella, and counting such categories as economic infrastructure as both aid to "build productive capacity" and to assist trade makes attributing changes in trade performance to aid difficult. One study finds that countries with low levels of trade performance and trade logistics tend to receive a higher share of Aid for Trade in GDP than those with lesser need, controlling for governance-related factors.[19] While this is encouraging, it is also the case that those countries with poor trade performance and trade logistics are among the poorest countries and those most likely, controlling for governance-related factors, to receive higher development assistance. In view of the level of double counting in the Aid for Trade program, it is impossible to tell whether support for trade was the motivation for the aid allocations.

One obvious change should be to link Aid for Trade to improvements in the infrastructure, institutions, and skills that impact export performance. This would both help to align incentives between donors and governments toward boosting exports and reduce the scope for double counting. Because there is a widely accepted measure of trade logistics performance published by the World Bank, it should be possible for donors to agree to align aid commitments with the specific infrastructure and institutional components of the trade logistics index. This would result in a substantial decline in the apparent donor commitments to Aid for Trade. On the other hand, it would also make it possible to see whether donor assistance is directed at the critical logistical constraints to exports.

Trade policy in Africa's main trading partners—especially those in Asia—has an important role to play in easing the entry of

18. One study suggests that aid to "build productive capacity" may have played a role in fostering exports in mining and manufacturing. See Cali and te Velde (2008). A World Bank (2008b) study on the effectiveness of eighty-eight trade development programs in forty-eight countries found that exports in sectors receiving trade-related technical assistance have increased.

19. Gamberoni and Newfarmer (2009).

nontraditional African exports into global markets. Although Asia's tariffs on African exports are gradually declining, the trend is weak, especially for Africa's least developed countries. An essential step is to reduce escalating tariffs directed at higher stage processing of commodity exports. These tariffs discourage the development of agro-industrial value chains. A poignant example is an Indian-owned cashew firm in Tanzania that cannot profitably export roasted nuts to India because India imposes higher tariffs on processed nuts than on raw nuts.[20] China could play a leading role here by shifting its preferential trading agreements with Africa from country-by-country bilateral deals to a single well-publicized, Africa-wide initiative. This might push its Asian trading partners to offer similar tariff reductions.

Higher income countries should develop a common, time-bound system of preferences for Africa's nontraditional exports. At present, different OECD countries have different trade preference schemes, and most of them are not well designed or effective. Indeed, the multiplicity of schemes is a needless source of complexity. An obvious improvement would be for the European Union and the United States to harmonize and liberalize their individual preference schemes for Africa, the Economic Partnership Agreement (EPA) and the African Growth and Opportunity Act (AGOA), respectively.

A global system of preferences would be best. The current preferences offered by the WTO to least developed countries (LDCs) are not relevant to the majority of Africa's newly industrializing countries. They have, happily, moved beyond LDC status, even if they are still struggling to break into global markets in industry. To address this problem, the United Nations could create a separate class of Least Developed Manufacturing Countries, which are low- and lower-middle-income countries with little manufacturing. This category could then be used by WTO members in devising a common preferential trading scheme that would apply to all such economies,

20. Broadman (2007).

including the vast majority of African countries.[21] To recognize the reality of task-based trade, these preferences should feature liberal and simple rules of origin, and stability in the eligibility for preferences should be a priority.

Helping to Build More Capable Firms

The aid community can play a supportive role in helping to build more capable firms in Africa. Because firm-to-firm interactions are the main channel by which capabilities are transferred, there is limited scope for development assistance to support capabilities transfer directly. Effective support for an export push is one obvious way for donors to help countries build capabilities. Attracting more foreign direct investment (FDI) is another. This is an area where properly designed investment climate reforms can have a large payoff by making it easier to attract FDI. Donors can also give priority to helping to develop effective foreign investment promotion agencies and world-class open architecture special economic zones (SEZs) at the country level.

A potentially promising area for donor engagement is support for management information and training. Donor agencies in Eastern Europe and Central Asia, for example, have created networks of related manufacturing companies and provide regular advice to them on achieving international standards in terms of quality and production.[22] Donors could play a similar role in establishing and supporting similar networks in Africa, working with governments and the private sector.

The management training experiments for large-scale firms in India, discussed in chapter 5, offer a new opening for aid to support capability building. This is an area that challenges donors to do something they generally do not do well: start small, evaluate impact

---

21. See Collier and Venables (2007) and UNIDO (2009) for such proposals.
22. Sutton (2005).

carefully, and then scale up in a consistent manner based on lessons learned. Substantially more work will be needed to understand the incentive structures and circumstances that make training in operational management both effective and scalable. The impact evaluations of MSME training show that donors are not getting these programs right. That should serve as a warning with respect to plunging into training of larger firms.

Helping to Create Clusters

Africa's traditional suppliers of aid have tended to neglect spatial economic policies. Indeed, the prevailing wisdom in the World Bank until recently was that export processing zones (EPZs) were costly, inefficient substitutes for economywide reforms in trade policy and regulation.[23] China, on the other hand, building on its own success with SEZs, has launched an initiative to build export-oriented special economic zones in Africa. China's Ministry of Commerce is supporting the development of six economic and trade cooperation zones in five African countries—Egypt, Ethiopia, Mauritius, Nigeria (two zones), and Zambia. In addition to contributing to China's Africa initiative, the zones are intended to help China's own restructuring by encouraging labor-intensive industries, such as textiles, leather goods, and building materials, to move offshore. Chinese enterprises have also set up industrial zones outside the official ministry program in Botswana, Nigeria, Sierra Leone, Uganda, and South Africa.

The official zones involve three parties: the Chinese government, Chinese developers, and African governments. The zones in Ethiopia and Mauritius are 100 percent Chinese-owned, while the others are joint ventures with national or local governments as minority partners. Most of the zones are designed to support clusters in

---

23. A World Bank study takes a broader view of EPZs as industrial agglomerations and provides a balanced account of their strengths and weaknesses in practice. See Farole (2011). The results of the study are slowly finding their way into World Bank operational policy.

textiles, home appliances, and other light industries, and the Chinese zone developers are obliged to construct high-standard infrastructure, promote the zone, and bring in world-class professional management. Host governments are expected to provide infrastructure outside the zones, including guaranteed supplies of electricity, water, and gas, as well as roads leading up to the zones and improved port services. While the Chinese government has not involved itself in the design or direct operation of the EPZs, it has organized marketing events in China to promote investment in the zones.[24]

Despite China's expertise, there are some early warning signs that the potential of the new EPZs may not be realized fully. For example, there is no evidence that any of the host governments have made efforts to develop supplier programs or other close links between the domestic private sector and the zones. In contrast to trends in China, none of the African zones appear to have been specifically designed to encourage synergies with local universities or technology institutes.[25] While it is too early to say whether this new initiative will succeed, traditional donors should observe it closely. There are many poorly functioning SEZs across the region and lessons learned from the Chinese experiment can be mainstreamed into new approaches by multilateral development banks (MDBs) and other donors.

Strengthening Regional Integration

Africa is a continent of small countries, many of them landlocked, which makes regional approaches to many of the constraints to industrial development imperative. We noted in chapter 4 that better functioning regional infrastructure and institutions were essential to export success in landlocked countries, and we pointed out some of the cost penalties associated with poorly functioning regional trade corridors. In chapter 5 we highlighted the costs to capability building of restrictive immigration policies that prevent the temporary entry

24. Brautigam and Tang (2011; 2014).
25. Brautigam and Tang (2011).

of skilled engineers and managers. In chapter 6 we raised the concern that political fragmentation may keep Africa's cities smaller than desirable from the point of view of competing globally. Stronger regional integration can go a long way toward addressing these problems.

While African governments can and must do more themselves to deepen their Regional Economic Communities (RECs), Africa's development partners have not aggressively supported regional infrastructure and institutions. Aid agencies are often better structured and equipped to deal with national partners. This has limited financial commitments to transborder projects with the RECs. Even when projects are approved, implementation and disbursement are particularly slow at the regional level. The regional organizations often lack the financial, institutional, and technical capacity to develop bankable projects and to make member countries implement their commitments. They are understaffed and their procedures are cumbersome. Where aid agencies are under pressure to disburse, the perception that supporting regional projects is slower and more complex can be a disincentive.

Donors should make the RECs the lead institutions in the dialogue on regional strategies and programs. They can build the capacity of RECs to develop bankable projects and to carry out monitoring and evaluation. Donors also need to make stronger efforts to harmonize their support to regional organizations and decrease the use of their own systems to channel aid flows to regional programs. The Infrastructure Consortium for Africa (ICA) is potentially an important tool to implement this agenda. It is designed to catalyze donor and private-sector financing for infrastructure. The ICA already facilitates collaborative work, donor harmonization, and sharing of best practice. It could serve as a framework to implement more effective donor support to regional infrastructure and institutions.

Both AGOA and the EPAs are doing too little to encourage regional integration. Tight rules of origin have undermined the role of EPAs in strengthening regional integration, and the current AGOA eligibility rules—which include governance performance criteria—discourage the development of regional value chains. Removing a country from AGOA punishes not only the offending country; its regional trading partners suffer as well. This was dramatically demonstrated in the case of Madagascar, which had developed regional supply chains in garments, including the supply of zippers from Swaziland, denim from Lesotho, and cotton yarn from Zambia and South Africa. Following a change of government, Madagascar became ineligible for AGOA preferences, ending these supply chain relationships.

Supporting Diversification in Resource-Abundant Economies

The Continent's newly resource-abundant economies face two major challenges. The first is managing their resource wealth in a way that supports long-term, widely shared growth: in other words, avoiding the resource curse. The second is finding ways to diversify their economies away from natural resources. In general, the aid community has chosen to focus on the first challenge and, in particular, questions of natural resource revenue management. The problem of economic diversification has received far less donor attention.

Most of the donor dialogue with newly resource-abundant economies in Africa centers on transparency in revenue management and how much to save or spend. While these are important questions, the quality of public spending is equally important. Donors can help to improve the quality of public spending by supporting the mainstreaming of cost-benefit analysis in public expenditure management programs. To do so, they will need to begin by putting their own houses in order. Most donor agencies do not have staff capable of helping developing countries improve cost-benefit analysis because they do not adequately do cost-benefit analysis themselves.

Reforming the donor community's approach to investment climate reform is certainly a significant first step toward supporting diversification. In particular, helping to implement a well-designed program of regulatory reform during the time before resource revenues begin to flow and create vested interests could pay high dividends.

Donors can also assist regional organizations to develop standards of good practice in regulation that provide a benchmark against which national reform efforts can be measured. There is sometimes a temptation among donors to believe that resource revenues are a substitute for development assistance in building infrastructure and skills. This is wrong: for most emerging resource exporters, revenues are both uncertain and a reasonably long way off, and that makes the donor's role in providing bridging finance highly relevant.

Resource-abundant countries such as Ghana have turned to global capital markets to accelerate the pace of infrastructure investment. Surprisingly, the role of the multilateral development banks— and in particular the World Bank—has been to warn of excessive debt accumulation, rather than to think creatively about how to use their considerable untapped lending potential to offer "hybrid" loans with longer maturities and lower interest rates than the capital markets.[26] In addition, the technical expertise of donors can be a significant help in priority setting and the evaluation of public investments in both infrastructure and skills development. The IFI experience with project design, procurement, and implementation also has much to offer newly resource-rich economies in terms of "investing to invest."

Donors have a role to play beyond the investment climate in helping countries to design and implement their diversification strategies. Many of the things they can do are similar to the kinds of support for industrialization in non-resource-rich countries we outlined previously. In addition, agencies can support south-south learning between successful resource-abundant countries such as Botswana, Chile, Indonesia, and Malaysia and Africa's newly

---

26. The International Bank for Reconstruction and Development (IBRD) is the "hard" lending window of the World Bank. The African Development Bank also has an "ordinary capital" lending window. Both lend mainly to middle-income countries on terms that are generally more favorable than they can obtain on international capital markets. In recent years concerns have been raised that the World Bank is not using its lending capacity under IBRD fully. See Kapur and Raychaudhuri (2014).

resource-rich economies. This may be particularly relevant in the area of investing in knowledge.

There is an opportunity for donors to help resource-rich economies to design and, just as important, evaluate spatial policies linked to the resource, such as growth corridors. Many of these proposals today read like wish lists and lack a clear sense of the complementarities among investments and their potential impact. Finally, donors can support the creation of institutions designed to integrate domestic producers into resource-based value chains. For many development agencies a major change of mind-set is required. Balancing effectiveness with transparency will, in the short run, most likely involve a degree of discretion that moves beyond the comfort zone of the "level playing field."

Is Small Beautiful? Aid and Small Enterprises

There is one area of industrial development in which the aid industry has been consistently and deeply engaged in Africa: the promotion of micro and small enterprises (MSEs). The overwhelming majority of enterprises in Africa are micro, small, and medium-scale firms. Small firms are big business for donors. At the end of 2010, the global commitments of multilateral development banks, bilateral donor agencies, and development finance institutions (DFIs) to MSEs totaled around US$24.5 billion. Official development assistance to micro and small firms is estimated to have exceeded US$1 billion in 2009. Forty-eight percent of this ODA went to Asia, 19 percent to the Middle East and North Africa, and 18 percent to sub-Saharan Africa.[27]

---

27. Siegesmund and Glisovic (2011). These estimates are approximate. There are data gaps in what donors and DFIs self-report, and the information is not reported consistently across organizations. In addition, there are a large number of nongovernmental organizations (NGOs) that deal with micro, small, and medium enterprises. Some of these MSMEs are financed by official development assistance, but a growing number are funded wholly or partly by private philanthropy.

Why? In a word: jobs. At the 2012 spring meetings of the International Monetary Fund (IMF) and World Bank, Andrew Mitchell, then the U.K. Secretary of State for International Development, and Lars Thunell, chief executive officer of the International Finance Corporation, announced a joint initiative to finance small and medium enterprises in developing countries declaring that "small and medium enterprises are a vital engine of job creation in developing countries."[28] Undeniably, micro and small firms are "where the jobs are" in Africa. While the definition of "small" varies by country and by income level, when microenterprises—virtually all of which operate outside the formal sector—are included, more than 90 percent of manufacturing firms and the vast majority of workers in Africa are found in MSMEs.[29] But in fact we know little about small enterprises and job creation.

This is largely because there are serious analytical challenges that complicate attempts to understand job creation by firms.[30] The most critical of these is the need to distinguish between gross and net job creation. While small firms indisputably create new jobs, as we saw in chapter 4, they can also destroy jobs through higher failure rates. Assessing the impact of turnover on net job creation requires data that record firm entry and exit. One of the few studies of net job creation in Africa used panel data from World Bank Enterprise Surveys in five countries covering a three-year period in the early 1990s. It found that large firms (defined as larger than 100 employees) were the "job creators." They contributed 56 percent of net job creation in Ghana, 74 percent in Kenya, 76 percent in Zimbabwe, and 66 percent in Tanzania. High rates of small enterprise failure were an important factor determining the difference between gross and net job creation.[31] A second study, using data on

28. See Elliot (2012).

29. Page and Söderbom (2015).

30. For a discussion of some of the methodological problems associated with attempts to measure job creation by SMEs, see Haltiwanger, Jarmin, and Miranda (2013). See also WIDER' s position paper on aid and employment (http://recom.wider.unu.edu/article/position-papers-how-does-aid-work).

31. Biggs (2002).

manufacturing firms in nine sub-Saharan countries, found that firms with 100 workers or more grew employment more rapidly than smaller firms.[32]

In Tanzania, we found that the exit rates of registered micro and small enterprises were sharply higher than those for medium and large firms. We were able to use Ethiopia's detailed data to analyze net employment growth across firms of differing size. There we found that net job growth for large and small firms was the same.[33] We also found that in Ethiopia, as in other countries outside of Africa where these types of studies have been undertaken, it is growing firms of all sizes that are the job creators.[34]

The focus on job creation begs another important question: What is the quality of jobs created? To answer this question we used data on nine African countries from the World Bank Enterprise Surveys.[35] We found that workers in small African firms are paid far less than employees in larger firms. The earnings of the average worker in a 100-worker firm are about 80 percent higher than the earnings of someone working in an enterprise employing five workers. We know that a sizable portion of the wage gap is due to differences in workers' characteristics: large firms tend to hire better-educated and more experienced workers than small firms. Nevertheless, conditional on skills and experience, there is still a large, statistically significant wage difference between small and large firms.[36]

These results lead us to an unsettling conclusion. If one of the objectives of development is—as it should be—to create good jobs, donors have been aiming at the wrong target. Aid needs to target those firms that are successful at creating more and better jobs. Our evidence tells us, not surprisingly, that growing firms of all sizes are

32. Van Biesebroeck (2006).
33. Page and Söderbom (2014).
34. Haltiwanger, Scarpetta, and Schweiger (2010).
35. Ethiopia (2002; 186 firms); Ghana (2007; 293 firms); Kenya (2007; 416 firms); Mozambique (2007; 347 firms); Nigeria (2007; 1,001 firms); Rwanda (2006; 77 firms); Senegal (2007; 262 firms); Tanzania (2006; 302 firms); and Uganda (2006; 358 firms).
36. Oi and Idson (1999); Söderbom, Teal, and Wambugu (2005).

the best job creators. They are firms that create net new employment and offer the potential for wage growth. At the same time, size alone cannot predict which firms will grow. This argues for policies and programs that encourage the growth of all firms, regardless of size.

Summing Up

Africa's lack of industrial development has been a missed opportunity for aid. Since the 1990s donor attention has primarily focused on the regulatory and institutional aspects of the investment climate. While these issues are undeniably important, the principal instrument guiding the policy dialogue, the World Bank *Doing Business* indicators, is not appropriate. League tables—in public policy just as in sports—are a way of drawing attention to comparative performance. They are poor guides to policy reform.

Africa's traditional donors have neglected two equally if not more critical aspects of the investment climate: infrastructure and skills. Official development assistance to infrastructure has declined as a share of total ODA continuously since the 1970s. The focus on achieving the MDG of universal primary enrollment, while a major success story in Africa, has left African governments with little budget space to improve quality, fund postprimary education, and reduce a growing skills gap with the rest of the world. Reversing the declining trend in aid to infrastructure and postprimary education is critically important to learning to compete in the future.

Beyond the investment climate, aid can play a catalytic role in accelerating industrial development. Aid and supporting trade policies can contribute to creating an export push, building firm capabilities, and supporting agglomerations. This will require the development community to be more attuned to the needs of recipient governments in the areas of trade logistics, foreign direct investment, value chain development, and spatial industrial policies. Donors can also play a much more active role in supporting regional integration.

Aid agencies need to move beyond the themes of transparency in revenue management and savings rules to engage with the region's newly resource-abundant economies on a wider range of issues that can help them diversify beyond the natural resource base. Here again, many of the aid industry's traditional concerns with the investment climate are relevant, but the donors will need to adapt to the changing circumstance of the resource-abundant. The IFIs, for example, can use their privileged position in global capital markets to help finance investments in infrastructure and education before resource revenues start to flow and add their project management skills to strengthen investing to invest. Donors can also contribute to the push for diversification.

Aid programs designed to support MSEs on the grounds that they are "job creators" are aiming at the wrong target. While micro and small enterprises may be "where the jobs are" in Africa, large firms and small firms create the same amount of net employment over the medium term. Growing firms are the region's real job creators, and growing firms come in all sizes. Donors need to think more carefully about how to promote the growth of productive firms of all sizes in Africa. That, in large measure, has been the subject of this book.

AFTERWORD

Leopards and Laggards

P art IV outlined an agenda for industrial development that we believe can place Africa on a path toward sustained growth, good jobs, and reduced poverty. Before closing, we wanted to share some final thoughts on how Africa's economy may evolve over the next several decades. Every student of Africa hears at some point the admonition: "Africa is not a country." That was never more true than today. One of the least appreciated features of the African growth miracle has been the difference in economic performance between countries across the Continent. We expect these differences to continue and become more pronounced in the coming years. Africa is likely to become a continent of leopards and laggards.[1]

The leopards will be those countries that manage to adapt their development strategies to domestic endowments and international

---

1. There is an amusing search for an appropriate African analogy to Asia's "tigers." We are aware of at least three species indigenous to the Continent that have been nominated for the honor—lions, leopards, and cheetahs. While each has its proponents, we prefer leopards. They are more industrious than their feline cousins in Africa.

opportunities. In doing so, they will need to declare policy independence from the donor community and, as earlier generations of tigers in Asia did, find their own way. We believe that some—perhaps those favored by coastal locations and more capable firms—will definitely industrialize. We would, however, be very surprised if the successful African economy in 2030 looked like Vietnam today. Natural resources—including the climatic and geographical advantages that underpin agriculture and tourism—play too large a role in the continent's endowments. The leopards of the future are likely to have economic structures that contain some natural resource extraction, high value added agriculture and agro-industry, and tradable services, in addition to a more robust manufacturing base.

To us, this is not disappointing news. We began Learning to Compete in the hope that it would help contribute to the debates and policy decisions that will support Africa's quest for sustained growth and poverty reduction. Tradable services, tourism, horticulture, and agro-industry are all industries without smokestacks. They offer prospects of good jobs and higher productivity growth. The strategies we have outlined in this book apply equally to them as to manufacturing. If some governments use these strategies and succeed in creating robust growth of industries outside of the manufacturing sector, this is good news. Just as Africa is not a country, industrialization is not just the growth of mass manufacturing. It is structural change toward high productivity, tradable activities, wherever they are found in the economic statistics.

The laggards will each have their own story to tell. Some of them will have succumbed to the maladies of conflict and the burden of disease. While both conflict and disease have diminished in importance on the Continent, neither has disappeared, as the 2015 outbreak of Ebola demonstrates. Some laggards will have issues of governance. Others will have failed to escape the resource curse, and some will simply have suffered from bad luck. All will remain, at least for some time, dependent on donors for money and ideas. We are persuaded that over time the laggards will be a diminishing fraction of the region's economies.

Neighborhood effects are powerful in both economic and political terms. Rising prosperity in some countries will open up opportunities for their less prosperous neighbors. The proximity of leopards will make it increasingly difficult for political leaders in the laggards to excuse their lack of economic and social progress. With leopards in the neighborhood, it is time to pay attention and do the right things. Leopards are highly adaptable and they run fast. Laggards will have to learn to run as well, and aid donors will have to come to grips with these new realities if they are to remain relevant.

References

Country Case Studies

Ackah, Charles, Charles Adjasi, and Festus Turkson. 2014. "Scoping study on the evolution of industry in Ghana." WIDER Working Paper 2014/075 (Helsinki: UNU-WIDER).

Ayadi, Mohamed, and Wided Mattoussi. 2014. "Scoping of the Tunisian economy." WIDER Working Paper 2014/074 (Helsinki: UNU-WIDER).

Chete, Louis N., John O. Adeoti, Foluso M. Adeyinka, and Olorunfemi Ogundele. 2014. "Industrial development and growth in Nigeria: Lessons and challenges." WIDER Working Paper 2014/019 (Helsinki: UNU-WIDER).

Chhair, Sokty, and Lunya Ung. 2013. "Economic history of industrialization in Cambodia." WIDER Working Paper 2013/134 (Helsinki: UNU-WIDER).

Cissé, Fatou, Ji Eun Choi, and Mathilde Maurel. 2014. "Scoping Paper on Industry in Senegal." WIDER Working Paper 2014/157 (Helsinki: UNU-WIDER).

Cruz, António Sousa, Dina Guambe, Constantino Pedro Marrengula, and Amosse Francisco Ubisse. 2014. "Mozambique's industrialization." WIDER Working Paper 2014/059 (Helsinki: UNU-WIDER).

Gebreeyesus, Mulu. 2013. "Industrial policy and development in Ethiopia: Evolution and present experimentation." WIDER Working Paper 2013/125 (Helsinki: UNU-WIDER).

Ngui, Dianah, Jacob Chege, and Peter Kimuyu. 2014. "Scoping Paper on Kenyan Industry." WIDER Working Paper 2014/136 (Helsinki: UNU-WIDER).

Nguyen Thi Tue Anh, Luu Minh Duc, and Trinh Duc Chieu. 2014. "The evolution of Vietnamese industry." WIDER Working Paper 2014/076 (Helsinki: UNU-WIDER).

Obwona, Marios, Isaac Shinyekwa, and Julius Kiiza. 2014. "The evolution of industry in Uganda." WIDER Working Paper 2014/021 (Helsinki: UNU-WIDER).

Wangwe, Samuel, Donald Mmari, Jehovanes Aikaeli, Neema Rutatina, Thadeus Mboghoina, and Abel Kinyondo. 2014. "The performance of the manufacturing sector in Tanzania: Challenges and the way forward." WIDER Working Paper 2014/085 (Helsinki: UNU-WIDER).

Other References

ACET. 2014. *2014 Africa Transformation Report: Growth with Depth* (Accra: African Center for Economic Transformation).

Ackah, C., A. Acquah, C. Adjasi, and F. Turkson. 2014. "Education, Skill Accumulation, and Productivity: Evidence from Ghanaian Manufacturing Firms." WIDER Working Paper 2014/073 (Helsinki: UNU-WIDER).

AEO. 2013. *Global Value Chains and Africa's Industrialization*. African Development Bank, OECD and UNDP (Paris: OECD).

_____. 2014. *Structural Transformation and Natural Resources*. African Development Bank, OECD and UNDP (Paris: OECD).

AfDB. 2010. *African Development Report, 2010: Ports, Logistics, and Trade in Africa* (Tunis: African Development Bank).

_____. 2012. "Youth Employment in Africa: A Background Paper for the 2012 African Economic Outlook" (Tunis: African Development Bank).

Aghion, P., M. Braun, and J. Fedderke. 2008. "Competition and Productivity Growth in South Africa." *Economics of Transition* 16(4): 741–68.

Amiti, M., and J. Konings. 2007. "Trade liberalization, intermediate inputs, and productivity: evidence from Indonesia." *American Economic Review* 97(5): 1611–38.

APO. 2013. *Asia Productivity Data Book* (Tokyo: Asia Productivity Organization).

Arbache, J. S., and J. Page. 2008. "Patterns of Long-Term Growth in Sub-Saharan Africa," in *Africa at a Turning Point? Growth, Aid, and External Shocks*, edited by D. Go and J. Page (Washington: World Bank).

_____. 2009. "How Fragile Is Africa's Recent Growth?" *Journal of African Economies* 19(1): 1–24.

Arndt, C., and C. F. Bach. 2011. "Foreign Assistance in a Climate-Constrained World." WIDER Working Paper 2011/66 (Helsinki: UNU-WIDER).

Arndt, C., A. F. Garcia, F. Tarp, and J. Thurlow. 2012. "Poverty Reduction and Economic Structure: Comparative Path Analysis for Mozambique and Vietnam." *Review of Income and Wealth* 58(4): 742–63.

Arrow, K. 1969. "Classificatory notes on the production and transmission of technological knowledge." *American Economic Review* 59(2): 29–35.

Au, C. C., and J. V. Henderson. 2006. "Are Chinese Cities Too Small?" *Review of Economic Studies* 73(3): 549–76.

Ayadi, M., and W. Mattoussi. 2014. "Disentangling the Pattern of Geographic Concentration in Tunisian Manufacturing Industries." WIDER Working Paper 2014/072 (Helsinki: UNU-WIDER).

Balassa, B. 1971. *The Structure of Protection in Developing Countries* (Baltimore: Johns Hopkins University Press).

Barry, F. 2004. "Export Platform FDI: The Irish Experience." *EIB Papers* 9(2): 8–37.

Baumol, W. J. 1985. "Productivity Policy and the Service Sector," in *Managing the Service Economy: Prospects and Problems*, edited by R. P. Inman (Cambridge University Press).

Ben Jelili, R., and M. Goaied. 2009. "Entry, Exit, and Productivity in Tunisian Manufacturing Industries," in *Market Dynamics and Productivity in Developing Countries*, edited by Khalid Sekkat (New York: Springer).

Bennedsen, M., K. M. Nielsen, F. Perez-Gonzalez, and D. Wolfenzon. 2007. "Inside the Family Firm: The Role of Families in Succession Decisions and Performance." *Quarterly Journal of Economics* 122(2): 647–91.

Bernard, A. B., J. B. Jensen, and P. K. Schott. 2006. "Trade Costs, Firms, and Productivity." *Journal of Monetary Economics* 53(5): 917–37.

Bevan, D., C. Adam, J. Okidi and F. Muhumuza. 2003. *Poverty Eradication Action Plan Revision 2002/3: Discussion Paper on Economic growth, Investment, and Export Promotion* (Kampala: Ministry of Finance, Planning and Economic Development).

Bhagwati, J. N. 1978. *Anatomy and Consequences of Exchange Control Regimes* (Cambridge, Mass.: National Bureau of Economic Research).

_____. 1984. "Splintering and Disembodiment of Services and Developing Nations." *World Economy* 7(2): 133–44.

Biggs, T. 2002. "Is Small Beautiful and Worthy of Subsidy? Literature Review" (Washington: International Finance Corporation).

Bigsten, A., P. Collier, S. Dercon, M. Fafchamps, B. Gauthier, J. W. Gunning, A. Oduro, R. Oostendorp, C. Pattillo, M. Söderbom, F. Teal, and A. Zeufack. 2004. "Do African Exporters Learn from Exporting?" *Journal of Development Studies* 40(3): 115–41.

Blalock, G., and P. J. Gertler. 2004. "Learning from Exporting Revisited in a Less Developed Setting." *Journal of Development Economics* 75(2): 397–415.

Blalock, G., and F. Veloso. 2007. "Imports, Productivity Growth, and Supply Chain Learning." *World Development* 35(7): 1134–51.

Bloom, N., M. Draca, and J. Van Reenen. 2011. "Trade Induced Technical Change? The Impact of Chinese Imports on Innovation, IT and Productivity." NBER Working Paper No. 16717 (Cambridge, Mass: National Bureau of Economic Research).

Bloom, N., B. Eifert, A. Mahajan, D. McKenzie, and J. Roberts. 2013. "Does Management Matter? Evidence from India." *Quarterly Journal of Economics* 128(1): 1–51.

Bloom, N., A. Mahajan, D. McKenzie, and J. Roberts. 2010. "Why Do Firms in Developing Countries Have Low Productivity?" *American Economic Review: Papers & Proceedings 2010* 100(2): 619–23.

Bloom, N., and J. Van Reenen. 2007. "Measuring and Explaining Management Practices across Firms and Countries." *Quarterly Journal of Economics* 122(4): 1341–1408.

_____. 2010. "Why Do Management Practices Differ across Firms and Countries?" *Journal of Economic Perspectives* 24(1): 203–24.

Brautigam, D., and X. Tang. 2011. "African Shenzhen: China's Special Economic Zones in Africa." *Journal of Modern African Studies* 49(1): 27–54.

_____. 2014. "Going Global in Groups: Structural Transformation and China's Special Economic Zones Overseas." *World Development* 63: 78–91.

Broadman, H. G. 2007. "Connecting Africa and Asia." *Finance and Development* 44(2): 31–44.

Cadot, O., C. Carrère, and V. Strauss-Kahn. 2011. "Export Diversification: What's Behind the Hump?" *Review of Economics and Statistics* 93(2): 590–605.

Cali, M., and D. W. te Velde. 2008. "Towards a Quantitative Assessment of Aid for Trade." Economic Paper 83 (London: Commonwealth Secretariat).

Chenery, H. 1986. "Growth and Transformation," in *Industrialization and Growth: A Comparative Study,* edited by H. Chenery, S. Robinson, and M. Syrquin (Oxford University Press).

Chhair, S., and C. Newman. 2014. "Clustering, Competition, and Spillover Effects: Evidence from Cambodia." WIDER Working Paper 2014/065 (Helsinki: UNU-WIDER).

Chhair, S., and L. Ung. 2014. "Exporting and Foreign Direct Investment Spillovers." UNU-WIDER Working Paper 2014/079 (Helsinki: UNU-WIDER).

Chong, A., and M. Gradstein. 2010. "Firm-level Determinants of Political Influence." *Economics and Politics* 22(3): 233–56.

Clarke, G. R. G. 2005. "Beyond Tariffs and Quotas: Why Don't African Firms Export More?" Policy Research Working Paper 4317 (Washington: World Bank).

Collier, P. 2010. *Plundered Planet* (Oxford University Press).

———. 2011a. "Building an African Infrastructure." *Finance and Development* 48(4): 18–21.

———. 2011b. "Managing Uganda's Oil Discovery." *Joseph Mubiru Memorial Lecture* (Kampala: Bank of Uganda).

Collier, P., and B. Goderis. 2007. "Prospects for Commodity Exporters: Hunky Dory or Humpty Dumpty?" *World Economics* 8(2): 1–15.

Collier, P., and A. Hoeffler. 2008. "Testing the Neo-Con Agenda: Democracy and Natural Resource Rents." *European Economic Review* 53(4): 293–308.

Collier, P., M. Kirchberger, and M. Söderbom. 2013. "The Cost of Road Infrastructure in Developing Countries" (Oxford: Centre for the Study of African Economies).

Collier, P., F. van der Ploeg, M. Spence, and A. J. Venables. 2010. "Managing Resource Revenues in Developing Countries." *IMF Staff Papers* 57(1): 84–118.

Collier, P., and A. J. Venables. 2007. "Rethinking Trade Preferences: How Africa Can Diversify Its Exports." *World Economy* 30(8): 1326–45.

———. 2008. "Trade and Economic Performance: Does Africa's Fragmentation Matter?" *Annual World Bank Conference on Development Economics* (Washington: World Bank).

Commission on Growth and Development. 2008. *The Growth Report* (Washington: World Bank).

Dadush, U. 2010. *In 2050, a World Transformed* (Tunis: African Development Bank).

Davis, S. J. and J. Haltiwanger. 1999. "On the Driving Forces behind Cyclical Movements in Employment Movement and Job Reallocation." *American Economic Review* 89(5): 1234–58.

De Vries, G. J., M. P. Timmer, and K. de Vries. 2013. "Structural Transformation in Africa: Static Gains, Dynamic Losses." GGDC Research Memorandum 136 (University of Groningen). Africa sector database: http://www.rug.nl/research/ggdc/data/africa-sector-database.

Dihel, N., A. M. Fernandes, R. Gicho, J. Kashangaki, and N. Strychacz. 2011. "Africa Trade Policy Notes: Can Kenya Become a Global Exporter of Business Services?" (Washington: World Bank).

Dinh, H. T., and G. R. G. Clarke, eds. 2012. *Performance of Manufacturing Firms in Africa: An Empirical Analysis*. Directions in Development: Private Sector Development (Washington: World Bank).

Dinh, H. T., V. Palmade, V. Chandra, and F. Cossar. 2012. *Light Manufacturing in Africa: Targeted Policies to Enhance Private Investment and Create Jobs* (Washington: World Bank).

Dinh, H. T., T. G. Rawski, A. Zafar, L. Wang, and E. Mavroeidi. 2013. *Tales from the Development Frontier: How China and Other Countries Harness Light Manufacturing to Create Jobs and Prosperity* (Washington: World Bank).

DNEAP. 2013. "Inquérito as Indústrias Manufatureiras 2012 (IIM2012): Descriptive Report" (Maputo: National Directorate for Studies and Policy Analysis [DNEAP]).

Dongier, P., and R. Sudan. 2009. *Information and Communications for Development* (Washington: World Bank).

Easterly, W. 2002. *The Elusive Quest for Growth: Economists' Adventures and Misadventures in the Tropics* (Cambridge, Mass.: MIT Press).

———. 2009. "Can the West Save Africa?" *Journal of Economic Literature* 47(2): 373–447.

Ebling, G., and N. Janz. 1999. "Export and Innovation Activities in the German Service Sector Empirical: Evidence at the Firm Level" (Mannheim: Centre for European Economic Research).

Edwards, L., and R. Lawrence. 2011. "AGOA Rules: The Intended and Unintended Consequences of Special Fabric Provisions." Paper presented at the CSAE Annual Conference, Oxford University.

Eichengreen, B., D. Park, and K. Shin. 2011. "When Fast Economies Slow Down: International Evidence and Implications for China." Working Paper 16919 (Cambridge, Mass.: National Bureau of Economic Research).

Eifert, B., A. Gelb, and N. B. Tallroth. 2003. "The Political Economy of Fiscal Policy and Economic Management in Oil-Exporting Countries," in *Fiscal Policy Formulation and Implementation in Oil Producing Countries*, edited by J. M. Davis, R. Ossowski, and A. Fedilino (Washington: International Monetary Fund).

Eifert, B., A. Gelb, and V. Ramachandran. 2005. "Business Environment and Comparative Advantage in Africa: Evidence from the Investment Climate Data." CGD Working Paper 56 (Washington: Center for Global Development).

_____. 2008. "The Cost of Doing Business in Africa: Evidence from Enterprise Survey Data." *World Development* 36(9): 1531–46.

Elliot, L. 2012. " 'A Million Jobs for World's Poorest' with UK Cash Boost for Entrepreneurs." *The Guardian*, April 15, 2012 (www.theguardian .com/global-development/2012/apr/16/uk-funds-million-jobs-world -bank).

Escribano, A., J. L. Guasch, and J. Pena. 2010. "Assessing the Impact of Infrastructure Quality on Firm Productivity in Africa: Cross-Country Comparisons Based on Investment Climate Surveys from 1999 to 2005." Policy Research Working Paper 5191 (Washington: World Bank).

Faccio, M. 2010. "Differences between Politically Connected and Nonconnected Firms: A Cross-Country Analysis." *Financial Management* 39(3): 905–28.

Farole, T. 2011. *Special Economic Zones in Africa: Comparing Performance and Learning from Experience* (Washington: World Bank).

Feenstra, R., and J. Romalis. 2012. "International Prices and Endogenous Quality." NBER Working Paper 18314 (Cambridge, Mass: National Bureau of Economic Research).

Fernandes, A. 2007. "Trade policy, trade volumes, and plant-level productivity in Columbian manufacturing industries." *Journal of International Economics* 71: 52–71.

Filmer, D., and L. Fox. 2014. *Youth Employment in Sub-Saharan Africa* (Washington: World Bank).

Fink, C., A. Matoo, and I. C. Neagu. 2002. "Assessing the Impact of Communication Costs on International Trade." Policy Research Working Paper 2929 (Washington: World Bank).

Foster, L., J. Haltiwanger, and C. Syverson. 2008. "Reallocation, Firm Turnover, and Efficiency: Selection on Productivity or Profitability?" *American Economic Review* 98(1): 394–425.

Foster, V., and C. Briceño-Garmendia, eds. 2010. *Africa's Infrastructure: A Time for Transformation* (Washington: World Bank).

Fosu, A. 2011. "Growth, Inequality, and Poverty Reduction in Developing Countries: Recent Global Evidence." CSAE Working Paper 2011-07 (Oxford: Centre for the Study of African Economies).

Gamberoni, E., and R. Newfarmer. 2009. "Aid for Trade: Matching Potential Demand and Supply." Policy Research Working Paper 4991 (Washington: World Bank).

Gebreeyesus, M., and M. Iizuka. 2010. "Discovery of the Flower Industry in Ethiopia: Experimentation and Coordination." Working Paper 2010-025 (Maastricht: UNU-MERIT).

Gelb, A., ed. 1988. *Oil Windfalls: Blessing or Curse?* (Oxford University Press).

Gelb, A., C. Meyer, and V. Ramachandran. 2013. "Does Poor Mean Cheap?" CGD Working Paper 357 (Washington: Center for Global Development).

_____. 2014. "Development as Diffusion: Manufacturing Productivity and Africa's Missing Middle" (Washington: Center for Global Development).

Ghani, E., and H. Kharas. 2010. "The Service Revolution in South Asia: An Overview," in *The Service Revolution in South Asia*, edited by E. Ghani (Oxford University Press), 1–32.

Gibbons, R., and R. Henderson. 2012. "Relational Contracts and Organizational Capabilities." *Organizational Science* 23(5): 1350–64.

Gill, I., H. Kharas, with D. Bhattasali et al. 2007. *An East Asian Renaissance: Ideas for Economic Growth* (Washington: World Bank).

Grossman, G., and E. Helpman. 1991. *Innovation and Growth in the Global Economy* (Cambridge, Mass.: MIT Press).

Grossman, G., and E. Rossi-Hansberg. 2006. "The Rise of Offshoring: It's Not Wine for Cloth Anymore." *Federal Reserve Bank of Kansas City Proceedings Economic Policy Symposium–Jackson Hole*, 59–102.

Gylfason, T., T. T. Herbertsson, and G. Zoega. 1999. "A Mixed Blessing: Natural Resources and Economic Growth." *Macroeconomic Dynamics* 3: 204–25.

Hallak, Juan Carlos, and Peter K. Schott. 2011. "Estimating Cross-Country Differences in Product Quality." *Quarterly Journal of Economics* 126(1): 417–74.

Haltiwanger, J., R. S. Jarmin, and J. Miranda 2013. "Who Creates Jobs? Small vs. Large vs. Young." *Review of Economics and Statistics* 95 (2): 347–61.

Haltiwanger, J., S. Scarpetta, and H. Schweiger. 2010. "Cross-Country Differences in Job Reallocation: The Role of Industry, Firm Size, and Regulations." Working Paper 116 (London: European Bank for Reconstruction and Development, Office of the Chief Economist).

Harding, A., M. Söderbom, and F. Teal. 2004. "Survival and Success among African Manufacturing Firms." Working Paper WPS/2004-05 (Oxford: University of Oxford, CSAE).

Harding, T., and B. Javorcik. 2011. "Roll Out the Red Carpet and They Will Come: Investment Promotion and FDI Inflows." *Economic Journal* 121(557): 1445–76.

Harrison, A., and A. Rodriguez-Clare. 2010. "Foreign Investment, and Industrial Policy for Developing Countries," in *Handbook of Development Economics*, vol. 5, edited by D. Rodrik and M. Rosenzweig (Amsterdam: North-Holland).

Harrison, A. E., J. Y. Lin, and L. C. Xu. 2012. "Performance of Formal Manufacturing Firms in Africa," in *Performance of Manufacturing Firms in Africa: An Empirical Analysis*, edited by H. T. Dinh and G. R. G. Clarke (Washington: World Bank).

_____. 2013. "Explaining Africa's (Dis) Advantage." *World Development* 63(C): 59–77.

Hausmann, R., J. Hwang, and D. Rodrik. 2007. "What You Export Matters." *Journal of Economic Growth* 12(1): 1–25.

Heath, R., and A. M. Mobarak. 2014. "Manufacturing Growth and the Lives of Bangladeshi Women." NBER Working Paper 20383 (Cambridge, Mass.: National Bureau of Economic Research).

Henderson, J. V. 1997. "Externalities and Industrial Development." *Journal of Urban Economics* 42(3): 449–70.

_____. 2003. "Marshall's Scale Economies." *Journal of Urban Economics* 53(1): 1–28.

_____. 2005. "Urbanization and Growth," in *Handbook of Economic Growth*, vol. 1, edited by P. Aghion and S. Durlauf (Amsterdam: Elsevier).

Henderson, J. V., T. Lee, and Y. J. Lee. 2001. "Scale Externalities in Korea." *Journal of Urban Economics* 49(3): 479–501.

Henderson, J. V., Z. Shalizi, and A. J. Venables. 2001. "Geography and Development." *Journal of Economic Geography* 1(1): 81–105.

Henn, C., C. Papageorgiou, and N. Spatafora. 2013. "Export Quality in Developing Countries." IMF Working Paper 13/108 (Washington: International Monetary Fund).

Henstridge, M., and J. Page. 2012. "Managing a Modest Boom: Oil in Uganda." OxCarre Research Paper 2/6 (Oxford: Oxford Centre for the Study of Resource Rich Economies).

Howard, E., C. Newman, J. Rand, and F. Tarp. 2014. "Productivity-Enhancing Manufacturing Clusters: Evidence from Vietnam." WIDER Working Paper 2014/071 (Helsinki: UNU-WIDER).

Howard, E., C. Newman, and F. Tarp. 2012. "Measuring Industry Agglomeration and Identifying the Driving Forces." WIDER Working Paper 2012/84 (Helsinki: UNU-WIDER).

Howard, E., C. Newman, and J. Thijssen. 2011. "Are Spatial Networks of Firms Random? Evidence from Vietnam." WIDER Working Paper 2011/087 (Helsinki: UNU-WIDER).

Hsieh, C. T., and P. Klenow. 2009. "Misallocation and Manufacturing TFP in China and India." *Quarterly Journal of Economics* 124(4): 1403–48.

Hummels, D. 2007. "Transportation Costs and International Trade in the Second Era of Globalization." *Journal of Economic Perspectives* 21(3): 131–54.

Hummels, D., and P. J. Klenow. 2005. "The Variety and Quality of a Nation's Trade." *American Economic Review* 95(3): 704–25.

Humphrey, J., and O. Memedovic. 2006. "Global Value Chain in the Agrifood Sector" (Vienna: UNIDO).

Iddrisu, A., Y. Mano, and T. Sonobe. 2012. "Entrepreneurial Skills and Industrial Development: The Case of a Car Repair and Metalworking Cluster in Ghana." *Journal of Knowledge Economics* 3: 302–26.

ILO. 2011. *Global Employment Trends 2011* (Geneva: International Labor Organization).

_____. 2014. *Global Employment Trends 2014* (Geneva: International Labor Organization).

Imbs, J., and R. Wacziarg. 2003. "Stages of Diversification." *American Economic Review* 93(1): 63–86.

IMF. 2013. *Article IV Consultation for Mauritius, 2013* (Washington: International Monetary Fund).

_____. 2014. *Regional Economic Outlook: Asia and Pacific* (Washington: International Monetary Fund).

Jensen, H. T., S. Robinson, and F. Tarp. 2010. "Measuring Agricultural Policy Bias: General Equilibrium Analysis of Fifteen Developing Countries." *American Journal of Agricultural Economics* 92(4): 1136–48.

Kapos, S. 2005. "The Employment Intensity of Growth: Trends and Macroeconomic Determinants" (Geneva: International Labor Organization).

Kapur, D., and A. Raychaudhuri. 2014. "Rethinking the Financial Design of the World Bank." CGD Working Paper 352 (Washington: Center for Global Development).

Kasahara, H., and J. Rodrigue. 2008. "Does the use of imported intermediates increase productivity? Plant-level evidence." *Journal of Development Economics* 87: 106–18.

Kauffman, D., A. Kray, and M. Mastruzzi. 2010. "The Worldwide Governance Indicators: Methodology and Analytical Issues." Policy Research Working Paper 5430 (Washington: World Bank).

Khandelwal, A. 2010. "The Long and Short of Quality Ladders." *Review of Economics Studies* 77(4): 1450–76.

Killick, T. 1978. *Development Economics in Action* (New York: St. Martin's Press).

Krueger, A. O. 1974. "The Political Economy of the Rent-Seeking Society." *American Economic Review* 64(3): 291–303.

———. 1978. *Liberalization Attempts and Consequence* (Cambridge, Mass.: National Bureau of Economic Research).

Kuznets, S. 1955. "Economic Growth and Income Inequality." *American Economic Review* 45(1): 1–28.

Kweka, J., and L. Fox. 2011. "The Household Enterprise Sector in Tanzania: Why It Matters and Who Cares." Policy Research Working Paper 5882 (Washington: World Bank).

Kweka, J., and C. Ugarte. 2013. "SMEs at the Center Stage of Competitiveness and Job Creation: What Do We Know and Need to Know for Tanzania?" (Dar es Salaam: World Bank).

Lewis, W. A. 1954. "Economic Development with Unlimited Supplies of Labour." *Manchester School* 22(2): 139–91.

Limão, N., and A. J. Venables. 2001. "Infrastructure, Geographical Disadvantage, and Transport Costs." Policy Research Working Paper 2257 (Washington: World Bank).

Lin, J. 2011 "From Flying Geese to Leading Dragons: New Opportunities and Strategies for Structural Transformation in Developing Countries." Policy Research Working Paper 5702 (Washington: World Bank).

Little, I. M. D., T. Scitovsky, and M. F. G. Scott. 1970. *Industry and Trade in Some Developing Countries* (Oxford University Press).

Manova, K., and Z. Zhang. 2012. "Export Prices across Firms and Destinations." *Quarterly Journal of Economics* 127(2): 379–436.

Marshall, A. 1920. *Principles of Economics* (London: Macmillan).

McKenzie, D., and C. Woodruff. 2012. "What Are We Learning from Business Training and Entrepreneurship Evaluations around the Developing World?" Policy Research Working Paper 6202 (Washington: World Bank).

McMillan, M., and K. Hartgen. 2014. "What Is Driving the Africa Growth Miracle?" NBER Working Paper 2077 (Cambridge, Mass.: National Bureau of Economic Research).

McMillan, M., and D. Rodrik. 2011. "Globalization, Structural Change, and Productivity Growth." NBER Working Paper 17143 (Cambridge, Mass.: National Bureau of Economic Research).

McMillan, M., D. Rodrik, and I. Verduzco-Gallo. 2014. "Globalization, Structural Change, and Productivity Growth, with an Update on Africa." *World Development* 63(1): 11–32.

Meier, G. M., and W. F. Steel. 1989. *Industrial Adjustment in Sub-Saharan Africa* (Oxford University Press).

Mengiste, T., and C. Patillo. 2004. "Export Orientation and Productivity in Sub-Saharan Africa." *IMF Staff Papers* 51(2): 327–53.

Mingat, A., B. Ledoux, and R. Rakotomalala. 2010. "Assessing the Financial Sustainability of Alternative Pathways." *Africa Human Development Series* (Washington: World Bank).

Moran, T. 2001. *Parental Supervision: The New Paradigm for Foreign Direct Investment and Development* (Washington: Institute for International Economics).

Moriset, B. 2004. "The Rise of Call Center Industry: Splintering and Virtualization of the Economic Space." Paper presented at Centennial Meeting of the Association of American Geographers, Philadelphia.

Mottaleb, K. A., and T. Sonobe. 2011. "An Inquiry into the Rapid Growth of the Garment Industry in Bangladesh." GRIPS Discussion Paper 11-10 (Tokyo: National Graduate Institute for Policy Studies).

Muto, M., Y. C. Y. Chung, and S. Shimokoshi. 2011. "Location Choice and Performance of Furniture Workshops in Arusha, Tanzania." JICA-RI Working Paper 28 (Tokyo: Japan International Cooperation Agency).

Ndulu, B. J. 2007. "The Evolution of Global Economic Paradigms and Their Influence on African Economic Growth," in *The Political Economy of Growth in Africa,* vol. 1, edited by B. J. Ndulu, R. Bates, S. A. O'Connell, P. Collier, and C. Saludo (Cambridge University Press).

Nellis, J. R. 1986. "Public enterprises in sub-Saharan Africa" (Washington: World Bank).

———. 2003. "Privatization in Africa: What Has Happened? What Is to Be Done?" Working Paper Number 25 (Washington: Center for Global Development).

NEPAD, AU, and AfDB. 2011. *Revision of the AU/NEPAD AFRICAN ACTION PLAN 2010–2015: Advancing Regional and Continental Integration Together through Shared Values Abridged Report 2010–2012* (Johannesburg: New Partnership for Africa's Development).

Newman, C., J. Page, J. Rand, A. Shimeles, M. Söderbom, and F. Tarp. Forthcoming 2016. "Identifying Direct FDI Linkages through Triangulation." WIDER Working Paper 2016/XX (Helsinki: UNU-WIDER).

Newman, C., J. Rand, T. Talbot, and F. Tarp. 2015. "Technology Transfers, Foreign Investment, and Productivity Spillovers." *European Economic Review* 76: 168–87.

Newman, C., J. Rand, and F. Tarp. 2013. "Firm Switching in Developing Countries: The Case of Vietnam." *World Bank Economic Review* 27(2): 357–88.

———. 2015. "Imports, Supply Chains, and Productivity." Mimeo (Dublin: Trinity College).

Newman, C., J. Rand, F. Tarp, and N. T. Tue Anh. 2014. "Exporting and Productivity: The Role of Ownership and Innovation in the Case of Vietnam." UNU-WIDER Working Paper 2014/070 (Helsinki: UNU-WIDER).

Nicita, A., and M. Orreagada. 2007. "Trade Production and Protection Database, 1976–2004." *World Bank Economic Review* 21(1): 165–71.

OECD. 2010. *Measuring Globalisation: OECD Economic Globalisation Indicators 2010* (Paris: Organization for Economic Cooperation and Development).

OECD-DAC CRS. 2013. International Development Statistics (IDS) online databases (www.oecd.org/dac/stats/idsonline.htm).

Oi, W. Y., and T. L. Idson. 1999. "Firm Size and Wages," in *Handbook of Labor Economics*, vol. 3B, edited by O. Ashenfelter and D. Card (Amsterdam: North-Holland), 2165–214.

Oluyomi-Abiola B. 2008. "The Nnewi Automotive Components Cluster in Nigeria," in *Knowledge, Technology, and Cluster-based Growth in Africa*, edited by Douglas Zhihua Zeng (Washington: World Bank).

O'Toole, C. M., and F. Tarp. 2014. "Corruption and the Efficiency of Capital Investment in Developing Countries." *Journal of International Development* 26(5): 567–97.

Overman, H., and A. J. Venables. 2005. "Cities in the Developing World," CEP Discussion Paper 695 (Centre for Economic Performance, London School of Economics and Political Science).

Pack, H., and J. Page. 1993. "Accumulation, Exports, and Growth in the High-Performing Asian Economies." *Carnegie-Rochester Conference Series on Public Policy* 40: 199–235.

Page, J. 2009. "Seizing the Day: The Global Economic Crisis and African Manufacturing." Working Paper 102 (Tunis: African Development Bank).

_____. 2012a. "Can Africa Industrialize?" *Journal of African Economies* 21(2): ii86–ii124.

_____. 2012b. *Jobs, Justice, and the Arab Spring* (Tunis: African Development Bank).

_____. 2012c. "Aid, Structural Change, and the Private Sector in Africa." WIDER Working Paper 2012/21 (Helsinki: UNU-WIDER).

_____. 2013. "Should Africa Industrialize?" in *Prospects for Industrialization in the 21st Century*, edited by L. Alcorta, W. Naude, and E. Szrmai (Oxford University Press).

_____. 2014. "Industrial Policy in Practice: Africa's President's Investors Advisory Councils." Wider Working Paper 2014/117 21 (Helsinki: UNU-WIDER).

_____. 2015a. "Structural Change and Africa's Poverty Puzzle," in *The Last Mile: Challenges to Eradicating Extreme Poverty*, edited by L. Chandy, H. Kato, and H. Kharas (Brookings).

_____. 2015b. "The East Asian Miracle and Development Policy: A 20-Year Retrospective," in *Japan's Development Assistance: Foreign Aid and the Post-2015 Agenda*, edited by H. Kato, J. Page, and Y. Shimomura (Basingstoke: Palgrave Macmillan).

Page, J., and S. Plaza. 2006. "Migration, Remittances, and Economic Development: A Review of Global Evidence," Special issue 2, *Journal of African Economies* 15: 245–336.

Page, J., and A. Shimeles. 2015. "Aid, Employment, and Poverty Reduction in Africa," *Africa Development Review* 27(S1): 17–30.

Page, J., and M. Söderbom. 2012. "Is Small Beautiful?" WIDER Working Paper 2012/94 (Helsinki: UNU-WIDER).

_____. 2014. "Are Small Firms Job Creators in Low-Income Countries? Evidence from Ethiopia" (Washington: Brookings).

_____. 2015. "Is Small Beautiful? Small Enterprise, Aid, and Employment in Africa." *African Development Review* 27(S1): 44–55.

Porter, M. E. 1990. *The Competitive Advantage of Nations* (New York: Free Press).

Raddatz, C. 2008. "Have External Shocks Become More Important for Output Fluctuations in African Countries?" in *Africa at a Turning Point? Growth, Aid, and External Shocks,* edited by D. S. Go and J. Page (Washington: The World Bank).

Ramachandran, V., and M. Shah. 2007. "Why Are There So Few Black-Owned Firms in Africa? Preliminary Results from Enterprise Survey Data." CDG Working Paper 104 (Washington: Center for Global Development).

Rasiah, R., Y. Lin, and Y. Sadoi. 2013. *Innovation and Industrialization in Asia* (New York: Routledge).

Rhee, Y. W. 1990. "The Catalyst Model of Development: Lessons from Bangladesh's Success with Garment Exports." *World Development* 18(2): 333–46.

Rivoli, P. 2005. *The Travels of a T-Shirt in the Global Economy: An Economist Examines the Markets, Power, and Politics of World Trade* (Hoboken, N.J.: John Wiley & Sons).

Rodrik, D. 1997. "Trade Policy and Economic Performance in Sub-Saharan Africa" (Cambridge, Mass.: Kennedy School of Government, Harvard University).

_____. 2007. "Normalizing Industrial Policy." Paper prepared for the Commission on Growth and Development, Harvard University.

_____. 2013. "Unconditional Convergence in Manufacturing." *Quarterly Journal of Economics* 128(1): 165–204.

_____. 2014. "An African Growth Miracle?" (Princeton, N.J.: Institute for Advanced Studies).

Romer, P. M. 1994. "The Origins of Endogenous Growth." *Journal of Economic Perspectives* 8(1): 3–22.

Rosenthal, S. S., and W. C. Strange. 2004. "Evidence on the Nature and Sources of Agglomeration Economies," in *Handbook of Regional and Urban Economics*, vol. 4, edited by J. V. Henderson and J. F. Thisse (Amsterdam: North-Holland).

Sachs, J. D., and A. M. Warner. 1995. "Natural Resource Abundance and Economic Growth." NBER Working Paper 5398, rev. 1997, 1999 (Cambridge, Mass.: National Bureau of Economic Research).

Sala-i-Martin, X., and A. Subramanian. 2003. "Addressing the Natural Resource Curse: An Illustration from Nigeria." NBER Working Paper 9804 (Cambridge, Mass.: National Bureau of Economic Research).

Saliola, F., and M. Seker. 2011. "Total Factor Productivity across the Developing World." World Bank Enterprise Note Series 23 (Washington: World Bank).

Schmitz, H. 1995. "Collective Efficiency: Growth Path for Small-scale Industry." *Journal of Development Studies* 31: 529–66.

Schott, P. 2004. "Across-product versus Within-product Specialization in International Trade." *Quarterly Journal of Economics* 119(2): 646–77.

Siba, E., and M. Gebreeyesus. 2014. "Learning to Export and Learning by Exporting: The Case of Ethiopian Manufacturing." WIDER Working Paper 2014/105 (Helsinki: UNU-WIDER).

Siba, E., M. Söderbom, A. Bigsten, and M. Gebreeyesus. 2012. "Enterprise Agglomeration, Output Prices, and Physical Productivity: Firm-Level Evidence from Ethiopia." WIDER Working Paper 2012/85 (Helsinki: UNU-WIDER).

Siegesmund, P., and J. Glisovic. 2011. "Estimating Funder Support for Small and Medium Enterprises (SMEs)" (Washington: World Bank, Consultative Group to Assist the Poor).

Söderbom, M., F. Teal, M. Eberhardt, S. Quinn, and A. Zeitlin. 2014. *Empirical Development Economics* (London: Routledge).

Söderbom, M., F. Teal, and A. Wambugu. 2005. "Unobserved Heterogeneity and the Relation between Earnings and Firm Size: Evidence from Two Developing Countries." *Economics Letters* 87(2): 153–59.

Sonobe, T., and K. Otsuka. 2006. *Cluster-Based Industrial Development: An East Asian Model* (Basingstoke: Palgrave Macmillan).

Sraer, D., and D. Thesmar. 2007. "Performance and Behavior of Family Firms: Evidence from the French Stock Market." *Journal of the European Economic Association* 5(4): 709–51.

Steel, W. F., and J. Evans. 1989. "Growth Trends in Manufacturing," in *Industrial Adjustment in Sub-Saharan Africa*, edited by G. M. Meier and W. F. Steel (Oxford University Press).

Stern, N. 2001. *A Strategy for Development* (Beijing: China People's University).

_____. 2002. *The Investment Climate, Governance, and Inclusion in Bangladesh*. World Bank Office of the Senior Vice President, Development Economics (Washington: World Bank).

_____. 2003. "The Investment Climate: Lessons and Challenges." *Distinguished Lecture Series 19* (Cairo: Egyptian Center for Economic Studies).

Subramanian, U., and M. Matthijs. 2007. "Can Sub-Saharan Africa Leap into Global Network Trade?" Policy Research Working Paper 4112 (Washington: World Bank).

Sutton, J. 2004. "Competing in Capabilities: Globalization and Development." Clarendon Lectures in Economics (London School of Economics).

_____. 2005 "Competing in Capabilities: An Informal Overview" (London School of Economics).

_____. 2012. *Competing in Capabilities: The Globalization Process* (Oxford University Press).

Sutton, J., and N. Kellow. 2010. *An Enterprise Map of Ethiopia* (London: International Growth Centre).

Sutton, J., and B. Kpentey. 2012. *An Enterprise Map of Ghana* (London: International Growth Centre).

Sutton, J., and G. Langmead. 2013. *An Enterprise Map of Zambia* (London: International Growth Centre).

Sutton, J., and D. Olomi. 2012. *An Enterprise Map of Tanzania* (London: International Growth Centre).

Syverson, C. 2004. "Product Substitutability and Productivity Dispersion." *Review of Economics and Statistics* 86(2): 534–50.

Syverson, C. 2007. "Prices, Spatial Competition, and Heterogeneous Producers: An Empirical Test." *Journal of Industrial Economics* 4(2): 197–222.

_____. 2011. "What Determines Productivity?" *Journal of Economic Literature* 49(2): 326–65.

Tarp, F. 1993. *Stabilization and Structural Adjustment: Macroeconomic Frameworks for Analysing the Crisis in Sub-Saharan Africa* (London and New York: Routledge).

Timmer, M. P., and G. J. de Vries. 2009. "Structural Change and Growth Accelerations in Asia and Latin America: A New Sectoral Data Set." *Cliometrica* 3(2): 165–90.

Tolonen, A. 2015. "Local Industrial Shocks, Female Empowerment and Infant Health: Evidence from Africa's Gold Mining Industry" (Gothenburg: University of Gothenburg).

Tyler, G. 2005. "Critical Success Factors in the African High Value Horticulture Sector." Background paper for the Competitive Commercial Agriculture in Sub-Saharan Africa Study (Washington: World Bank).

Uganda Bureau of Statistics. 2011. *Construction Price Indices* (Kampala: Government Printer).

UNCTAD. 2012. *Who Is Benefiting from Trade Liberalization in Lesotho? A Gender Perspective* (Geneva: United Nations Conference on Trade and Development).

_____. 2013. *World Investment Report 2013: Global Value Chains: Investment and Trade for Development* (Geneva: United Nations Conference on Trade and Development).

UNIDO. 2003. *Industrial Development Report 2002/2003: Competing through Innovation and Learning* (Vienna: United Nations Industrial Development Organization).

———. 2009. *Industrial Development Report 2009* (Vienna: United Nations Industrial Development Organization).

———. 2013. *Industrial Development Report 2013* (Vienna: United Nations Industrial Development Organization).

_____. 2014. *Manufacturing Value Added Database* (Vienna: United Nations Industrial Development Organization) (www.unido.org/en/resources/statistics/statistical-databases.html).

_____. 2015. *Industrial Development Database 2015* (Vienna: United Nations Industrial Development Organization) (www.unido.org/en/resources/statistics/statistical-databases.html).

Van Biesebroeck, J. 2006. "Exporting Raises Productivity in Sub-Saharan African Manufacturing Firms." *Journal of International Economics* 67(2): 373–91.

Van der Ploeg, F. 2011. "Natural Resources: A Curse or a Blessing?" *Journal of Economic Literature* 49(2): 366–420.

Veit, P., S. Lupberger, and A. Ashraf. 2010. *Challenges of Natural Resources for Africa* (Tunis: African Development Bank).

Verhoogen, E. 2008. "Trade, Quality Upgrading and Wage Inequality in the Mexican Manufacturing Sector." *Quarterly Journal of Economics* 123(2): 489–530.

Wiebelt, M., K. Pauw, J. M. Matovu, E. Twimukye, and T. Benson. 2011. "Managing Future Oil Revenues in Uganda for Agricultural Development and Poverty Reduction: An CGE Analysis of Challenges and Options." Working Papers 1696 (Kiel Institute for the World Economy).

WIDER. 2014. "Aid, Growth, and Employment," ReCom Position Paper (Helsinki: UNU-WIDER).

Williamson, J. 1990. "What Washington Means by Policy Reform," in *Latin American Adjustment: How Much Has Happened?* edited by J. Williamson (Washington: Institute for International Economics).

Wood, A., and K. Jordan. 2000. "Why Does Zimbabwe Export Manufactures and Uganda Not?" *Journal of Development Studies* 37(2): 91–116.

World Bank. 1983. *World Development Report 1983* (Oxford University Press).

———. 1991. *World Development Report, 1991* (Oxford University Press).

———. 1992. *World Bank Structural and Sectoral Adjustment Operations: The Second OED Overview* (Washington: World Bank).

———. 1993. *The East Asian Miracle: Economic Growth and Public Policy* (Oxford University Press).

———. 2000. *Can Africa Claim the 21st Century?* (Washington: World Bank).

———. 2004. *Competing in the Global Economy: An Investment Climate Assessment for Uganda* (Washington: World Bank).

———. 2007a. "Expanding the Possible in Sub-Saharan Africa: How Tertiary Institutions Can Increase Growth and Competitiveness" (Washington: World Bank).

———. 2007b. *Country Economic Memorandum: Uganda* (Washington: World Bank).

———. 2008a. *World Development Report, 2008: Agriculture for Development* (Washington: World Bank).

———. 2008b. *Doing Business: An Independent Evaluation.* Independent Evaluation Group (Washington: World Bank).

———. 2008c. "Has Product Specific Aid for Trade Increased Exports?" International Trade Department, *Trade Note 36* (Washington: World Bank).

_____. 2009a. *Investment Climate Assessment of Mozambique* (Washington: World Bank).

_____. 2009b. *World Development Report 2009* (Washington: World Bank).

_____. 2009c. *Transforming Africa's Infrastructure* (Washington: World Bank).

_____. 2009d. *Cambodia—A Better Investment Climate to Sustain Growth* (Washington: World Bank).

_____. 2010. *Africa's Trade in Services and Economic Partnership Agreements* (Washington: World Bank).

_____. 2011a. "Curbing Fraud, Corruption, and Collusion in the Roads Sector" (Washington: World Bank).

_____. 2011b. *Country Economic Memorandum, Mozambique* (Washington: World Bank).

_____. 2013. *World Development Report 2013* (Washington: World Bank).

_____. 2014a. *Doing Business 2014* (Washington: World Bank).

_____. 2014b. *Connecting to Compete, 2014* (Washington: World Bank).

_____. 2014c. *Productive Jobs Wanted: Tanzania Country Economic Memorandum* (Washington: World Bank).

_____. 2014d. *World Development Indicators (WDI) Database* (Washington: World Bank) (www.data.worldbank.org/data-catalog/world-development-indicators).

_____. 2014e. *Africa Development Indicators 2014* (Washington: World Bank) (www.data.worldbank.org/data-catalog/africa-development-indicators).

_____. 2015. *Enterprise Survey Database* (www.enterprisesurveys.org/data).

Yepes, T., J. Pierce, and V. Foster. 2008. "Making Sense of Sub-Saharan Africa's Infrastructure Endowment: A Benchmarking Approach." Africa Infrastructure Country Diagnostic, Working Paper 1 (Washington: World Bank).

Yoshino, Y. 2008. "Domestic Constraints, Firm Characteristics, and Geographical Diversification of Firm-Level Manufacturing Exports in Africa." Policy Research Working Paper 4575 (Washington: World Bank).

Yoshino, Y., with O. Cadot, F. Ratsimbazafy, and J. Regolo. 2013. "Uncovering Drivers for Growth and Diversification of Tanzania's Exports and Exporters" (Washington: World Bank).

Young, A. 2012. "The Africa Growth Miracle." *Journal of Political Economy* 120(4): 696–739.

Zafar, A. 2011. "Mauritius: An Economic Success Story" (Washington: World Bank).

Index